The Emptiness of Asia

The Emptiness of Asia

Aeschylus' *Persians* and the history of the fifth century

THOMAS HARRISON

BLOOMSBURY ACADEMIC
LONDON • NEW YORK • OXFORD • NEW DELHI • SYDNEY

BLOOMSBURY ACADEMIC
Bloomsbury Publishing Plc
50 Bedford Square, London, WC1B 3DP, UK
1385 Broadway, New York, NY 10018, USA

BLOOMSBURY, BLOOMSBURY ACADEMIC and the Diana logo are trademarks of Bloomsbury Publishing Plc

First published 2000
Paperback edition published by Bloomsbury Academic 2019

A catalogue record for this book is available from the British Library.

ISBN: PB: 9781350113411

The quotation from Louis MacNeice's *Autumn Journal* is taken from *The Collected Poems of Louis MacNeice* (London: Faber & Faber, 1996) and reproduced by kind permission of David Higham Associates.

Typeset by Ray Davies

Contents

For R. D. R. and A. M. R.

The Glory that was Greece: put it in a syllabus, grade it
    Page by page
To train the mind or even to point a moral
    For the present age
...
But I can do nothing so useful or so simple;
    These dead are dead

Louis MacNeice, *Autumn Journal*

Acknowledgements

This book began unpromisingly as the first paper that I wrote as a postgraduate student, over the Christmas vacation of 1990-1. My then supervisor, the late David Lewis, pronounced subsequently that he had found it 'enormously entertaining and stimulating' but that he was left with the impression that I did not quite 'play by the rules'. As I left the room, he threw out the comment that I should read Edith Hall; he expected I would find her 'rather harder to nail'. It is not for me to say whether my ideas have retained their entertainment value, or indeed whether that would be a good thing. Though I cannot claim to have 'nailed' Edith Hall – or seriously to have felt the need to do so – one central conviction survives from my first encounter with the *Persians*: that the play has been largely ill-served by its critics, that the rules followed to this point have been unhealthily restrictive.

A large number of others have helped me through my intervening academic adolescence. Paul Cartledge, Christy Constantakopoulou, Amélie Kuhrt, Robin Osborne, and Robert Parker have all suffered reading the complete book in manuscript; all have greatly improved it. David Colclough and Lucinda Platt have listened under duress to the ideas expressed here, and have frequently imposed a stern sense of perspective. I am particularly grateful also to Giovanna Ceserani and Emma Dench for their advice and reassurance. The ideas expressed here have been aired on a number of occasions in conference and seminar papers: in Oxford, at a Warwick colloquium organised by Fiona McHardy, and at a conference in Kraków, organised by Edward Dabrowa, Stanislaw Kalita and Slawomir Sprawski. A much shorter precursor of chapters 3-8 of the current book, 'Aeschylus, Atossa and Athens', has been published in the proceedings of that conference: E. Dabrowa (ed.), *Ancient Iran and the Mediterranean World, Electrum* vol. 2 (Kraków, 1998), 69-86. I am very grateful to all those who contributed to the discussion of these papers – particularly to Maria Brosius and Heleen Sancisi-Weerdenburg for their sharp criticisms in Kraków – but above all to David Gribble, a piece of encouragement from whom long ago has had this unintended, and quite disproportionate, consequence.

The greatest part of the work for this book was carried out during two years' teaching in the School of Greek, Latin and Ancient History of the University of St. Andrews. I should like finally to thank all those friends and colleagues who made my time there so enjoyable and so fulfilling. To two of those friends – in thanks for their company – this book is dedicated.

October 1999 T.H.

Abbreviations

All references in the form 398-407 or 3.134.1-2 are, unless specified, to Aeschylus' *Persians* and to Herodotus' *Histories* respectively. The translations of the *Persians* are, with some small modifications, those of Edith Hall (Warminster, 1996), reprinted here by kind permission of the publisher, Aris and Phillips. Secondary literature is referred to by the surname of the author and the date of publication. Abbreviations of journals are as in *L'Année Philologique*.

A[eschylus]	*Ag[amemnon], Cho[ephoroe], Eum[enides], P[rometheus] V[inctus], Sept. = Seven Against Thebes, Suppl[iants]*
Ar[istophanes]	*Ran. = Frogs, Vesp. = Wasps*
[Arist][otle]	*Ath[enaion] Pol[iteia]*
Arist[otle]	*EN = Nicomachean Ethics, Poet[ics], Pol[itics], Rhet[oric]*
Diod[orus] Sic[ulus]	
E[uripides]	*Alc[estis], And[romache], El[ectra], Her[acles], Heracl[idai], I[phigenia in] A[ulis], Suppl[iants], Tro[iades]*
Hes[iod]	*Erg. = Works and Days*
Hipp[ocrates]	*A[irs] W[aters] P[laces]*
Isoc[rates]	*Paneg[yricus]*
Lys[ias]	
Paus[anias]	
P[indar]	*Isthm[ian], Nem[ean], Pyth[ian]*
Pl[ato]	*Leg. = Laws*
Pliny	*N[atural] H[istory]*

Plut[arch]	*Alc[ibiades], Alex[ander], Arist[ides], Cim[on], Per[icles], Nic[ias], Philopoem[en], Sol[on], Them[istocles], Thes[eus]*
Soph[ocles]	*Ant[igone], Aj[ax], El[ectra], O[edipus] C[oloneus], O[edipus] T[yrannus], Phil[octetes], Trach[iniai]*
Thuc[ydides]	
Xen[ophon]	*Anab[asis], Cyrop[aedia]*
[Xen][ophon]	*Ath[enaion] Pol[iteia]*
Campbell	D. Campbell (ed.), *Greek Lyric* (5 vols., Cambridge Mass., 1982-93)
CAH	*Cambridge Ancient History*
DK	H. Diels (ed.), rev. W. Kranz, *Die Fragmente der Vorsokratiker* (Berlin, 1951-2)
Dover	K.J. Dover (ed.), Aristophanes *Frogs* (Oxford, 1993)
FGrHist	F. Jacoby, *Die Fragmente der griechischen Historiker* (Berlin and Leiden, 1923-58)
Hornblower	S. Hornblower (ed.), *A Commentary on Thucydides* (2 vols., 1991-6)
Lobel-Page	E. Lobel and D.L. Page (eds.), *Poetarum Lesbiorum Fragmenta* (Oxford, 1955)
IG	*Inscriptiones Graecae* (Berlin, 1873-)
ML	R. Meiggs and D.M. Lewis (eds.), *A Selection of Greek Historical Inscriptions to the end of the fifth century B.C.* (revised edn., Oxford, 1988)
OCD	S. Hornblower and A.J. Spawforth (eds.), *Oxford Classical Dictionary* (3rd edn., Oxford, 1996)
PA	J. Kirchner (ed.) *Prosopographia Attica* (2 vols., Berlin, 1901-3)
P.Oxy.	B. Grenfell and others (eds.), *The Oxyrhynchus Papyri* (London, 1898-)
PMG	D.L. Page (ed.), *Poetae Melici Graeci* (Oxford, 1962)
TGrF	S. Radt (ed.), *Tragicorum Graecorum Fragmenta*, III: Aeschylus (Göttingen, 1985)
West	M.L. West (ed.), *Iambi et Elegi Graeci* (2 vols., Oxford, 1971-2)

Introduction

This book is a study of the historical value of Aeschylus' play, the *Persians*: its value both for the history of events and for Athens' 'ideological history', its worth as a source both of the Athenians' conception and portrayal of their enemy, the Persians, and – implicit in that portrayal – of their image of themselves.

Aeschylus' *Persians* is doubly unique among extant ancient dramas. Performed in 472 BC, seven years after the withdrawal of the main Persian army from mainland Greece, it is now recognised as the earliest extant Greek tragedy. Though we know, moreover, of the existence of earlier plays that took events from recent history as their subject-matter – Phrynichus' *Capture of Miletus*, for example, which dramatised the sack of Athens' ally during the Ionian revolt against Persian rule, or his *Phoenician Women*, on which Aeschylus is said to have based his play – the *Persians* is the only such 'historical tragedy' to survive in more than fragments or paraphrase. In one sense indeed, the *Persians* itself might be thought of as fragmentary: the three plays, all of them with mythological subject matter, together with which the *Persians* was performed – the *Phineus*, the *Glaucus Potnieus*, and the *Prometheus*, offer at best no more than tantalising glimpses of any thematic unity to the tetralogy.[1]

These distinctions have in many respects proved curses rather than blessings. Historical critics have tended to take the play's historical status as a licence to operate in an unhampered fashion deemed impossible in the case of other tragedies: to assume, for example, that Aeschylus felt obliged to provide an accurate historical record of the events of Salamis, or to take for granted the play's effectiveness as a vehicle for political propaganda, without asking how such political messages may be transmitted through the medium of drama.[2] Many literary critics, on the other hand – with some notable recent exceptions such as Edith Hall or Simon Goldhill[3] – have proceeded as if Aeschylus exercised his art in a vacuum. This book is written in the conviction that any but the most minimalist historical conclusions based on the evidence of the play depend upon a sensitive literary reading, and conversely that no literary study can safely ignore the historical context in which the play was written and first performed. Such observations are transparently banal: their only justification is that critics have failed to live up to them.

It may be useful to begin by sketching the bare bones of the play's action. (Contentious questions will be left on one side for the time being.) Like the *Phoenician Women*, the *Persians* tells how the news of Persian defeat in Greece reached Asia. The play opens with a Chorus of Persian elders – only women and old men are left behind in the Persian capital, Susa – listing the great individuals and the peoples of Asia currently on campaign (1-154), and ruminating darkly on the likely outcome of Xerxes' expedition. Their gloomy prognostications are interrupted by the arrival of the Queen, Xerxes' mother, on a chariot. She also voices her anxieties, in particular through her account of a dream (foreshadowing the outcome of the play) in which her son attempts and fails to yoke two women – one representing Greece, the other the 'land of the barbarians' (187) – to a chariot (176-200), and through a subsequent omen of an eagle being torn apart by a weaker hawk (201-10). The Chorus soothe the Queen, and answer a number of questions concerning Athens: her location, the source of her wealth, the number of her men and so on (230-45). These general inquiries are interrupted, however, by the arrival of a Persian messenger with more certain information. Initially quick bursts of headline news are interspersed with the Chorus' laments. The Queen, at first silent from shock, then begins to ask more detailed questions: she learns (with open delight) of the survival of Xerxes, then of the death of a whole stream of Asian nobles and of the relative strengths of the navies at Salamis; she then leads the Messenger into a largely unbroken narrative of the events of Salamis, of the subsequent land engagement on the nearby island of Psyttaleia, and of Xerxes' flight from Europe (353-514).

The Messenger's departure is followed shortly by that of the Queen, who sets out to prepare offerings to the Earth and to the dead. Before leaving, however, she instructs the Chorus to take counsel, and to console Xerxes should he arrive in her absence (527-31): the King's arrival, it transpires now, is expected imminently. Far from taking counsel, the Chorus, left to their own devices, give themselves up to even greater displays of grief and anxiety, attributing the blame for the Persians' reversal to Xerxes (contrasting him to his father Darius), and forecasting the end of Persian rule over Asia (532-96). On the Queen's return, this time on foot, another dramatic dawning takes place: her propitiation of the dead is more particularly, we now discover, a propitiation of Darius; indeed she orders the Chorus to sing hymns – again contrasting the former King's virtues with the failures of his son – to raise Darius from the Underworld.

On his appearance, Darius scents that not all is well; but it is only after failing to elicit the truth of the situation from the Chorus that he learns it from his widow, the Queen (681-738). Darius, it transpires, had known from oracles that such events would occur at some point in the future, though he had not guessed how soon (739-41). He blames Xerxes' failure on a madness that had afflicted him (750-1), and on the encouragement and reproaches of 'wicked men' (753-8). To emphasise the greatness of the disaster that has befallen Persia, he recites the achievements of his predecessors, none of whom 'would ever have been responsible for so much suffering' (786). Asked finally for his wisdom on the best course of action for the Persians, he instructs them never again to lead an expedition into Greece, tells the Chorus to encourage Xerxes to 'behave temperately' (829-30) and the Queen to calm him with kind words and to replace the robes he had rent in anguish at Salamis (832-8). He also takes the time to prophesy the final fate of the Persians at Plataea (800-20).

On Darius' disappearance, the Queen leaves to fetch new clothes for her son, never to speak again in the play (849-51). The Chorus return to the theme of the golden age of Darius' reign, and of his conquests in the Greek world (853-906). In the wake of this praise of his father, Xerxes then arrives in his rags. The play closes with a lengthy lament of both King and Chorus – on the Chorus' part tinged initially with a tone of accusation (908-1078).

A whole book on the historical value of a play of only a little over a thousand lines of verse may seem at first sight to be stretching scholarship too far. It is important to stress at the outset just how scarce is the evidence for this period of history.[4] Though the surviving corpus of

Greek tragedies provides ample evidence of the evolving conception of the generic barbarian (of whom the Persian was a substantial ingredient), no other surviving drama – comedy or tragedy – is concerned so exclusively with the Persians: we have only scattered allusions to stereotyped or exotic features of Persian culture – or rather what was imagined (perhaps only half-jokingly) to be Persian.[5] Vase-paintings again conflate Persian characteristics with those of other, often mythical, peoples.[6] For comparison with the play's portrayal of the Persians, we have also a number of vignettes preserved in the course of Herodotus' account of Persian history and customs, written under the shadow of the first years of the Peloponnesian war (431-404).[7] A number of fifth-century histories of Persia survive in no more than a handful of fragments.[8]

For a history of events, the prospects may seem even bleaker. As David Lewis observed, 'we frequently run short of events to fill the period'.[9] What little we know of the period following the Persian wars must be harvested also from a very disparate body of sources. Thucydides provides us with a sketchy account of the fifty years between the Persian wars and the Peloponnesian wars between Athens, Sparta and their allies (1.89-118), an account focussing on the growth of Athens' hold over her allies, her foreign expeditions under the leadership of Cimon, the son of Miltiades, the hero of Marathon, and on Sparta's increasing wariness of Athenian power. This is supplemented by a digression on Themistocles and Pausanias, the Athenian and Spartan commanders at Salamis and Plataea respectively, taking on their stories from where Herodotus had left off through to their deaths: in the case of Themistocles in Persian exile, in that of Pausanias at the hands of his fellow-Spartans (1.128-38). Scraps of the narrative of Diodorus Siculus (writing in the mid-first century BC, but deriving his material in large part from the fourth-century Ephorus of Cyme) occasionally supplement Thucydides' account of the relations between the Greek cities – for example in the detail of the so-called Hetoimaridas debate in which the Spartans in the early years of the 470s were by a narrow margin persuaded against war with Athens (11.50) – and are unavoidable on the many difficult questions of chronology that scar the period. Plutarch's lives of Athenian politicans turn up circumstantial biographical detail, often tendentious, concerning many of the leading figures of the period (Themistocles, Cimon, Aristides) as well as scraps of partisan contemporary sources (Ion of Chios or Stesimbrotus of Thasos, for example), embedded in a cake of retrospective moralism. The Aristotelian *Constitution of the Athenians* (or *Athenaion Politeia*) gives again a sketchy and schematic account of the politics of the period, pairing in any period a popular and an aristocratic figure as the two leading men in the city: Miltiades and Xanthippus (the father of Pericles), Themistocles and Aristides, Ephialtes and Cimon (the son of Miltiades), Pericles and Thucydides (the son of Melesias) (*Ath. Pol.* 28.2). Apparently at a loss for solid information (at least for internal affairs) on the years following the Persian wars, the author of the *Athenaion Politeia* characterises them, in terms of the events that they precede, as the 'Areopagite constitution': since the reforms of Ephialtes in 462 removed a number of (largely unknown) powers from the ancient council of the Areopagus, that council is deemed in the years leading up to the reforms to have been predominant (*Ath. Pol.* 23-25.1),[10] this predominance the result of prompt action taken to evacuate Attica in advance of the Persian invasion. Finally, there is a spattering of epigraphic and artistic material, invariably with difficulties of dating. In the case of a number of pieces of monumental art, the works themselves no longer survive: we are dependent on the descriptions of the second-century AD traveller Pausanias.

Should we then surrender in the face of this lack of evidence? The ancient historian, inclined by inclination and long practice to make a meal out of the most meagre crumbs, sees it only as a challenge. In the often quoted description of Iris Murdoch's from her novel *The Nice and the Good*, early Greek history 'is a game with very few pieces where the skill of the player lies in complicating the rules. The isolated and uneloquent fact must be exhibited within a tissue of hypothesis subtle enough to make it speak ....'[11] In the case of this book, the main way in which the rules will be complicated will be through an attempt to marry literary and historical approaches. This is in part in order to discover a more historically plausible reading, one that does not jar with the play's historical and ideological context or with its main themes. But it is hoped that it will have another result: that is, to reveal the *Persians* as a more sophisticated work than it has yet been seen to be.

The *Persians* has indeed often been deemed a disappointment.

> A Queen and a number of old men stand or move about listening to bad news. [The *Persians*] is little more than a lamentation for the fall of great and ancient Persia as a notable instance of God's vengeance upon earthly pride. No doubt it was chiefly valued in antiquity, as it is valued now, for the superb description of the battle of Salamis.

With such faint praise J.A.K. Thomson damned the *Persians* in his splendidly titled *Irony. An Historical Introduction.*[12] Thomson's verdict on the *Persians* is not ostensibly ironic. Nor is such a damp reaction atypical of twentieth-century critics of the play. 'The *Persians*', wrote H. Weir Smyth in his 1924 *Aeschylean Tragedy*, 'is far from revealing its author at the topmost pitch of excellence'; the best idea of the play, he added, its innovative setting in Persia, is one that Aeschylus derived from Phrynichus.[13] 'What would it be', asks Richmond Lattimore, 'without the poetry?'[14]

Explicit pronouncements on the relative quality of ancient dramas are no longer the fashion. But a certain uneasiness still underlies even the most rewarding of recent approaches to the play. The back of Edith Hall's 1996 edition promises the following highlights:

> A ghost summoned with bizarre rituals from the underworld, the elaborate protocol of the Persian court, desperate lamentation, self-mutilation, and a thrilling eye-witness account of the battle of Salamis – these are some of the features of Aeschylus' *Persians* which make it one of the most exciting examples of ancient theatre.

As 'the only extended account of the Persian wars by an author who fought in them', the publicity material continues, 'it is a unique document of the Athenian historical imagination.' The commentary will focus on 'visual and aural effects', Aeschylus' 'extraordinarily rich imagery', and 'the play's unrivalled contribution to Athenian democratic ideology'. Probably few would deny the value of the play as historical evidence – whether it be as evidence of 'hoplite citizen ideology' or of the topography of the battle of Salamis – but the play's historical value surely contributes nothing to its dramatic or literary worth. Nor would anyone now doubt the importance of the visual in Attic drama. Plays, after all, require performance. Its visual and aural effects, however, like its historical value, seem often to be appealed to in compensation for a lack of more conventional dramatic virtues. 'Certainly', wrote R.M. Hickman, 'this play would be dull without the ghost.'[15] As this comment comes in the course of a book entitled *Ghostly Etiquette on the Classical Stage*, there may be an element of special pleading. Arguably, however, a similar reliance on the visual underlies even the more recent – and important – discussion of Oliver Taplin. According to Taplin, Aeschylus has deliberately not introduced any preparation for the raising of the ghost of Darius into earlier scenes: 'Since the ghost-raising is the most exotic and exciting event in the play it could easily come to dominate the whole work. Aeschylus wishes to avoid this and to give the disaster of the Persian army and of Xerxes full play.'[16] By conceding the possibility that one episode of the play might overbalance the remainder, and by failing to find any thematic or ideological context for Darius' appearance in the play, Taplin is in danger of reducing the play to little more than a series of unconnected tableaux, of conflicting images elbowing for room on the stage.[17]

There are, without doubt, obstacles to criticism which are unique to the *Persians*. As the first extant Greek drama, it is perhaps destined to be the victim of deterministic theories of the evolution of tragedy, of spurious comparisons with predecessors of whose works we know nearly nothing.[18] These snares are common to the play's defenders as well as its critics. Christian Meier, for instance, has complimented the *Persians* by comparison with Phrynichus' *Phoenician Women*: 'Aeschylus clearly set about his subject in a more fundamentally dramatic fashion than his predecessor' – whatever that may mean.[19] Others, turning on its head the idea of the play as 'primitive pageantry',[20] have praised it precisely for its simplicity of theme. According to Conacher, the reason that critics have resorted to patriotism as a structuring theme of the play is that its actual theme, that of *hybris*, is so simple that they become bored with it:

> Thus, though the theme of the *Persae* can be quickly understood or at least mentally pigeon-holed by any schoolboy who can read a handbook, it cannot be experienced as Aeschylus meant us to experience it in this instance, until every fibre of its simple but powerful structure has been grasped as bearing, each time from

> some new direction, on the same central pathos which we are asked to share with Xerxes.[21]

The effect of the play being 'fully founded' upon *hybris* is one of 'complete adequacy', according to Jones, 'without the portentous, teasing superfluities of the other plays'.[22]

To praise the *Persians* for its simplicity, however, or in comparison with a predecessor that is no longer extant, implies a rather strained attempt to vindicate Aeschylus. If the play 'seems static and undramatic ... in terms of our conventional notions of what a tragic plot has to offer',[23] should we then reclassify the *Persians* as something other than conventional tragedy – a proto-tragedy or a historical tragedy perhaps? The play has in fact made cameo appearances as the sole representative of a seemingly endless series of genres. Sidgwick pronounced that it is 'not so much a play in the modern sense, as a picturesque presentment of a single striking incident in a setting of poetic description and lyric song'.[24] Gravenhorst described the play likewise as 'a dramatised dirge of epico-lyrical character'.[25] Gilbert Murray saw the *Persians* as 'not so much to be compared with a modern play about, say, Mary Queen of Scots, as with a Thanksgiving Service at Westminster Abbey to commemorate the Armistice of 1918 except that the service would of course be a service and the *Persae* is, after all, a drama'.[26] And the Persians has also been characterised through a whole range of musical analogies, 'nearer oratorio than drama', a cantata, or as a 'symphonic tone-poem':[27]

> the theme [of pathos] is developed, as if in a symphonic tone-poem, from premonitory hints of disaster in the parodos (soon to be lost in a rush of triumphant brass), through the central portions of the play where every instrument is tuned to the disaster, to the final lament of the King himself as he sings his grief and guilt antiphonally with the Chorus' questioning.

The attempt to see the play on its own terms can only be applauded, but such catch-all and impressionistic descriptions are really no more than a substitute for proper criticism; they take for granted and reinforce the assumption of the play as a naive, intellectually simplistic work. Other critics likewise appear to envisage the act of criticism as a mere tracing of 'dominating motifs, ... consistently elaborated and recapitulated',[28] without attention to the connections between such themes, or to the political charge of many of these apparently abstracted motifs.[29]

The *Persians*' status as the only extant play with a historical subject-matter gives rise to further problems: can it be judged by the same criteria as other plays? That Aeschylus succeeds in 'universalising' his subject-matter appears to be a universal consensus among literary critics; but if the emergence of transcendent truths is an essential characteristic of tragedy, then the selection of raw material so rooted in a particular historical context constitutes at least a severe obstacle to the *Persians* attaining the status of true tragedy.[30] A parallel difficulty lies in the play's portrayal of the Persians. When H.D. Broadhead insists on the play's status as a 'genuine tragedy',[31] it is on the grounds of its 'comparative absence of patriotic bias'. As he puts it in another context, 'if the *Persae* was meant to be a genuine tragedy, we expect to find that the poet has done his best to view the scene through Persian eyes, and that whatever his feelings towards the Persian invader, he has, as a dramatist and a delineator of character, entered with imaginative insight into the heart of the Persian tragedy'.[32] Any such definition of tragedy, when applied to the *Persians*, is perhaps bound to lead to a degree of apologetic: the comparative absence of patriotism may save the *Persians* for tragedy, but the implied presence of any patriotism is presumably still a regrettable qualification. Gilbert Murray made explicit his feeling that patriotism and art rest uncomfortably alongside one another when he judged the *Persians* the 'only celebration of a victory in war which reaches the rank of the highest poetry'.[33]

More often today such discomfort with the patriotic nature of the play lies unspoken. Even a critic such as Edith Hall, who addresses the chauvinism of the play directly – indeed, who seeks to redress a reluctance to discuss such 'arrogant and insistent chauvinism'[34] – seems still to find herself in an uncomfortable balancing-act between the nineteenth-century view of the play as 'mere xenophobic self-congratulation' and the usual modern view that it is relatively sympathetic to its Persian subjects. She finds genuine tragic pathos in the play, and takes issue with those who see the play as not a genuine tragedy. But the solution to the problem of these two conflicting interpretations that she offers is surely not so very far from 'xenophobic self-congratulation': 'Aeschylus presents Persian characteristics as vices exactly correlative to the cardinal democratic Athenian values. Portrayal of the enemy has thus become self-definition and self-praise.' Self-praise but not self-congratulation; self-definition but not xenophobia.[35]

How – and indeed whether – such a balancing-act can be maintained will be one of the main issues addressed in this book. In the course of answering these questions it will be necessary also to confront, and dispense with, many of the preconceptions of the nature of 'genuine' tragedy against which the *Persians* has struggled.

Part I

Framing the Play

1

Aeschylus the historian?

In what does the historical value of Aeschylus' *Persians* consist? The play is, of course, the only extant 'historical' tragedy from classical Athens. Such a statement can mean many things, however. It could mean, for example, simply a tragedy capable of exploitation by the modern historian. It is apparently this sense of the word that lies behind Angus Bowie's recent survey of historical tragedies:[1]

> Thus, in this 'historical' category, we have up to eleven 'historical' plays on Persian subjects; four on Macedon, but none certainly historical; one each on Sicily, Mausolus and Alexander; *Eumenides* on Athens; plus the strongest candidates among the other extant plays, Sophocles' *Philoctetes*, and Euripides' *Supplices* (?424-420, relatable to Delium), *Troades* (415, relatable to the massacre at Melos), and *Orestes* (409, relatable to recent events in Athens).

As Bowie's parentheses show, the historical status of any tragedy depends for him on the presence, often only implicit, within a play of some contemporary reference, or at least some contemporary resonance. This presupposes a sadly restricted definition of history: historians may legitimately search only those texts which openly declare that they are carrying politically relevant material; they may then only examine select 'historical' passages. Do other tragedies – those with no easily datable references, with exclusively mythological subject matter, and with no parallels evident between their characters and contemporary politicians – tell us nothing of historical significance?

Another, surely uncontroversial, definition of the historical tragedy – and one by which the *Persians* is restored to its unique status – would be simply as a tragedy 'dealing with', or based upon, a historical theme.[2]

This is only uncontroversial, however, by avoiding certain important questions. Does such a distinction have, or require, any ancient authority? Were plays with a historical subject seen as a discrete sub-genre within tragedy?[3] (It is surely significant, in this context, that the *Persians* was performed alongside three 'mythological' plays.[4]) Was there even a clear distinction drawn between 'history' and 'myth'?[5] Most importantly, *how* is it that the play or the playwright 'deals with' this historical theme? As we have seen, on the back of Edith Hall's 1996 edition it is announced that, 'as the only extended account of the Persian Wars by an author who fought in them, it is a unique document of the Athenian historical imagination'. In what sense, however, can it be said that the play provides, let alone that it *is*, an account? Did Aeschylus intend to offer a historical account? If so, is it only the play's descriptions of Salamis, of Psyttaleia, and of the return of Xerxes through Greece – studded with assurances of the Messenger's first-hand knowledge[6] – that qualify the play as a historical tragedy?

The idea that Aeschylus' purpose in writing was, either primarily or in part, informed by a historical duty, is an article of faith amongst many twentieth-century readers.[7] The most extreme expression of this view is that of Gilbert Murray:[8] 'with the *Persae* we seem to be on firmer ground .... For one thing it is not only a play: it is a direct, historical record ....' For Murray, the fact that the *Persians* is a play, and that Aeschylus is a poet, is no obstacle to the historical value of his account, but rather the opposite: Aeschylus was 'not only an eyewitness but a combatant, and one who, beside his Greek sense of poetry, had also the peculiar Greek power of describing what he saw'. A similar line is pursued by Jacqueline de Romilly: 'on pourrait penser qu'Eschyle a traité l'évènement avec la liberté d'un poète: il n'en est rien. Sa tragédie est, en fait, une de nos sources – la seule à émaner d'un temoin direct et authentique, qui s'était battu à Salamine, comme il s'était battu à Marathon. Il était là. Il avait vu. Et son évocation a le relief et l'intensité de l'expérience immédiate.'[9] The objections to such a fundamentalist position scarcely need stating. The projection of a historical purpose onto Aeschylus too easily becomes a *carte blanche* for the cavalier treatment of his play as a historical source. It is surely too comfortable and convenient an assumption that Aeschylus' poetic powers of description should have been harnessed *exclusively* to the task of creating an accurate eye-witness account – as opposed, for example, to that of creating dramatic impact, or ensuring dramatic unity.[10] More generally, even if we can take for granted Aeschylus' intention to write history (and that surely is a great 'if', given that the same cannot even be said unequivocally for Herodotus, writing half a century later), good intentions cannot guarantee success. We all know now – and I think it possible that some people knew it in 1940 – that no account can ever be 'zero-focalised', that bias does not consist solely in malevolent or sycophantic interpolations or excisions operated upon an otherwise seamless historical account.

The argument that Aeschylus' purpose was, at least in part, historical has come to be presented more subtly, in such a way as to account for these objections. The fact that the *Persians* is a play may result, in this view, in a certain amount of literary distortion, but a distortion that is strictly limited and identifiable, a sort of shell that can be cracked open to reveal the gleaming kernel of an eyewitness historical account. So, according to de Romilly again, 'Eschyle s'est contenté de très légères déformations, portant, non pas sur des faits, mais sur leur interprétation'.[11] Macan was happy to declare that Aeschylus 'must remain the regulative witness' of the accounts of Salamis, only 'making all allowance for poetic treatment and dramatic situation'.[12] The difficulty of reading tragedy is envisaged by historians in terms of a set of limited caveats: the temptation, for example, must be resisted to substitute historical for mythical characters;[13] we cannot blame Aeschylus for failing to be comprehensive, as we might (surely wrongly?) blame Herodotus or Thucydides;[14] 'the poet may be expected to heighten the ferocity of the struggle, but he will not alter its nature. The valour (or birth) of the combatants may be magnified; their military identity will not be disguised.'[15]

A corollary of this argument is the idea of the constraining effect represented by his audience. This view envisages Aeschylus' historical purpose as secondary: Aeschylus may have aimed primarily for dramatic effect, but he could surely not have got away with any substantial alterations in front of an audience made up of veterans.[16] As Kitto colourfully observed, 'we cannot indeed assert that the Athenian audience, regaled with such inaccuracy, cheered like mad, but they did give the first prize to the trilogy of which the *Persians* formed part, which makes it likely that the play was not received with dissent and with cries of: 'Hey, Mister! It didn't happen like *that*!'[17] There are, as it were, margins of credibility beyond which Aeschylus simply could not go if he wanted to keep his audience in their seats.

This must be true. Only those margins could be very wide.[18] Aeschylus, for example, may well exaggerate the importance of Psyttaleia vis-à-vis Salamis;[19] he appears to misrepresent Darius as guiltless by comparison with his son Xerxes;[20] his lists of Persian names have been found to be 'to a great extent fictitious', created with 'the plain intention to create an impression of enormous losses';[21] most remarkably Aeschylus can, as we will see in more detail, portray the Persian empire as all but annihilated, waiting for a single knock-out blow – a grotesque exaggeration perhaps, but one surely in which his audience might have indulged him, in which he may himself in some sense have believed.[22] Broadhead suggests comfortingly that the points of a narrative emphasised by our dramatist 'would be precisely those best remembered by the audience', and that therefore these points 'would be least likely to suffer serious distortion':[23] Aeschylus may – as an illustration of divine Providence – have invented the story of the Persians' flight across the frozen river Strymon (495-507), reassuringly removed from the experience of his audience, but would not so blithely have tampered with the record of Salamis for fear of correction. But how confident can we be of this? Aeschylus' 'account' of the events of the Persian Wars clearly allows a striking degree of latitude in interpretation. It has been suggested, for example, that the events on the island of Psyttaleia recorded by Herodotus were the fabrication of an 'anti-Themistoclean tradition'.[24] Aeschylus cannot provide us with the evidence conclusively to squash this doubt.

Even the advocates of some residual form of historical duty must acknowledge the existence of other competing pressures. The poet, according to Conacher, will highlight only such 'historical events as provide ... a striking example ... of some great truth or insight about life which he finds fundamental to his own view of tragic experience ...'.[25] Broadhead likewise maintains that Aeschylus, while he has 'adhered broadly to the historical facts', has 'striven to raise the historical to the level of the poetic and philosophic'.[26] For Harry Avery, one of the main problems for Aeschylus was to combine 'exalting the Greek victory and at the same time not doing violence to the historical circumstances which obtained in 472'.[27] These critics arguably underestimate, however, the tension that exists between these pressures and a supposed historical duty.[28] One of the means by which, according to Broadhead, Aeschylus attains to 'the level of the poetic and philosophic' is – in plain contradiction of the facts of Marathon – by transforming Darius into his own blameless mouthpiece. Avery succeeds in resolving the apparently irreconcilable clash between patriotism and historical truth only by speculating that in the course of the play's final scene the Queen returns bringing Xerxes a new set of clothes – clothes that symbolise the resurgence of Persia after her defeat at the hands of the Greeks.

None of these critics, moreover, considers the possibility of what we might call crudely unconscious or unintentional distortion. Surely, however, other constraints, ideological rather than historical, may have outweighed historical concerns both with Aeschylus and his audience? This is particularly clear in the case of Aeschylus' evidence for the Persian court. The ostensibly Persian standpoint of the play might seem at first, as Richardson suggests,[29] to make care over historical detail important. One could equally argue the opposite position, however: that the portrayal of the Persian court *demanded* reference to caricatured Persian features, as much to ensure the recognition of the Athenian audience as to indulge their prejudices.[30] As Hall has sensibly observed, 'a balance must be struck between the misguided use of the play as a truthful empirical source for Persia and denial that it contains any features which derive from observation of the distinctive protocols and practices of the Persian court'. How that balance can be struck, the question of whether in any instance a practice is authentic or the result of Greek ignorance or prejudice, is, Hall concedes, 'one of the challenges this drama presents'.[31]

Even if, as we must, we dispense with the comforting belief that Aeschylus felt obliged to provide an accurate historical record, Aeschylus may still provide us with certain limits to our historical reconstructions of events: 'it would be odd', as Pelling has written, for example, if Psyttaleia played no role at all' in the events of Salamis.[32] More specific historical conclusions are also possible. We may, for example, argue that the list of Darius' conquests in the Greek world (857-906) has been tailored to represent Xerxes' subsequent losses. 'Now there is no doubt', the Chorus conclude, 'that through wars we are enduring the gods' reversal of our fortunes' (904-5). As Kebric has commented, 'the implication is that all these possessions were now in the danger of being lost, and, if Aeschylus were attempting to heighten the dramatic irony of his play by having the chorus reflect upon areas his Greek audience knew *had already been taken from the Persians*, then the date of the performance … can be used as a *terminus post quem* for the recovery of Cnidus and all the locations mentioned in the list'.[33] That Cnidus or Cyprus was free from Persian control by 472 may not be a conclusion to everyone's taste, but it is beyond any serious question that this sort of deduction – which takes account of, indeed relies upon, the dramatic function of the passage, and which does not require a catch-all historical purpose on Aeschylus' part – is a reasonable, if not a conclusive,[34] line of argument. The only serious question is how best Aeschylus might best have made ironic use of historical circumstances. We must, however, recognise that Aeschylus was free to do more than merely embroider the historical facts of the war, to apply a 'wide choice of detail and emotional colouring', in the words of Podlecki:[35] the emotional, the patriotic, the artistic colouring of the play has in many instances had the effect of distorting the 'known facts'.

2

Politics and partisanship

The other main historical 'application' of the play – on which I will have more to say than on its value as evidence for Persia or for Salamis – also centres on the intentions of Aeschylus, more particularly his political intentions: was the play written in support of any single political figure, either the moderate Aristides[1] – according to Herodotus, the leader of the Athenian force on Psyttaleia (8.95) – or, as is more commonly claimed, Themistocles?

The question rests partly on Aeschylus' choice of Salamis as a subject: in the context of Themistocles' imminent (or recent) ostracism,[2] against the background of an alleged dispute in Athens over the relative importance of Salamis and Marathon, 'could a playwright whose sympathies were not with Themistocles ... have chosen to write a play on this theme?'[3] But the question of Aeschylus' political commitment depends also on one's opinion of the relative emphasis given to Themistocles or Aristides in the play – neither man is named – and on a number of specific allusions to incidents in the career of Themistocles recorded by Herodotus.[4] The Chorus' description, for example, of the Athenians' 'spring of silver, a treasury in the earth' (238) has been seen by A.J. Podlecki as a reference to Themistocles' advice, duly accepted by the Athenians, that a new vein of silver from the Laureion mines should be used to build two hundred warships rather than distributed amongst the citizens (7.144.1).[5] These ships, built ostensibly for a war against the Athenians' island neighbours, the Aeginetans, proved invaluable at Salamis; indeed Herodotus goes further in saying that this local war saved Greece through forcing the Athenians to become seamen (7.144.2). The Messenger's remark on the hatefulness of the name of Salamis (284-5) has been interpreted similarly as an allusion to the Delphic oracle which advised the Athenians to take refuge from the

Persians behind a 'wooden wall' (7.141.3). When there had been a dispute as to whether the wooden wall referred to her navy or to a stockade that had formerly surrounded the Acropolis, Themistocles introduced the clinching argument. The god had spoken also of 'divine Salamis', that the island would 'destroy the children of women' (7.141.4), but the oracle, he argued, would surely have read 'wretched Salamis' (*ô skhetliê Salamis*) rather than 'divine Salamis' if the island's inhabitants were destined to die there (7.143.1).[6]

There is also evidence external to the play suggestive of the alignment of politically like-minded poets and politicans. Pericles, seen by the *Athenaion Politeia* as the political successor of Themistocles and Ephialtes (28.2), acted while still a young man as the *choregos* or sponsor for the *Persians* in 472 (*IG* II^2 2318 = *TGrF* I DID A1). Aeschylus is said in the hypothesis to the *Persians* to have based his play on Phrynichus' *Phoenician Women* and, just as Pericles served as *choregos* for Aeschylus, the *Phoenician Women* was (probably[7]) the play for which Themistocles acted as *choregos* in 476 (Plut. *Them.* 5.4).[8] Two plays of similar plot then, and perhaps – in so far as we can tell – of similar slant, were produced by men of similar political leanings. Arguably also Aeschylus' preference for politicians 'of the left' (to use an inappropriate modern term) is reflected also in his later plays. The Argive monarchy of the *Suppliant Women*, performed probably in 463,[9] reveals a distinct emphasis on the sovereignty of the people.[10] His *Eumenides*, performed in 458 in the aftermath of the reforms of Ephialtes, is commonly seen as expressing his approval of those reforms – an approval tempered in some readings with a caution – through its staging of the original constitution of the council of the Areopagus as a homicide court, precisely the chief role left to it in the wake of Ephialtes ([Arist.] *Ath. Pol.* 57.3).[11] As Aeschylus was the court poet of the left, so the right also had its representative – in Sophocles. Plutarch preserves a story of how Cimon, the son of Miltiades, and the panel of other generals took the place of the judges at the Dionysia and preferred the young Sophocles to Aeschylus, who a little later left in indignation for Sicily (Plut. *Cim.* 8.78-9).

In addition to our reconstructing these internal political genealogies, we may also be able to detect an alignment between foreign and home policy: on the one hand an affinity between democratic radicalism and a hawkish anti-Spartan policy, and on the other between a commitment to the 'dual hegemony' of Athens and Sparta and a political conservatism. Cimon is reported in all ancient sources as a lover of Sparta (Plut. *Cim.* 10.7, 14.3, 16.3), naming one of his sons, for example, Lacedaimonius[12] (and others Eleius and Thessalus) (Plut. *Cim.* 16.1). When an earthquake prompted a revolt of the Spartans' indigenous slave population, the Messenian helots (Thuc. 1.101.2) – the so-called Third Messenian War – Cimon led an Athenian expedition to help in quashing this uprising, proclaiming (in Plutarch's allusion to the ideal of the dual hegemony) that Greece should not be allowed to become lame (Plut. *Cim.* 16.10). The reforms of Ephialtes, however, coincided – the precise chronology is virtually unfathomable – with the dramatic failure of Cimon's policy of *rapprochement* with Sparta. He and his forces were dismissed from the Peloponnese – ostensibly, Thucydides tells us, because there was no longer a need of help, but in reality out of a Spartan fear that the Athenians might combine with the rebels (Thuc. 1.102.3-4)[13] – and, after making an unsuccessful attempt, according to Plutarch, to overturn Ephialtes' reforms, Cimon was ostracised (Plut. *Cim.* 15.3-5, 17.3, *Per.* 9.5). The Athenians reacted to the dismissal of Cimon's force by breaking off their alliance with the Spartans and forging other friendships with Sparta's enemies, Argos and Thessaly (Thuc. 1.102.3-4). At the time of the subsequent battle of Tanagra (458) between Athenians and Spartans, four years after the reforms of Ephialtes, Thucydides tells us of the existence of a pro-Spartan third column within Athens, urging the Spartans on in secret, hoping to put an end to the democracy (Thuc. 1.107.4). Aeschylus' *Eumenides*, by its setting in Argos rather than Mycenae and by its emphasis on the perpetuity of the mythical alliance between Athens and Argos, has often been seen as celebrating the modern-day treaty, and as corroborating the connection between domestic politics and foreign policy suggested by other sources.[14]

This political schism also has a mythological dimension. For even Theseus is drawn in. According to Plutarch, Theseus was held in greater esteem in Athens in the period after the Persian wars because he had been sighted at Marathon (Plut. *Thes.* 35.8).[15] Themistocles was haunted by the success of Miltiades just as Theseus had been driven by the desire to emulate Heracles (Plut. *Thes.* 6.8-9).[16] Cimon then, Miltiades' son, was responsible for the recovery of the bones of Theseus from the island of Scyros (Plut. *Cim.* 8.6, *Thes.* 36),[17] and may 'have been believed to have been a descendant of Theseus'.[18] Theseus was also 'a favourite subject of the painter Polygnotus' (Paus. 1.15.3, 10.29.3), whose 'connections with Cimon were very close' – in that he is said to have had an affair with Cimon's sister Elpinice (Plut. *Cim.* 4.5) and so to have modelled a Trojan captive on her in his paintings in the Stoa Poikile or Painted Colonnade. 'Was Miltiades being sold to the Athenians as a second Theseus?', asks Podlecki.[19]

That Aeschylus chose Salamis then, in preference to Marathon, as the centre-piece for his play is thought to be evidence of his support for Themistocles, of a 'propaganda battle'[20] waged between the supporters of Cimon and Themistocles as to the relative importance of the two battles. 'Each side enlisted the help not only of poets, but also of painters and sculptors, to impress its own version of the facts on public opinion.'[21] This 'battle of the battles' provides a kind of axis around which to order the politics of the *Athenaion Politeia's* 'Areopagite Constitution' into two convenient and comprehensible party platforms: on the one side you have Plataea and Marathon, Miltiades and Cimon, a muted Panhellenism and pro-Spartan *tendence* and a balanced hoplite democracy, and on the other Salamis, Themistocles and Ephialtes, an anti-Spartan imperialism and a radical naval democracy.[22] The *Athenaion Politeia* includes a story of a conspiracy between Themistocles and Ephialtes (25.4), a story that has usually been judged chronologically impossible.[23] But might Aeschylus himself – through his *Persians* and *Eumenides* – provide a bridge between the two men, and give some substance to this myth of their association?

There are a number of problems with this approach. We can, to begin with, pick and prod at particular joints in this great structure, the association of Themistocles with the *Phoenician Women*, for example, or the anecdotal nature of the story of Sophocles and Cimon. Can we assume then that a *choregos*, especially perhaps one as young as Pericles in 472, was responsible for the 'political texturing' of a play,[24] or that Marathon and Plataea, in so far as they may be said to have been played down, have not been played down for sound aesthetic rather than political reasons, the desire to continue to play on the 'land-and-sea theme', or to avoid the clumsiness of a double climax.[25] Of course, aesthetic reasons do not exclude political ones. There are more profound objections to this picture, however.

First, the picture that it creates is simply too tidy. Podlecki speaks of 'a convergence of scattered lines of evidence',[26] but is it anything more than wishful thinking that persuades us that they converge? The tendency to create tidy patterns is, of course, a tendency of our ancient sources: so, the young love turned to rivalry of Themistocles and Aristides (Plut. *Them.* 3.1-3) or of Peisistratus and Solon (Plut. *Sol.* 1),[27] or the neat grid of popular versus aristocratic politicians provided by the *Athenaion Politeia* (28.2-3). As the story of Themistocles' and Ephialtes' collaboration may demonstrate, an idea that a politician was, in some sense, the political heir to another can easily become transformed into a narrative tradition that connects them explicitly. For this reason we should be sceptical, for example, of Plutarch's casual observation that it was Aristides more than anyone who promoted Cimon as a foil to Themistocles (Plut. *Cim.* 5.4), or that Themistocles took his own life out of despair at no longer being able to eclipse the brave undertakings of Cimon (Plut. *Cim.* 18.6). For the same reason we can be more confident of the contribution of the otherwise unknown Archestratus to the reforms of Ephialtes (*Ath. Pol.* 25.2) than we can be of Pericles'.[28]

Despite the schematising character of ancient sources, it is worth noting, moreover, that not all the details preserved fit the pattern so neatly. A tradition recorded in Plutarch's life of Cimon portrays our conservative hero playing a vital role in motivating the Athenians to put into practice Themistocles' plan of evacuation, and acquitting himself brilliantly in the battle of Salamis (Plut. *Cim.* 5.2-3). Either party lines were more fluid than has been imagined,[29] or, far from a battle between Salamis and Marathon, we have here a battle *for* Salamis. It was Pericles, according to Plutarch, who proposed the motion that Cimon should be recalled from exile (17.6). (Can we be confident then of Pericles' political leanings in 472?[30]) Similarly it was Themistocles who, relying on his prestige in Sparta, engineered the rushed rebuilding of the walls of Athens, and then forged the uneasy peace with Sparta after the war (Thuc. 1.90-2). Themistocles' observation in Thucydides that equal counsel depended on equal strength (Thuc. 1.91.6-7) has overtones arguably of the idea of dual hegemony ascribed to Cimon. We may then, through our reliance on 'secondary' ancient authors, and through our own desire for order, be being lulled into an over-schematic vision.

I have, of course, pruned the evidence for this propaganda battle savagely to its main branches. The battle of the battles might more aptly be described as a war on several fronts: the murals of the Theseion[31] and of the Stoa Poikile (Paus. 1.15),[32] the Marathon group of sculptures at Delphi (Paus. 10.10.1-2),[33] the murals of the Cnidian Lesche at Delphi,[34] Bacchylides 18,[35] the Persian War epigrams[36] and even Pindar.[37] However, the more closely one looks at any of the branches of this evidence, the less likely it appears that they belong to the same tree.

Particularly problematic is the propaganda battle fought on the field of myth. Cimon's recovery of the bones of Theseus, for example, has been seen by Podlecki as part of a programme of the manipulation of myth by which 'Salamis and Themistocles, whose star had been for some time on the wane, were finally and firmly eclipsed'.[38] Many of the myths of Theseus, Podlecki speculates, may have originated as 'embellishments of the material in the traditional *Theseia*' contemporary to Cimon and Themistocles. It is very possibly the case that certain elements of the Theseus myth 'originate' in some sense in the political context of the first half of the fifth century. Theseus' building of a fleet (Plut. *Thes.* 19.9), for example, or the identification of the king of the Scyrians responsible for the death of Theseus as Lycomedes (Plut. *Thes.* 35.6; cf. *Cim.* 8.5-7), uncannily reminiscent of the genos of the *Lycomidai* of which Themistocles was a member (Plut. *Them.* 1.4).[39] But in what way were such details generated? The story related in scholia that Theseus was ostracised as the result of a false charge of aiming for tyranny can be explained, for Podlecki, in terms of the 'supporters of the exiled and disgraced Themistocles' turning 'Cimon's Theseian propaganda back against himself'. But not every fragment of a myth can have been a weapon. It is at least equally possible that such details are the product of what we might describe as a secondary industry of embellishment, the spontaneous reflection – uncharged by partisan political meaning – of a political controversy in a mythological idiom. A parallel might be the way in which the portrayal of Minos or of Midas in fifth-century art was coloured – with, for example, Midas being assimilated to the Great King – by the experience of the Persian wars.[40]

It is hard, after all, to see how such subtle allusions might have constituted effective political weapons. Francis comments that 'it would have been easy enough for Cimon to hint at the coincidence' of Lycomides and the Lycomidai:[41] but this is to presume that the Athenians sat in wait for such allusions, and that such mythical slanders were the stock-in-trade of contemporary politics, the equivalent of accusations of undeclared directorships or donations. Similar doubts can be raised over other such mythical allusions. Clearly such clever allusions as the word-plays that have been detected in Bacchylides 18 by John Barron (on Eion, recaptured by Cimon from the Persians, or on the names of Cimon's sons)[42] or what we might call pictorial puns such as Polygnotus' supposed modelling of Priam's daughter Laodice on the sister of Cimon, Elpinice (Plut. *Cim.* 4.6), or the naming of two Amazons on a bell-krater by Polygnotus as Dolope (for Cimon's Dolopian pirates?) and Peisianassa (for Cimon's brother-in-law, Peisianax?)[43] would not have propelled crowds to man barricades. Sly reminders of Cimon in highly-wrought verse, or of his brother-in-law through rare and refined pottery, are more likely to raise appreciative smiles than alter political persuasions. Of course, that Bacchylides' Cimonian echoes adorn the myth of Theseus' arrival from Troizen may be significant in the light of Cimon's return of Theseus from Scyros, but – even if that were so – it is surely the return of Theseus itself, and Cimon's possible rebuilding of the Theseion to house him, that would have bought Cimon any popularity, not the reflection of that action in verse. There is no such broader context for the identification of Laodice and Elpinice. Why Laodice, a Trojan captive? Why should such an identification have assisted Cimon or flattered Elpinice?[44] (Not, presumably, in so far as it reminded a broader public of her liaison with the painter?) It is surely more likely, in fact, that the identification of Elpinice with Laodice, like the identification of Pericles in the shield of Athena Parthenos,[45] and the accompanying tradition of Elpinice's relationship with Polygnotus, are both second-generation embellishments based on the known collaboration of Polygnotus and Cimon.[46]

The effectiveness of such very abstruse forms of propaganda has, in general, however, been taken for granted by a number of scholars,[47] for whom consequently the expansion of the Cimonian propaganda battle has become a kind of 'intellectual dot-to-dot'.[48] All Athenian buildings built within a certain period are dubbed Cimonian ('we may assume', Erika Simon tells us, 'that Kimon rebuilt the sanctuary of Poseidon and Athena'[49]). Religious devotion (to Theseus) translates directly into political support (for Cimon). All Amazons are straightforwardly Persians,[50] and 'bringing in the Amazons wherever possible had propagandistic value' (again exclusively for Cimon, it seems).[51] We can also put the pieces of the jigsaw together, and fill in the psychological motives of the characters and the order in which the propaganda moves were made: Cimon's actions in Eion and Scyros were in response to Themistocles' support of Phrynichus' *Phoenician Women*;[52] Themistocles' building of the temple of Artemis Aristoboule was an attempt to stem the decline in his popularity;[53] this temple-building in turn prompted Cimon's seeking out of Theseus' bones,[54] and it was to the transfer of Theseus finally that Cimon 'owed most of his popularity'.[55]

Of course, rival politicians must have advertised their achievements. Herodotus indeed tells us of how the friends of Miltiades reminded people at the time of his trial of Marathon and of his capture of Lemnos (6.136.2).[56] Poets, painters and (perhaps less plausibly) potters may very well have formed entourages around prominent politicians: we may be able to reconstruct something approaching a 'Cimonian circle'[57] comprising some or all of Pindar, Ion of Chios, Melanthius, Archelaus, Pheidias, Pherecydes, Sophocles, Timocreon and Simonides.[58] Though some of what has been termed Cimonian propaganda must be dismissed as either fanciful or ineffectual, and though we must abandon any illusion that it is possible to reconstruct a full narrative of Athenian politics in the period, there is surely a kernel of events (the return of Theseus' bones) and buildings or monuments (the Theseion, for example, or the Marathon group of sculptures at Delphi) that can securely be identified with Cimon, and which might have translated into political support. However – and this is the crucial point – such activities would surely only have been politically successful in so far as they harnessed broader, pre-existing feelings of piety or patriotism.[59] Moreover, if the object of such initiatives had ever been seen to be too overtly political, it would surely have undermined their political effect. The elevation of Theseus and of Miltiades must then have been seen as motivated by family or religious devotion; the connection that the same values were alive and well in Miltiades, or in his son Cimon, was more likely a connection that was made by others.[60]

We may not, at any rate, on the basis of other such evidence, prejudge the nature of any political stance taken by Aeschylus in the *Persians*, nor indeed whether Aeschylus is likely to adopt any such stance. When we turn to the evidence of the *Persians* for such a propaganda battle, very similar questions must be asked. The evidence of the play in may ways belies any black and white political interpretation. As Hans van Wees has observed, it is striking that in the course of the Queen's interrogation of the Chorus on the Athenians and their resources, it is the spears and shields of Athens that are emphasised rather than her ships and oars (240).[61] Moreover, even if we were to accept the play's pro-Themistoclean stance, another question awaits: how might such advertisement have been realised through a play? The political propaganda described by Podlecki – like much of the supposed propaganda through poetry and pottery that we have seen – is arguably rather subtle.[62] 'Partisan politics in tragedy', as Malcolm Heath has written, 'apparently works by stealth.'[63] To take a rather weaker example than those quoted above, when Xerxes blames some *daimon* for the disaster that has overtaken the Persians, or when Darius says that the gods have taken their revenge for the Persians' 'burning and overturning of the gods' images', these are intended, we are assured, as echoes of well-known Themistoclean sentiments reported in Herodotus: 'the theme of "divine cooperation" in the *Persians* might have reminded the audience of him.'[64] This assumes not only that Aeschylus' audiences were adept at picking up on such references, but also that Themistocles' emphasis of the theme of divine cooperation, or of sacrilege, was sufficiently unique – a deliberate archaism? – as to allow of 'reference'.[65] Were the ancient Athenians ever so political, they were still human.

How, moreover, would such a series of scattered allusions have inspired an audience to support Themistocles? Podlecki pays regular lip-service to Aeschylus' literary genius, but the political significance that he finds consists of allusions to contemporary events that appear to work on an entirely different level from the rest of the play.[66] Podlecki talks of these allusions as themes, yet he makes no attempt to anchor these to other themes integral to the play.[67] If such political allusions were no more than asides, they would surely have undermined the dramatic impact of the play, and would very probably have had little effect in themselves. (We might compare the way in which playwrights felt it necessary to veil anachronistic references to the theatre for fear of being too modern.[68]) If, as Forrest states – uncompromisingly and unmistakably – Aeschylus had no qualms whatever about his plays being used as 'vehicles of propaganda on specific political issues', then the *Persians* would surely have seemed little more than a rigged bout of political wrestling.[69] The less overtly political a play, however, surely the more politically effective.[70]

3

Aeschylus, Atossa and Athenian ideology

It is tempting to suppose, given the failings of such narrowly political readings of tragedy, that any such attempts to describe the political dimension of the play are bound to be similarly flawed. The fact that a case can be made out for Aeschylus' support of Aristides as well as of Themistocles leads Conacher to comment on the dangers that 'historical critics' will face when they try to 'burden the playwright with specific historical causes'.[1] 'The ransacking of tragedy for indications of the political views of tragic poets', Kenneth Dover writes with authority, 'is seldom profitable and may be disastrous.'[2] That something is done badly, however, does not mean that it cannot be done better. If we accept that any 'political message' must be rooted in the central themes or arguments of the play in order to be effective, ransacking is no longer at issue. We will return to the question of Aeschylus' political commitment in Part III – in the light of the discussion of the play's main themes in Part II – and suggest a political reading that runs with, rather than against, the grain of the play. The sum of the historical value of the play, however, would never consist solely in the author's expressed opinions – even if they ever were so expressed. The *Persians* has a far greater value than this, but one from which both literary critics and historians have been distracted by the concentration on the play as a 'historical account': that is, its value as evidence of ideological assumptions shared by both audience *and* playwright. In this sense, there can be no absolute distinction of 'historical' and 'non-historical' sources: no source is out of bounds for the historian.

Many classicists will ascribe everything to the ingenuity of the author. By his use of the word *theos*, one critic has written, Aeschylus 'exploits the traditionally "religious" weather language of the Greeks to express in a single description the idea of Persian description by natural phenomena and by divine nemesis'.[3] Such traditional language, of course, is unlikely to have been the object of a great deal of deliberate attention on Aeschylus' part. Another likely example of such a shared ideological assumption is Aeschylus' habit of speaking of Persian society in terms of a Greek city.[4] Susa he describes as the city of the Persians (511-12). 'What sorrow is the city suffering?', Darius enquires, as he makes his first appearance in the play (682). At the same time, Aeschylus evidently knew that there were more cities in the Persian empire, if not in Persia, than Susa (16-17, 36, 45, 52, 535, 961).[5] Such ideological assumptions are of value in their own right; but the attempt to sketch them is also an essential preliminary to the discussion of other areas of thought more subject to what we might call the playwright's autonomous voice, for example Aeschylus' political intentions.[6]

Of course, not all critics of the play have been so blind to its value as evidence of ancient ideology. One reading of the play that must be singled out for mention is that of Edith Hall, especially in her *Inventing the Barbarian*.[7] The *Persians* represents, according to Hall, 'the first unmistakable file in the archive of Orientalism, the discourse by which the European imagination has dominated Asia ever since by conceptualising its inhabitants as defeated, luxurious, emotional, cruel, and always as dangerous'.[8] We may perhaps question first whether the direct equation of ancient and modern chauvinism, indeed the assumption of an unbroken line of inheritance between them – Hall describes the 'Other' as one of the most important and influential of the Greeks' 'ideological inventions'[9] – is particularly helpful or enlightening. As Edward Said has described, the binary oppositions 'dear to the nationalist and imperialist enterprise', the sense – first revealed by the Greeks – of an 'us' and a 'them', 'each quite settled, clear, unassailably self-evident', has begun to be broken down by a modern scholarship that envisages identity as something much more fluid, not as an essentialisation but, in Said's phrase, a 'contrapuntal ensemble'.[10] It is important to be alive to a similar fluidity in the history of identity. Because the Greeks were the first to write in terms of such binary oppositions, we may be in danger of exaggerating their responsibility for the later pervasiveness of such ideas, of fitting the Greeks too easily into a modern model. The Greeks were, after all – at least in their own estimation – the underdogs in their clash with Asia. Not all barbarians came from the East. The assumption of a continuous tradition of the Orient – and a corresponding idea of Europe[11] – may indeed play into the hands of those who ascribe very different values to East and West, who believe (with Gilbert Murray) that 'with all its faults and vulgarities, and with all that it has still to learn from certain Eastern nations' the Western community 'is nevertheless, in virtue of its Hellenic and Christian heritage, called upon to lead the world'.[12]

But there are more immediate difficulties in Hall's reading of the play. In a sense indeed she provides no reading of the play. The modern view of the play as sympathetic to the Persians has led, Hall notes, to a concentration on the play's theology or political purpose and, correspondingly, to the downplaying of the antithesis between Greek and barbarian, tyranny and freedom.[13] A result of this process has been, she says, a failure to 'assess the extraordinarily powerful and original nature of the techniques deployed in the evocation of the foreign setting and characters'. 'The tragedy is not ornamented by oriental colouring but suffused by it.'[14] Little clue, however, is given as to how such oriental colouring – whether it suffuses or merely ornaments, surely a relative distinction – is connected with the sequence of the play's action. Hall's attempted refutation of the idea of the play as static and repetitive merely emphasises this lack. It is a view, she says, which 'the evidence of the text alone completely refutes':[15]

> The following was the minimum exotic visual stimulation offered to the audience (there may have been much more): a mass prostration by the chorus, the arrival of the Queen on a gorgeous chariot and in gorgeous clothes, a distraught messenger who rushes on to the stage, moving his limbs in a manner distinctively 'Persian', the pouring of an elaborate libation, prayers, a necromantic sequence involving the beating and scratching of the ground, the appearance and disappearance of a deified ghost from Hades, complete with Persian royal regalia, the arrival of a ragged bowless Xerxes on a second Persian vehicle, a dirge of extreme emotional intensity involving a young man waving his quiver and rags at twelve old grey-haired men who beat their breasts, pluck their beards and tear at their clothes and hair, and finally a quasi-funeral procession in which the Persians walk in a strange 'soft' way indicating

> their ethnicity. Not only is this not bad for an hour's entertainment: the visual dimension affected the meaning of the text. Thalmann has shown how Xerxes' rags symbolise the complete ruin of the Persians' supremacy, the destruction of their empire.

The play's value consists apparently in the sum of its visual effects. To be fair, it should be admitted that this passage derives from a section in her 1996 commentary entitled 'Visual and Aural Dimensions', but the preceding section on the '*Persians* as Tragedy' adds little. Much of the section is taken up with a summary of past critical views of the play, but gradually Hall puts her weight behind a number of supposedly unifying elements. The play can be seen as the story of the unfolding of the news of Salamis, or of the homecoming of Xerxes.[16] Another unifying feature is the play's focus on the city of Susa. The *Persians* can also be seen as an '*emotional* progression' (her italics) from fear and foreboding, through panic, to the 'resigned pragmatism' of the Queen and the final 'catharsis of grief'.[17] The starkness of the polarity of Greek and Barbarian sketched by Hall seems also at times to exclude a more nuanced interpretation of the play.[18] Hall speaks correctly of the 'absolute polarisation' between Greek and Barbarian implied by particular passages (434).[19] However, the 'moral lesson' given by Darius, is, she tells us, delivered 'in terms so Greek that it is easy for critics to forget that this play is the earliest fully-fledged testimony' to the idea of 'the culturally other, the anti-Greek, the *barbarian*'.[20] In common with many other modern interpretations of the play, no attempt is made to explain the contrast between Darius and Xerxes – except to say simply that the one serves as a dramatic foil to the other.

What Hall provides – in general magnificently – is arguably not literary criticism but history, not the history of events certainly, or of Persian institutions, but of the 'Athenian collective imagination'.[21] Despite this focus, Hall appears sometimes to envisage the development of the polarity of Greek and Barbarian as exclusively the product of the poet's art: her aim is to show how 'the poets created a whole new "discourse of barbarism" '; we are then reminded that 'Aeschylus is creating a poetic discourse by which to define the difference between barbarian and Greek'.[22] More seriously though, Hall is occasionally led astray into discussions of the historical veracity of the play that are irrelevant to her main purpose. An example is the play's portrayal of the

Persians in religious terms. She rightly denies that the play reflects a 'concerted attempt to paint a picture of the authentic Zoroastrian religion'.[23] In support of this, however, it is argued that a number of similarities that have been alleged between Aeschylus' religious characterisation of the Persians and authentic Persian religious practice are unfounded. The question, for example, of whether posthumous deification of a king would have struck Aeschylus' audience as distinctly Persian is answered by seeking to establish whether there was evidence for Persian posthumous deification. There is probably no need to push further the point that Aeschylus felt no duty to portray the Persians' religion accurately: the requirements of dramatic effect and of his audience's recognition of his stereotyped Persians must surely have outweighed any such historical duty. In order, however, to distinguish which aspects of Aeschylus' presentation of the Persians are reflections of the 'Athenian collective imagination' and which Aeschylean innovations, to reveal the ways in which Aeschylus works upon and mediates broader cultural commonplaces, the study of Persian evidence is irrelevant;[24] it would be better to discuss the play within the context of other Greek *representations* of Persian monarchy.[25]

A first step would be to read Herodotus. This has, of course, been done before. The emphasis, however, has been largely on the examination of differences (or similarities) of detail. There is a much greater body of parallels, ideological parallels, between the two texts that has scarcely been tapped. As Winnington-Ingram wrote, Herodotus gives us 'the range of ideas within which the Aeschylean characters are moving'.[26] As an illustration of the relationship between the two authors, I will take their characterisation of the Persian Queen, the widow of Darius and the mother of Xerxes, Atossa. According to Herodotus, Atossa's position in Persia was a pivotal one: Xerxes would, he says, have succeeded Darius regardless of the advice of the deposed Spartan king, now refugee, Demaratus, because Atossa, Xerxes' mother, 'held complete power' (*hê gar Atossa eikhe to pan kratos*, 7.3.4).[27] Herodotus also portrays Atossa as approaching Darius as he lies in bed to plead with him to annexe Greece to the Persian empire, to prove thereby to the Persians that they are 'ruled by a man' (3.134.1-2). The reason for this attempt at persuasion is that Atossa is under an obligation to the Greek doctor Democedes;[28] her pretext for wanting the annexation of Greece, however (apparently a plausibly selfish motive for her to present to her husband), is that she has a passion for some female servants from Laconia, Argos, Attica and Corinth (3.134.5).[29]

A similar impression of Atossa is found in Aeschylus' play.[30] Aeschylus too evinces a fascination with the royal bed-chamber, though he has no opportunity for any such pillow-talk (157, 160, 709). More generally the same impression of the Queen's power is conveyed: though the Chorus of Elders have been chosen to oversee the King's territory in his absence (5-7), their behaviour towards the Queen in the course of the play, right from their reaction to her first appearance (150-8), rather belies their sense of their own importance. The Chorus promise to help her in any way in word or deed (173-5), but their advice when it is called for is noticeably ineffectual: 'we do not want, mother, to say anything either to frighten you too much or make you over-confident' (215-16).[31] It is the Queen who has the courage to engage with Darius in a discussion of Xerxes' defeat; the Chorus are so in awe of Darius that they cannot initially speak (694ff.). Most starkly, at the close of her description of her dream and of the omen of the eagle and the hawk, the Queen warns the Chorus not to imagine that Xerxes will be in danger of losing his position should he return defeated: he is 'not accountable to the city, but provided that he survives is still sovereign over this land' (213-14). It is clear that there are limits to the Elders' power: it is the Queen, Atossa, who is the real representative of the monarchy.

To identify Aeschylus' Queen as Herodotus' Atossa is itself controversial, however. As Sancisi-Weerdenburg has observed, there is 'nothing to suggest that explicit information about Persian queens was available to the poet':[32]

> In the tragedy Atossa is portrayed as a model of motherly care for her son Xerxes who has undertaken a foolish and ill-fated expedition against Greece: Xerxes is every bit the young daring rascal and Atossa is consistently portrayed as his counterpart, the wise old lady, comporting herself in a queenly dignified way.

Sancisi-Weerdenburg sensibly then dismisses Aeschylus' play as a reliable source of information on Atossa's position. However, in the context of this argument, she approves the suggestion of Broadhead that Atossa must have been 'hardly more than a name' to the average Athenian of Aeschylus' audience. Indeed, she adds, 'it may be doubted whether she was even that': the name of the Queen, known from the pages of Herodotus, may have been transferred from the scholia into the *dramatis personae*; 'she may well have been less than a name to the Athenian public and consequently her conduct in the tragedy more dependent on dramatic necessities than on real historical data'.[33] One might accept, however, the proposition that Aeschylus was not constrained by 'real historical data' – one might observe, in addition, how Atossa has become conflated with figures such as Semiramis[34] into the archetypal oriental queen, and how similar traits are ascribed to the royal Persian women of the fourth century[35] – without then supposing that his portrayal of the Queen was a completely free composition: Aeschylus may have been under other constraints than historical truth, not least the expectations of his audience of how the Queen *should behave*; in other words he may have been constrained by a false perception of Persia, and of Persian women. Indeed it is not unreasonable to suppose that Aeschylus must have been under some such constraints, for surely the Athenians of 472 must have had some image of the character of the Persians, whether true or false.[36]

It is in reconstructing this false image of Persia that Herodotus is of use. The overall shape of the Queen's characterisation is similar in both authors. (It tallies well also with the description of Atossa by Hellanicus of Lesbos as 'most warlike and manly in every deed'.[37]) The similarities, however, are not so precise as to suggest that Herodotus derived his impression of Xerxes chiefly, let alone exclusively, from Aeschylus.[38] Rather we should hypothesise the existence of a far larger body of anecdotes – and of an underlying structure of attitudes – concerning the Persian court on which both authors drew.[39] There are hints of such a larger background in Herodotus' references to other Persian royal women. The story of Amestris' robe forms a sustained illustration of the way in which Xerxes' court degenerates into an orgy of sex and slaughter after his defeat (9.108-114.1). Other anecotes are more brief. So, for example, we have an explanation for Cambyses' invasion of Egypt, that Cambyses' mother Cassandane felt that she had been displaced in her husband Cyrus' affection by the Egyptian newcomer Nitetis (3.3). We have Amestris' barbaric murder of fourteen noble Persian children by burying them alive (7.114.2). Then there is the story of the detection of the false Smerdis by Otanes' daughter Phaidimie (3.68-9). And finally we have a short notice of Darius' affection for Artystone: Darius loved her above all his wives and so had a statue made of her from hammered gold (7.69.2). Clearly all these stories reflect the same Greek fascination with the supposed harem-politics of Asia. The stories of Cassandane and Cambyses or of Amestris' robe, like the story of Atossa and Darius, reflect and develop a belief that in oriental monarchies political priorities may easily be affected by personal feeling.[40] Many of such stories, however, most clearly those of Amestris and the aristocratic children or of Artystone, beg questions; they presuppose a greater body of knowledge or imagined knowledge. It would be foolish then to assume that these examples constitute the sum of Greek perceptions of Persian royal women.

When and where did these stories originate? The possibility cannot, of course, be dismissed that they are primarily the product of Herodotus' imagination, but the truncated nature of some of these anecdotes suggests otherwise: that Herodotus has drawn selectively, sometimes choosing to elaborate (as for example in the story of Atossa and Darius) and on other occasions merely to report telegraphically his knowledge of a story. These anecdotes may sometimes, as Sancisi-Weerdenburg has suggested of the story of Amestris' robe,[41] originate distantly in Persian oral tradition. They have then been shaped and selected according to the principles of Greek prejudice. But whatever the balance of Greek and Persian elements in their make-up, it is surely more likely that the date either of their import or of their elaboration in Greece was nearer to the time of the Persian wars – when the domestic affairs of Darius and Xerxes were of more pressing importance – than to that of the composition of Herodotus' *Histories*.

The ideology of Aeschylus' *Persians* needs then to be read against the background of this larger pool of anecdotes, a sample of which survived to be written down in the pages of Herodotus' *Histories*; Aeschylus needs to be read against the background of Herodotus. The question of whether the name of Atossa was known to Aeschylus' audience is not in itself very important, but in view of the extent of (garbled) knowledge of Persia in the play, in view in particular of the many Persian names and of the royal genealogy[42] – arguably implying a degree of familiarity with such details on the part of Aeschylus' audience[43] – and of the fact that Xerxes too is never addressed by name, we might reasonably suppose that Atossa was indeed a household name, that she was not named in the play because she did not need to be.[44]

Confirmation of the potency of the ideological themes common to Herodotus' *Histories* and the *Persians* can be gained, finally, from another source, the work of Thucydides. Thucydides' ironic inversion of many of the motifs common both to Herodotus and Aeschylus will mark the chronological limit to the discussion of these themes in Part II. As has been suggested by many others,[45] Thucydides' account of Athens, and in particular of the Athenian expedition to Sicily, plays off Herodotus' account of Persian imperialism and of the Persian expedition to Greece. Thucydides, in the words of Francis Cornford, 'turned against Athens the tremendous moral which his countrymen delighted to read in the *Persians* of Aeschylus and the History of Herodotus'.[46] The question of what moral, if any, is attached to such parallels by Thucydides is a difficult one which I mean to address elsewhere.[47] How familiar we can suppose Thucydides' original readers or audience to have been with Herodotus or with Aeschylus is also debatable.[48] The proof of the existence of such echoes is cumulative: the whole shape of Thucydides' account of Athens' intervention in Sicily is built around the model of Xerxes' expedition. What requires emphasis in advance is also that these are not merely literary allusions but echoes of democratic Athenian slogans most likely in more common currency. Aeschylus' *Persians* then provides not only a guide to the parameters of the political culture of Aeschylus' day, but also to some of the most potent themes in fifth-century Athenian self-representation.

Part II

Finding Athens

4

The use and abuse of Persia

Modern critics of Aeschylus' *Persians* usually express surprise that the play is so lacking in patriotic fervour.[1] According to A.J. Podlecki, the play would have required from its audience a 'nearly total abstraction from natural stirrings of pride at bringing about the defeat of this bitter enemy. They had almost to forget who they were and to concentrate on the common humanity which they shared with their former enemy.'[2] Gilbert Murray went further still and drew, implicitly at least, a moral for his own age: 'to read the *Persae* during the Great War did indeed fill one with shame at the contrast between ancient Hellas and modern Europe.'[3]

It will be argued here that this consensus is fundamentally mistaken.[4] There are, first, a number of objections that can be made on the basis of the historical context. Is it really plausible that in the year 472, so shortly after the conclusion of hostilities in Greece, and at a time indeed when the battle of Eurymedon and other hostilities still lay in the future, Aeschylus would have thought to stage a domestic tragedy centred, just incidentally, on the Persian royal family?[5] (If the play were indeed written in support of Themistocles, we may also question whether a pro-Persian play would have helped to serve this purpose.) Is it plausible then that Aeschylus, himself a veteran of Salamis,[6] would have chosen to express his sympathy for the consequences of the Persians' defeat in a city, indeed in a theatre, that still bore the scars of Persian occupation,[7] in front of an audience that had experienced evacuation from Attica, and who sat (possibly) on seats made from the timber of the shipwrecked Persian fleet?[8] We might also take into account biographical considerations: Aeschylus' brother was killed in the aftermath of Marathon, his hand chopped off by an axe as he hung on to the stern of an enemy ship.[9] In order to maintain the thesis that the play was so sympathetic to the Persians we would also, more importantly, have to believe that at least one ancient Athenian who knew the play misunderstood its theme quite fundamentally: Aristophanes in his *Frogs* presents his character Aeschylus as having, through the *Persians*, taught the Athenians 'always to long for victory over their enemies'.[10]

All these external considerations might serve, of course, only to make Aeschylus' lack of patriotic pride, his conversion to pacifism, all the more extraordinary. Even some of the advocates of the play as sympathetic to the Persians admit that Aeschylus' impartiality is extraordinary: for McCall, for example, the demand that the play makes for sympathy towards the Persians was a great dramatic risk carried off by the expedient of Aeschylus casting himself in the role of Xerxes.[11] To turn to the evidence of the play itself, the very setting of the *Persians* in Susa has often been seen to suggest some sympathy for the Persians' plight. As Desmond Conacher has written, 'the scene is set in Susa in the Persian court for the obvious purpose that we may experience the action and share the sufferings of Xerxes as much as possible through Persian eyes and ears and minds and hearts'.[12] This imaginative empathy with the Persians' sufferings is often envisaged as being the necessary corollary of Aeschylus' historical duty:[13] Broadhead, for example, argues against the suggestion that Xerxes' tattered robes constitute a satire on Oriental decadence that 'the dramatist was bound to represent as faithfully as he could the Persian point of view'.[14]

If the setting in itself constituted proof of sympathy, however, it is surely striking how frequently Aeschylus finds the opportunity to highlight patriotic Athenian themes. So, for example, the dialogue between Darius and his wife, the Queen, allows Darius – the voice for now of Persian common sense – to assert how foolish it had been of his son to attempt to conquer Greece: Darius assumes that the destruction he has been told of must have been the result of a plague or of *stasis* within the city (715); he thinks that a god must have taken hold of his son to encourage him to undertake the campaign (725, 744ff.); and his advice, if the Persians are to prosper in future, is never again to take the field against the Greeks, whose land is their ally (790-2). Most blatantly perhaps, the Messenger's speech provides an opportunity to hear the chant of the Athenians before battle (398-407), memorably described by Émile Cahen as 'la Marseillaise de Salamine':[15]

> At great speed the whole fleet came clearly into view. First, in the lead, came the right wing, in disciplined and orderly fashion, and secondly the whole fleet came out against us; at the same time we could hear a great shout: 'O sons of the Greeks, come on, liberate your children, your wives, the shrines of your ancestral gods and the graves of your forefathers. Our struggle now is on behalf of them all!' This was met from our side by a clamour in the Persian tongue.

Broadhead finds this the 'only passage that betrays Greek national sentiment'.[16] This might be contested: the Queen's description of Athens as famous (347-8, 473-4) – though she had earlier not known where Athens was[17] – can hardly be explained simply in terms of a duty of historical accuracy or of sympathy; the references to the hateful name of Salamis (*ô pleiston ekhthos onoma Salaminos kluein*, 284) or to Athens' 'impregnable ramparts' (349), if they are references to the oracle of the wooden wall, as suggested by Podlecki, can also only have gratified the Athenian audience.[18]

A comparison with Herodotus, moreover, suggests that such glimpses of Greek 'patriotic fervour' constitute not so much lapses into a Greek perspective as part of a concerted strategy of patriotic stimulation. For Herodotus also is able occasionally to see the Persian defeat from the 'Persian point of view'. So, for example, there are a number of stories of Xerxes' retreat from Europe parallel to the account of Aeschylus' messenger (480-514). Instead of the account of the fleeing Persians drowning as the rising sun thawed the ice on which they were crossing the Strymon, Herodotus has a group of Persians drowned by a sudden floodtide at Potidaea, punishment (as Herodotus supposes) for the same group's earlier sacrilege against Poseidon (8.129).[19] He has Xerxes' army eating the bark from the trees from hunger (8.115.2), then eating so immoderately, when eventually they got the chance, that a large number died again (8.117.2). A variant story (which Herodotus judges incredible, 8.118-19) sees Xerxes returning by ship and, when a wind from the Strymon hit them, on the pilot's advice asking volunteers to throw themselves overboard to lighten the load: the pilot, in a wonderful example of paradoxical oriental justice,[20] is then rewarded with a golden crown for saving the King's life and immediately beheaded for causing the death of his subjects. Another story, told (Herodotus says) by the Abderites was that it was amongst them that Xerxes for the first time 'loosed his girdle', for only then did he feel he was in safety (8.20). This provides an excellent parallel for the theme of Xerxes' rags in the *Persians*.[21] Similar stories surround the later retreat of Artabazus after Plataea (9.89). Most significant, however, as background for Aeschylus' *Persians* are Herodotus' accounts of the news of Persian defeat being transmitted from Greece to Susa. Xerxes had sent one message home after occupying Athens to announce to Artabanus 'his present success' (*tên pareousan sphi euprêxiên*, 8.54).[22] Subsequently, one might almost say inevitably, he sends another message announcing his 'present misfortune' (*tên pareousan sphi sumphorên*, 8.98.1). After a digression on the Persian courier service, than which nothing mortal is faster,[23] Herodotus resumes (8.99):

> The first message that reached Susa, that Xerxes held Athens, so delighted those of the Persians that had been left there that they strewed all the roads with myrtle, burnt incense and gave themselves up to sacrifices and festivities. The second message when it arrived threw them into such consternation that they all rent their clothes and shouted and lamented endlessly, placing all the responsibility on Mardonius.

The theme of Persian messages clearly fascinated the Greek imagination to an unusual degree.[24] Phrynichus' *Phoenician Women* appears to have included – simultaneously with Xerxes' return in Persia – the arrival of the news of the battle of Mycale (and so perhaps of the supposedly simultaneous Plataea, 9.100; cf. 9.90[25]). In Herodotus again, we also have briefer glimpses of the message of Marathon that drove Darius into a fury (7.1.1), or of Mardonius' dream of sending home the news of his occupation of Athens by beacons across the islands (9.3.1); Mardonius' system of beacons seems to have provided the model for the beacons by which the news of Agamemnon's return is signalled in Aeschylus' play (A. *Ag.* 281-316), so lending a dangerous touch of barbarian excess to the destroyer of Troy.[26] The arrival of the news of Persian defeat (and the consternation to which it gave rise) is arguably evoked also by Thucydides in his description of the arrival in Athens of the news of the Sicilian expedition (8.1), just as their desperation for drinking water – leading to their drinking water mingled with their own blood – recalls the flight of the Persians from Greece (7.84).

These passages do not show clearly that Herodotus 'used' Aeschylus.[27] In Aeschylus' version, for example, the Queen is unsure as to whether Athens has been sacked (348).[28] In Herodotus' account, the reaction of the Persians of Susa was to transfer the blame for Persian defeat onto Xerxes' lieutenant, Mardonius. What such passages show is rather (to reiterate my point concerning Persian royal women) that Aeschylus and Herodotus both drew on a larger pool of stories with many common themes: rent garments, the emptiness of Susa, and the horrors of the retreat, or the shock of the news arriving in Susa.[29] The Greeks then were apparently quite comfortable in seeing the war from the Persian 'point of view'; only the themes highlighted are those which stress the devastation wrought on the Persians, not their common humanity.

Far from being simply patriotic asides,[30] still less lapses into a Greek perspective,[31] these passages reflect a double focus, a 'kind of "oratio obliqua" which pervades the whole play'.[32] The frequent stress on the unexpectedness of the Persian defeat, for example, doubles as a reminder of the unhoped-for nature of the Greek victory (e.g. 261, 265, 1006, 1026).[33] Devastation for the Persians is delight for the Greeks, as Aeschylus even hints to his audience (1034; cf. 843-4): 'Twofold, threefold are ... our afflictions. But they delight our adversaries' (*diduma gar esti kai tripla ... lupra; kharmata d'ekhthrois*).[34] When the Persians' own focus switches to the Greeks, moreover, the ostensible focus on the Persians becomes a means of highlighting the imagined reasons for Greek victory. The conversations of Demaratus and Xerxes in Herodotus' *Histories* (7.101-5, 234-7), for example, or of Tritantaechmes and Mardonius (8.26)[35] are convenient vehicles for demonstrating those differences between Greek and Persian character that will only be given their full proof in the following Persian defeats. When Tritantaechmes, for example, expresses his amazement that the Greeks compete in the Olympic games for no financial reward but only for virtue (8.26), it would clearly be futile to look for any Persian source or duty of historical accuracy behind the contrast between Greek freedom and Persian slavery.[36]

The clearest example of this exploration of the reasons for Greek victory in the *Persians* is the curiosity shown by Atossa the Queen concerning Athens (230-45):[37]

Q: But there is something I want to find out, my friends. In what part of the world do they say that Athens is situated?
C: Far away towards the west, where the lord Sun sets.
Q: Was this the city my son was so eager to make his prey?
C: Yes, for thus all Hellas would become subject to the King.
Q: Do they have such a large supply of men for their army?
C: Their army is large enough; it did the Medes great harm.
Q: Besides their men what else do we have? Is there plenty of wealth in their palace?
C: They have a spring of silver, a treasury in their earth.
Q: Do they wield bows and arrows in their hands?
C: Not at all. They have spears for close combat and are equipped with shields.
Q: Who leads them and is sole commander of the army?
C: They are called neither the slaves nor subjects of any single man.
Q: So how then can they withstand hostile invaders?
C: Well enough to have destroyed Darius' large and excellent army.

Broadhead comments that 'this period of *stichomythia* provided an interval during which the emotional tension could be relaxed'.[38] Atossa 'would have wanted to know the information': the passage is not therefore a 'dramatically illegitimate *parenthêkê*'. Some of the statements put into the mouth of the Chorus would, Broadhead concedes, have been 'very gratifying to Athenian ears, but we may not therefore tax Aeschylus with pure jingoism'. It may not be quite pure jingoism, an absurd suggestion,[39] but patriotic stimulation is at least a substantial ingredient here: the repeated harping on Athens and her qualities would surely have sparked tingles up the spine of a contemporary Athenian audience. (Though it hardly constitutes proof, unless we assume a universal Greek character and outlook over the centuries, I am assured that even today in performances of the *Persians* in Athens, the actors are at this point held up by applause.[40])

Patriotism, however, need not be unsubtle. Indeed even these few lines of *stichomythia* contain within them a number of complex ideological strands. Aeschylus, according to Kitto, was 'inviting his audience not to cheer but to think'.[41] The distinction is a false one. The *Persians* is not propaganda in the sense outlined by Kitto of 'taking others in'; rather it reflects and develops the shared prejudices and assumptions of author and audience. The remaining chapters of Part II will seek to draw out the main themes implied in these lines.

5

Where is Athens?

The Queen's opening question immediately establishes the Athenians as the plucky underdogs in the struggle between Asia and Europe (230-1):

> Q: But there is something I want to find out, my friends. In what part of the world do they say that Athens is situated?

Atossa's ignorance of the whereabouts of Athens has appeared puzzling to commentators.[1] For Sidgwick, the Queen's 'grotesque ignorance' of Atossa is symptomatic of Attic drama being 'still in its early stages'.[2] For Patin, in a much-cited passage, the Queen's questioning is rendered plausible by the cruel apprehensions under which she is suffering, and by the secluded life of women of the time.[3] However, such 'where on earth ...' questions are common in Herodotus: their function is to emphasise both the bravery and the success of the 'plucky little Greeks' in standing up to Persian power.[4] Cyrus, for example, on receiving a rather peremptory embassy from the Spartans, asks his attendants 'who these Lacedaimonians were, and how many they were that they should make these pronouncements to him' (1.153.1).[5] He then makes a mocking reference to the Greeks' habit of 'setting aside a place in the middle of the city in which to cheat one another under oath'[6] and swears that the Spartans will soon have sufferings of their own, no longer just those of the Ionians, to concern them. Two other similar stories concern the Athenians.[7] After their falling out with Cleomenes, Cleisthenes and the Athenians send envoys to Artaphernes in Sardis asking for an alliance. Artaphernes' first reaction to their request for an alliance was to ask: 'who were these men, and in what part of the world did they live that they should request to become the allies of the Persians?' (5.73.2).

His condition for an alliance, the symbolic submission of giving earth and water, is clearly a response to their negligible importance in his eyes.[8] The other passage (soon after) concerns Darius' reaction to the news of the destruction of Sardis in the Ionian revolt. The destruction of Sardis, he was told, had been the act of 'the Athenians and Ionians' (so omitting the Eretrians, implying that the Athenians were the leaders of the mission?).

> It is said that as soon as he discovered these things, taking no account of the Ionians, as he well knew that these would not go unpunished in their revolt, he asked 'Who were these Athenians?' and, being told, he called for his bow and placing an arrow on it, he released it up into the sky, and as he fired it into the air, said: 'Oh Zeus, grant me my revenge against the Athenians.' And after saying these things, he instructed one of his servants, whenever dinner was laid before him, to say three times: 'Oh master, remember the Athenians' (5.105).[9]

The Athenians doubtless had little difficulty remembering themselves and their achievements, especially when the very stories of their triumphs, even through the filter of their being ostensibly about the Persians, cleverly enjoined them to do so: so Aeschylus' messenger groans as he remembers Athens (285); Darius similarly instructs Aeschylus' Persians henceforth to 'consider what the penalties for these things are like, and remember Athens and Greece, so that no one may scorn the position god has put him in, lust after what belongs to others, and pour away great prosperity' (823-4).[10] At the same time, the Persians' memory of Athens is now turned to a different end: no longer to encourage reprisals, but as a warning that they should be avoided.[11]

Thus the Greek states deluded themselves that they were the Great King's chief 'foreign policy priority'[12] – this despite their simultaneous position as underdogs. Their perception that the Great King stayed awake at night, fixated by his desire for, and curiosity in, Greece, finds its most graphic illustrations in the detail that Darius followed the career of the Greek wrestler Milo (3.137.5),[13] or in the extraordinary assertion by Herodotus that Xerxes 'knew better all the things that were worthy of note in the shrine [of Delphi], as I discover, than he knew the contents of his own palace' (8.35.2).[14] Sometimes, such vignettes spill more clearly into humour. Other stories explain the Persian invasions in terms of the frivolous whims of individuals: the desire of Atossa for Greek servants (3.134.5) or of the Persian king, apparently Darius, for Attic figs (Dinon *FGrHist* 690 F 12).[15] The humour can also be self-directed. Some anecdotes of the prominent status of Greeks within the Persian court reveal a certain pride – so, for example, the frank speech of Demaratus (7.101-5, 234-7), or the jealousy incurred by Themistocles' intimacy with the King (Thuc. 1.138.1, Plut. *Them.* 29.5) – but others suggest a degree of ambivalence towards those Greeks in Persian service and a degree of irony directed at the Greeks in general. During his account of the Ionian revolt against Persian rule, Herodotus envisages Aristagoras impressing a group of Naxian rebels by dropping the name of Artaphernes (5.30.5):

> Artaphernes happens to be my friend. Artaphernes is the son of Hystaspes, and the brother of Darius the King, and he rules all those areas of Asia that border the sea, and has a large army and many ships. This man, I think, will do what we ask.

The theme of the Great King's interest in things Greek is also, finally, put to splendid ironic use by Aristophanes in the parabasis of his *Acharnians*. The central conceit of the passage is the assumption that the playwright is an essential asset as an adviser. His fame indeed has spread so far that the Great King is envisaged cross-examining Spartan envoys to the Persian court and asking two questions (648-51): 'which people has the greater force of ships, and then to which does this poet speak his harsh words of advice; for those men, he said, will be much better, and will conquer easily in the war, who have this man as an adviser.' The theme of the Persian King's fascination for the Greek world may possibly reflect and distort a genuine Persian policy of exploration preceding imperial expansion.[16] By taking his claim to a useful role so far, however, Aristophanes illustrates just how familiar to his audience, how embedded in Athenian self-representation, was the motif of Persian interest in Greece; he also reveals that claim to be absurd.[17]

6

Athens and Greece

The answer to the Queen's second question narrows the focus on Greece of the opening question down to one on Athens (233-4):

Q: Was this the city my son was so eager to make his prey?
C: Yes, for thus all Hellas would become subject to the King.[1]

Athens stands for Greece. Or rather Greece stands or falls with Athens. The fact that this was an Athenian claim provides a good illustration of why it was that Herodotus felt so self-conscious in delivering his verdict that Athens' contribution to the war had been crucial (7.139). For Herodotus' remark is made against the backdrop of an ongoing debate as to which city had been primarily responsible for the Greek victory, a debate itself overshadowed by Athens' behaviour as an imperial city. A very similar claim is 'reported' by Thucydides (1.73.4-74.2), and made by the speaker of Lysias 2 (Lys. 2.2).[2] But the debate, as one might expect, is one that grew up in the immediate aftermath of the Persian wars. The Persian War epigrams include similar claims on behalf of the contributions of the Athenians (Simonides 20-1 Campbell), the Tegeans (Simonides 54 Campbell), and the Corinthian Adeimantus (Simonides epig. 11 Campbell; cf. epig. 14).[3] That such claims were a commonplace already by 470 is shown by Pindar's First Pythian, with its praise of Syracuse for saving Greece from heavy slavery, and equation of the Syracusans' achievement at Himera with the Athenians' at Salamis and the Spartans' at Plataea (*Pyth.* 1.75ff.; cf. frs. 64-5 Bowra, tr. G.S. Conway):[4]

From Salamis, in thanks from men of Athens,
I shall seek my reward; in Sparta's city

Tell of Kithaeron's battle, where disaster
    Came to the Medes with curving bows.
But by the fertile shores of Himera
The sons of Deinomenes fill the song,
    Which for their valour
They won amidst the downfall of their foes.

The question of whose contribution to the war was most important is also one fought out on the pages of Herodotus. Herodotus' famous judgement on Athens is one which is reflected in a number of remarks by characters in the *Histories*: Themistocles tells Eurybiades that the freedom of Greece depends on his decision to remain at Salamis (8.62.1); Mardonius realises eventually that if he is to conquer Greece he must ally with the Athenians (8.136.2-3; cf. 8.140). Interestingly, however, the focus of such 'if it was not for ...' expressions is not always on the Athenians. Xerxes tells his nobles that the Greeks as a whole are such brave men that, if they succeed in conquering them, no army of men will ever oppose Persia again (8.53.2; cf. 7.8.γ, 53.2). Like the British in the dark days of the Second World War (standing alone – except with the peoples of the Empire) the Greeks are all that lie between Xerxes and world domination. A similar judgement is also implied concerning the contribution of the Spartans. Demaratus tells Xerxes firmly (7.209.4): 'Understand this. If you conquer these men and those that wait in Sparta, no other people of men remain, King, who will raise their hands to you.' Xerxes finds Demaratus' words unbelievable (7.209.5), though after Thermopylae he comes back to Demaratus to ask how many of these Lacedaimonians are left, and if they are all made of the same stuff (7.233.2). Such speeches or dialogues contain, embedded within them, implied judgements as to which city was most responsible for the Greek victory. Herodotus has included a number of stories of variant provenances without making any clear attempt to reconcile their different tendencies. In the light of this, it is hardly possible to distil from Herodotus' account any clear view as to the city most responsible for Greek victory.[5]

Another way of putting Athens centre-stage was to emphasise her role as the target of Persian aggression (5.105, 7.5, 7.8.α2-γ1, 7.138.1, 9.3.1; cf. Isoc. *Paneg.* 4.67). The same idea is reflected in the repeated focus on, and repetition of, the names of Salamis and of Athens in the

Persians.[6] It is this aspect of the fifth-century debate over the Persian wars that Thucydides makes greatest use of in his account of the Sicilian expedition. The Syracusan Hermocrates is made to argue that the Athenians' great name had been earned due to the Persian invasion having been directed against them (Thuc. 6.33.6). By a precisely similar pattern, it is implied, the ostensible object of the Athenians' campaign in Sicily was Syracuse. In both cases, the aggressors' real ambitions were much broader: as Thucydides and a number of speakers – Hermocrates, Alcibiades, Gylippus – emphasise, the Athenians' real aim was to subdue all of Sicily, then the Peloponnese and Greece, and (in the judgement of Thucydides' Alcibiades and Plutarch, at least) Carthage and Italy as well (6.6.1, 15.2, 33.2, 76.2, 90.2, 7.66.2; Plut. *Nic.* 12, *Alc.* 17.3), to have (in Gylippus' words) 'the greatest empire of any Greeks of our own or former times' (7.66.2); the Persians' aim was even more grandiose, to unite Asia and Europe, to create an empire 'bordering the aither of Zeus' (1.209.1, 7.8.γ.2-3, 19.1, 54.2, 8.53.2, 109.3; A. *Pers.* 189-99). Like Athens in the Persian wars, the Syracusans stand to gain credit from this position. Syracuse is the key to Sicily and to Italy (6.33.2, 91.3): this was actually the reason, according to Hermocrates, for their being the object of Athenian hostility (6.33.2). The Syracusans, like the Athenians, would, Hermocrates tells them, 'be regarded as the authors of the Sicilians' deliverance' (7.56.2). They are credited as the first Sicilians to stand up to Athenian forces (7.66; cf. 7.21.4, 55.2), just as the Athenians were the first of the Greeks to confront the Persians at Marathon (6.112.3; cf. 9.27.5, 9.46.2).

The Athenocentrism of the *Persians* is not merely a judgement on the past, however. The claim that the Athenians' courage against the Persians justified their empire was clearly sufficiently hackneyed for Thucydides, in his *Melian Dialogue*, to have the Athenians dispense with it (amongst other aspects of the Athenian strategy of self-justification) as a 'great mass of words that nobody would believe' (Thuc. 5.89; cf. 1.73.2, 6.83.1-2). It is implied likewise throughout Herodotus' account of the Persian wars that the Greeks are fighting not only against the Persians but amongst themselves, jostling for the position they will hold come the peace.[7] So, Miltiades before Marathon attempted to persuade the polemarch Callimachus to vote for battle by saying that if 'the city were to win through, she would be the first of the Greek cities' (6.109.3). Correspondingly, implicit in the *Persians*' celebration of Athens' achievements are Athens' imperial ambitions. This can be seen, for example, in Aeschylus' references to the Ionians. On occasion he refers to Ionia in the limited geographical sense of Ionia in Asia Minor; the Ionians are the Ionians of Asia Minor.[8] But more usually 'Ionia' and 'Ionians' take on a broader meaning as embracing Attica and the Athenians: when the Chorus assert that the 'Ionian people do not run away from battle' (1025; cf. 178, 563, 950-1, 1011) the Athenians are clearly not excluded.[9] Or rather, I suggest, it is the Athenians who are embracing the Ionians.[10] We may think here of the Athenians' angry response, in Herodotus' account, to the Spartan plan to evacuate Ionia (9.106) that 'the Athenians did not agree that ... the Peloponnesians should deliberate about their [the Athenians'] colonists'. The list of Darius' conquests provided by the Chorus, as well as highlighting the extent of Greek reconquest (under Athenian leadership) by 472, also very possibly marks the growth of the Delian League by the same date.[11] The *Persians* then provides, like the famous speech of Athena in Euripides' *Ion* (1569-94) prophesying the foundation of Athenian colonies and speaking of the glorious name of the Ionians (1588),[12] a charter for the Delian League – only (in our terms) a historical rather than a mythical one.[13]

This convenient blurring of the distinction between the Ionians of Asia Minor and of Attica goes hand-in-hand with another blurring, over the precise part played by Athens' new allies in the Persian Wars. Just as Herodotus' story of Darius' bridge over the Danube neatly illustrates the opposition of the cities of Asia Minor to Persian-sponsored tyranny (4.137.2), and just as his account of Themistocles' inscribed message to the Ionians to take as little active part as possible in the Persian fleet (8.22)[14] justifies the Athenians' allies against a charge of Medism, so Aeschylus shows a similar concern for the Athenians' colonists by omitting any mention of their participation in Xerxes' expedition (21-58), and by including the detail that Cyrus had defeated them by force (771).[15]

It is certainly true that Athenocentrism could be more blatant: as Hall points out, for example, 'there is an almost complete absence of references to Athena,[16] and in the central Salamis narrative, the Greek agents are always "Hellenes" rather than "Athenians" (353-432)'.[17] The 'Remember Athens' of Herodotus' Darius (5.105.2) becomes the 'Remember Athens and Greece' of Aeschylus' ghost (824). Nor are Dorians excluded or any opposition between Dorian and Ionian made plain: Aeschylus makes, at very least, a significant nod to the Spartans' achievement through Darius' prophecy of the effect of the 'Dorian lance' at Plataea (817).[18] Richmond Lattimore famously remarked that Plataea is relegated in the *Persians* to the status of a 'mopping-up operation'.[19] However, whilst there is no doubt that Salamis allowed Aeschylus greater opportunities for highlighting the Athenian contribution to the defeat of Persia than Plataea, there are surely literary grounds for arguing that to expect anything more than a prophetic glimpse of Plataea (itself ingeniously introduced) would be unrealistic. There is no reason, moreover, why the lauding of Athens' achievement should necessarily have been seen, or – more significantly – have been presented as being seen, as incompatible with the acknowledgement of Sparta's contribution. There is, it seems, a tension between a Panhellenic ideal and Athenian imperialism which is never fully resolved: never fully resolved, however, because Panhellenism like Panionianism itself provided a useful veil for such imperialism.[20]

7

The emptiness of Asia

Another theme heralded in the dialogue between Queen and Chorus is that of Persian numbers.[1]

> Q: Do they have such a large display of men for their army?
> C: Their army is large enough; it did the Medes great harm.

The Persians are obsessed with numbers. Later in the play similarly, the Queen asks the Messenger how many ships the Greeks had 'that they thought they could meet the Persians in a naval encounter' (333-6). The Messenger's reply makes clear that the Queen has missed the point (337-47):

> As far as the size of the fleet was concerned you can be sure that the barbarians would have won. The total number of ships came to three hundred, but ten of these were selected out separately from them. The size of Xerxes' fleet I know for certain was a thousand, and two hundred and seven of the ships were exceptionally fast. So much for the numbers. You are not under the impression that we were numerically undone in the battle? No, it was some god who destroyed us by loading the scales with an unequal weight of fate.

The same point is pushed almost subliminally by the repetition of *andro-* compounds, from *poluandros* (73) to *kenandros* (118) and *anandros* (166, 288, 298), and then, in the context of the Persian defeat, to *poluandros* again (533, 899).[2]

Again there are a number of parallels in Herodotus.[3] According to Herodotus, the belief that numbers constitute strength is actually a distinct characteristic of the Persians (*to pollon d'hêgeatai iskhuron einai*, 1.136.1).[4] Xerxes, like the Queen, is obsessed with the number of his ships as if numbers were a guarantee of victory. He reviews and – ingeniously – checks the numbers of his men (7.44, 59.2-60), and allows the Greeks' spies to observe his own army freely that they should be intimidated by its size (7.146-7).[5] The Persian obsession with numbers is most clearly expressed, however, in the series of conversations in book 7, especially those between Xerxes and Artabanus, concerning the wisdom of the Persian expedition. Mardonius has already argued that no one would oppose Xerxes leading such a mass (*plêthos*) of men (7.9.γ1). After the decision to launch the expedition had become irreversible, just after Xerxes' review of his soldiers (7.47-9), Artabanus confesses to being afraid of two great enemies. Xerxes replies (7.48):

> Mysterious man, what are these two great enemies you say exist? Do you think that our army is at fault in its number, and that the Greek force will appear much greater than ours? Or that our navy will fall short of theirs? Or both of these things? If you think that our affairs are at all deficient in this respect, it would be quite possible for someone to collect another army.[6]

He has, of course, also missed the point, as Artabanus tells him in words reminiscent of those of the messenger to the Queen in the *Persians* (7.49.1):

> King, no one of sense could find fault with this army, nor with the number of your ships. Indeed if you collected more, the two enemies of which I speak would be much greater. For these are the land and the sea.

He proceeds to detail the ways in which the land and sea will prove hostile (7.49.2-5): no harbours will be large enough to shelter the fleet in the event of a storm (for accidents rule men, not men accidents); the land will beget a famine.[7] After the battle of Thermopylae, it becomes clear to the Persians, even to Xerxes, that they have 'many people' but 'few men' (*polloi … anthrôpoi, oligoi … andres*, 7.210.2),[8] but still Achaemenes needs to reassure his king that numbers are not the problem (7.236.3).

The land and sea do then indeed conspire against the Persians. In Herodotus, the Persians are greeted by a number of natural miracles on their arrival, expressions of divine disapproval: the great wind that overwhelmed the Persians at Athos on the Marathon campaign (6.44.2); the thunder and lightning as they enter the territory of Troy (7.42.2), the storm that broke up the bridge painstakingly constructed over the Hellespont (7.34); the thunderbolts and rocks that fell upon them at Delphi (8.37-8); the endless rainstorms and violent thunder which descended from Pelion on the Persians at Aphetae (8.12.1).[9] More subtly, cliffs form themselves by optical illusion into ships to instil fear into the Persians (8.107.2). Artabanus' prophecy is fulfilled in precise detail, moreover, by the failure of the land to support the Persian numbers when the rivers of Greece are drunk dry (7.21.1, 187.1, 196). Aeschylus likewise has the island rocks echo back the Greeks' paean before Salamis (389-91); he has Darius warn the Persians (790-2) that if they are to prosper in future, they should 'not take an expedition into the territory of the Greeks, not even if the Median army is greater. For the very land itself is their ally.' There are also a number of quite gratuitous references to a land-sea duality, for example Darius' aphorism (707-8) that 'many evil things come from the sea, many from the land, to mortals'.[10]

The theme of land and sea was a sufficiently familiar and potent one to allow its ironic treatment by Thucydides in the context of Athens' empire. It was the war at Aegina, for Herodotus, which saved Greece by forcing the Athenians to become seamen (7.144.2). The Athenians learnt to row almost by accident as 'necessity drove every man to take up his oar' ([Xen.] *Ath. Pol.* 1.19-20). Each man, in the words of Aeschylus' messenger, 'was lord of his oar' (378). According to Thucydides, the Athenians had become sailors as a consequence of their evacuation of Attica (Thuc. 1.18.2; cf. 7.21.2-3). The whole world subsequently divided (as the Herodotean world divides into the continents of Asia and Europe) into the realms of sea and of land (2.62.2): with the control of the sea, Pericles is made to say – in language echoing Herodotus' Xerxes – no king or people can prevent the Athenians from going where they will.[11] The inversion of land and sea at Pylos and then at Syracuse (4.12.3, 4.14.3, 7.62)[12] herald the end of this special relationship between the Athenians and the sea: as Hermocrates reassures the Syracusans, Athenian naval superiority is a historical accident; nothing would last for ever (7.21.3). Step by step then the Syracusans believe this true; and step by step they overhaul the Athenians (7.12.3-5, 36, 41). Then it is even acknowledged by Athenians, in Nicias' curious boast that the Sicilians would not have dared fight Athens' navy at its peak (7.63.4; cf. 7.47.3), or most poignantly at the death of the expedition: asked to attempt a second break-out from Syracuse harbour, the Athenian sailors refuse – as they no longer believe they can win (7.72.4).

When the land and the sea turn against the Persians, their numbers, as prophesied by Artabanus, compound their problems. Herodotus makes this explicit in the context of Thermopylae and Salamis. Thermopylae seemed an appropriate position for the Greeks in that the Persians would not be able to use their numbers (*plêtheï*, 7.177) or their cavalry. At Salamis too, as Themistocles tells Eurybiades, the narrowness of the straits (compared to the open seas by the Isthmus) would be to the advantage of the Greeks (8.60.α-β). These plans work well: the Greeks hold their line, whereas the Persian fleet collapses in disorder (8.86). At Thermopylae, the Persians die in proportion apparently to their numbers: the Persian dead through the tactic of feigned retreats at Thermopylae are 'innumerable' (*plêthei anarithmêtous*, 7.211.3) and the Spartan dead few. The disaster at Aphetae is exacerbated by the bodies and wrecks of an earlier storm at Pelion (7.188.2) drifting into the ships' oars, causing a panic (8.12). At Artemisium, the Persians' strength in numbers cancelled itself out, for 'by virtue of its size and number' the fleet destroyed itself, ships running into one another (8.16.2):

> Many Greek ships were destroyed and many men, but many more barbarian ships and many more men (8.16.3).

The Persians, however, continued to fight out of shame (given perhaps their *nomos* that numbers equal strength) at being put to flight by so few ships.[13] More frivolously, even the bravura remark of the sage Dieneces at Thermopylae that the number of Persian arrows will allow them to fight in the shade reflects the same paradoxical turning of the Persians' strength into a weakness, 'holding the number of the Persians in contempt' (*en alogiêi poiumenon to tôn Mêdôn plêthos*, 7.226.2).[14]

In Aeschylus, the same idea, that the numbers of the Persians' ships will work against them, is present also (413-21):[15]

> When the mass of their ships was crowded together in a narrow strait, and they could not bring any assistance to one another, they struck each other with their bronze-mouthed beaks, and shattered all the rowing equipment; the Greek ships judiciously encircled them and made their strike, and ships' hulls were turned upside down, and it was no longer possible to glimpse the sea, which was brimming with wrecked ships and dead men. The shores and reefs were brimming with corpses.[16]

The land is the Greeks' ally in so far as it kills by famine any excess population (793-4). The messenger's remark that the Persians were dying of thirst in Boiotia (482-4) is presumably a reference to the idea of the rivers being drunk dry by the Persian hordes.[17] The Persians' numbers become a weakness figuratively as well as literally: the 'mass of men' becomes on numerous occasions a 'mass of woes' (*plêthos pêmatôn*, 477) a 'mass of sufferings' (*kakôn de plêthos*, 429), or the 'masses of corpses' that clog up Salamis (*plêthousi nekrôn*, 272-3).[18] The army is likened to a 'huge flood of men' (88)[19] or an 'invincible wave of the sea', presaging their defeat by the sea (so the later 'wave of disasters', 599-600),[20] or to a 'flower of men' (59) that will inevitably wilt (252, 925).[21]

This theme of the counter-productive nature of the great numbers of the Persian fleet is again one that Thucydides turns against the Athenians. He has Gylippus reassure the Syracusans and their allies (7.67.3; cf. 7.36.4-6, 49.2):

> For they will gain nothing by the number of their ships – in case any one of you is afraid because he will be fighting a sea battle against unequal numbers. For in a small space, on the one hand, many ships will be slower in performing whatever manoeuvres they intend and, on the other, it will be easier for our plans to inflict damage.

The Athenians, as Gylippus goes on to say, are so desperate that they plan to force their way out through the blockade (7.67.4; cf. 7.56.1-2, 59), a further ironic twist on their predicament at Salamis:[22] the Persians' blockade had been desirable in so far as it prevented the Greeks' withdrawal to the Isthmus of Corinth and forced the Persians to fight in a place where their numbers counted for nothing. Here the blockade – for similar reasons – worked against the Athenians.[23]

A theme parallel to that of the Persians' numbers is that of the emptiness of Asia.[24] At the opening of the play, the city is empty except for the old men and the women (1ff., 118), left mourning their menfolk in anticipation of their later more permanent state of mourning (cf. 286-9). The idea that only women are left in Persia can be seen reflected also in Xerxes' threat to Artabanus in Herodotus that he will be left behind with the women (7.11.1).[25] This theme of the emptiness of Persia may be associated with the Themistoclean sentiment – itself rooted in his interpretation of the Wooden Wall oracle[26] – that a city consists in its men rather than its walls: Themistocles famously replied to Adeimantus' taunt that he was a 'man without a city' (*apoli andri*, 8.61.2)[27] that the Athenians would have a city and a territory greater than the Corinthians so long as they had two hundred ships fully manned. The phrase – or, if we doubt a specific allusion to a historical remark recorded by Herodotus,[28] the underlying ideology that gave rise to it – is probably alluded to in the *Persians* by the Messenger's reply to the Chorus that 'while men remain to a city its ramparts are secure' (349).[29] Susa, by contrast, has walls but no men.[30] The theme is then inverted by both Herodotus and, with terrible pathos, Thucydides. Herodotus has Mardonius reassure Xerxes that the contest between Persians and Greeks is a contest of men and horses, not of mere wood (8.100.2).[31] Thucydides has Nicias tell the Athenians (in a speech designed to deter the Athenians from the Sicilian expedition) to understand that they must prepare to found a city in a foreign land (6.23.2); he himself describes the Athenian forces as like a besieged city in flight (7.75.5); finally, he has Nicias reassure his troops, in the expedition's final stages, that 'a city is its men, not its walls or its unmanned ships' (7.77.7: *andres gar polis, kai ou teikhê oude nêes andrôn kenai*).

It is interesting to note, finally, that this Athenian tradition has transformed the evacuation of Attica into a cause of pride.[32] This is made explicit by Thucydides' Athenian representatives in Sparta (1.74.2-4; cf. 1.144.4): if, like others, they had given in to their fears for their territory, the war would have been lost. The Athenian envoy to Camarina transformed the Athenians' willingness to sacrifice their land into a justification of Athens' empire (6.82.4). The same motif is then satirised by Aristophanes in the *Frogs* when he makes Aeschylus claim that the Athenians should consider 'their enemies' land their own and their own their enemies' ' and treat ships as if they were the only true wealth (Ar. *Ran.* 1463-5). Moreover, the Periclean defensive strategy for Athens of sitting tight behind their walls and relying on the strength of their own navy is also one founded upon the experience of the evacuation. When Archidamus argues that the Athenians would never allow themselves to become the slaves to their land (1.81.6), the evidence for this assertion is that they had famously turned their backs on it. This was, of course, a situation that had been envisaged by Themistocles when he advised the Athenians, should they ever be hard pressed by land, to 'go down to the Piraeus and oppose the world with their ships' (1.93.7). The same need not to become excessively attached to property is also expressed by Pericles in language reminiscent again of Themistocles' formulation: 'houses do not own men, but men houses' (1.143.5).[33] The one weakness in the Athenians' position, according to the Xenophontic *Athenaion Politeia* (2.14-16), is that Athens was not, in fact, an island.

The emphasis on the mass of Persian men on the expedition has an obvious implication: that the disaster that will overcome the Persians will be correspondingly massive.[34] Indeed the disaster is portrayed repeatedly (though not consistently[35]) as complete:[36] 'the whole barbarian force has perished' (255); 'the entire force is lost' (260); 'the entire force was defeated' (278-9); 'the gods have ordained utter catastrophe for the Persians' (282-3); 'a vast ocean of catastrophes has burst out upon the Persians and the entire barbarian people' (433-4);[37] a heavy weight has crushed 'the entire Persian race' (516); 'the entire land of Asia mourns, emptied of its men' (548-9);[38] Salamis 'holds all that was once Persia' (*ekhei ta Persan*, 595-7);[39] and so on throughout the play.[40] The same point is made by the lists of the peoples and commanders of the Persian army (16-58, 302-30, 956-1002): though superficially they may appear to be evidence simply of the magnificence of the Persian forces, by implication such magnificence reinforces the impression of the heaviness of the fall to come and of the achievement of the Athenians and Greeks in being the instrument of the Persians' destruction.[41] The same implication lies surely behind Herodotus' descriptions of the Persian forces. Asia was 'astir for three years' while the best men were chosen for the expedition against Greece (7.1.2). Xerxes' expedition was greater than any expedition before (7.21): 'for what nation did Xerxes not lead out of Asia against Greece? what stream, being drunk, did not fail him except that of great rivers?'[42] The crossing of the Hellespont took a whole seven days and seven nights (7.56.1), just as it would take Aeschylus' messenger ten days to retell the 'mass of woes' that the Persians suffered as a result (429-30). Herodotus himself expresses the thought that it was no wonder that the rivers of Greece were exhausted, given the size of Xerxes' army (7.187.1-2). Such grandiose descriptions of the Persians' forces may reflect (and doubtless distort) the language of Persian inscriptions, with their lists of subject peoples and their emphasis on the totality of Persian power in Asia.[43] The emphasis on the completeness of the Persians' destruction also puts Thucydides' inversion of the idea of a city consisting in its men into greater focus: a slogan that, alluding to the wooden wall oracle, celebrated the victory of the Greeks over the Persians, and the foundation of Athens' hegemony in Greece, becomes instead a proof of the completeness of Athens' destruction, destruction in circumstances analogous to those of the Persians. Like Herodotus, Thucydides employs a number of strategies to magnify the Athenians' fall: his famous description of the Athenians' preparations for their expedition (6.30-2), the fleet's departure, viewed by the whole population (6.30.2), his final review of the forces of both sides before the campaign's dénouement (7.57-8) or the pathetic flashback to the beginning of Athens' rise – her liberation from tyranny (6.53-9)[44] – all serve to emphasise the significance of her defeat. Just as the 'whole of Persia' was left behind on the shores of Salamis and Psyttaleia, so the whole of Athens is destroyed in Sicily. They, Nicias tells them, are 'the army and navy of the Athenians and all that is left of the city and the great name of Athens' (7.64.2).

The complete destruction of the Persians leads to another conclusion, however – one largely absent from the aftermath of Thucydides' account of the Sicilian expedition in which Athens, with its limited resources, rallies (8.1):[45] the imminent destruction of the Persian empire. Darius is afraid unless 'the great wealth I amassed by my labours may be plundered by the first comer' (751-2). (An impression of the wealth awaiting the Greeks has been built up gradually through the play by the accumulation of *khruso*-compounds.[46]) At the end of the play, the Persians are said to be deprived of defenders (1024). Xerxes himself has lost his bow, and his quiver is empty (1018-23).[47] The bow stands in the play as a symbol for Persia as the spear does for Greece (147-8, 278-9); Darius was called 'lord of the bow' (555-7).[48] Xerxes' torn clothes, prefigured in the Queen's dream (198-9), and also her later appearance without her finery (598),[49] signify the end of the monarchy. The imminent destruction of Persia is also perhaps implicit in three other passages. The first passage is also the most oblique, that is the vision of the eagle (perhaps known by Aeschylus' audience to have been a symbol of Persia and the Persian monarchy[50]) and the hawk seen by the Queen immediately after she wakes from her dream (205-11):

> But I saw an eagle seeking refuge at the hearth of Phoebus: my friends, I stood there speechless with terror. Next I saw a hawk rushing on beating wings towards the eagle, and tearing at its head with its talons. The eagle could do nothing but submit its body, cowering. These things are terrifying to me as witness, and to you as audience.

So, perhaps, with the Greeks and Persians: war is no longer even at issue as the Persians are impotent to resist.[51] The fact that the hearth is one of Phoebus may also reflect the tradition that the Persians were repelled from Delphi by the god (8.37-8).[52] Obviously, however, the omen may have been fulfilled simply and exclusively by the events of the Persian war. The second passage, already much discussed, is the list of the conquests of Darius recounted by the Chorus in his praise, and by implication, given that Darius' conquest's are his son's losses, to set Xerxes in a worse light (864ff.) The process of Persian decline and of Athenian imperial aggrandisement, will, it seems to be suggested, continue. The final passage bearing on the Persians' bleak future is the Chorus' prophecy of the end of the Persian empire (584-90):

> Not for long now will the inhabitants of Asia abide under Persian rule, nor pay further tribute under compulsion to the King, nor shall they be his subjects, prostrating themselves on the ground; for the kingly power is destroyed.

Could the Athenians, however, really have believed that Persian power was finished? Persia, writes Avery, 'had not been absolutely destroyed. The empire was still a threat to Greece and the ringing of bells and shouts of joy that marked the final peace were still some twenty years in the future.'[53] Avery recognises that Aeschylus puts great emphasis on the totality of the Persian defeat, and so for him the fact that it was not true presents Aeschylus with a problem 'of exalting the Greek victory and at the same time not doing violence to the historical circumstances which obtained in 472'.[54] The solution, as he sees it, lies in the final scene. He detects a shift in tone in the relationship of Xerxes and his chorus of Elders from confrontation to 'communal sorrow'. The explanation for this shift, he speculates, is that Xerxes has a new set of clothes brought to him: 'Symbolically the defeat is put aside and Xerxes emerges in his new clothes essentially undamaged in his royal power.'[55] To this final scene, and to the King's new clothes, I will return at greater length in discussing the themes of democracy and accountability in the play. But is it necessary to square the rhetoric of the play with reality so closely? Thucydides' Nicias envisages similarly – in the event of defeat in Sicily – that Athens will be defenceless against attack (7.64.1); Thucydides himself describes the Athenians' defeat as total – only for Athens awkwardly to pick herself up in book 8, and for Thucydides to introduce, almost casually, another worse setback in the revolt of Euboea (8.96.1).[56] Even Herodotus, writing with substantial hindsight, reflects the same ideology of the Persian wars as a fight to the death.[57] Xerxes portrays the coming war as a struggle that will lead either to the Greek world falling subject to the Persians or *vice versa* (7.11.3); the Greeks, he said, had not only burnt Sardis, but advanced into Asia (*êlasan es tên Asiên*, 7.11.2). On the occasion of Darius' Scythian campaign, he reminds Artabanus, the Ionians had had the power to destroy 'the whole Persian army' (*hê pasa Persikê stratiê*, 7.52.1). This is the same point that Artabanus had earlier introduced, though then it had been made in an attempt to dissuade him from the expedition (7.10.γ2): if Histiaeus had not helped Darius cross the Danube, 'the affairs of the Persians would have been finished' (*diergasto an ta Perseôn prêgmata*).[58]

In their cooler moments, the Athenians would doubtless have recognised such hyperbole for what it was.[59] The fact, however, that Aeschylus was able to present the Greeks' victory as total is perhaps further testimony to the heightened atmosphere in which his play was performed.

8

Democracy and tyranny

The last main theme which emerges from the Queen's questioning of the Chorus over Athens is the contrast between the Athenians' democracy and the Persian monarchy.[1] The Athenians are distinguished from the Persians in so far as they have no single 'shepherd' (241-4):

Q: Who is a shepherd over them, and is sole commander of the army?
C: They are called neither the slaves nor subjects of any single man
Q: So how then can they withstand hostile invaders?
C: Well enough to have destroyed Darius' large and excellent army.

The contrast between the Persians, the 'slaves' of the King, and the Greeks must surely have gained an added piquancy from a Greek perception that the Persian King used such language in describing his subjects.[2] For the Queen, however, despite her closing observation that 'what you say is terrible for the parents of our men to contemplate' (245), the Athenian lack of a single shepherd is simply incomprehensible. Similarly she takes for granted that there must be a palace in Athens (237).[3]

This gap of political understanding is not merely a small element in Aeschylus' characterisation of the Queen, but an integral theme of the play:[4] again and again there is an implicit comparison between Persia – with its monarchy resolved on maintaining its grip on power, and a servile population unable by nature or habit to emancipate themselves – and Athens in which all men, as we have seen, chant their paean in hearty chorus. A.H.M. Jones famously observed the curious fact that 'in the abundant literature produced in the greatest democracy of Greece there survives no statement of democratic political theory';[5] one might not too fancifully suggest that we have in Aeschylus' *Persians* just that. Aristotle in his *Politics* makes the point that the victory at Salamis was instrumental in strengthening the democracy due to the participation of the common people in the fleet (Arist. *Pol.* 1304a22-5). What the *Persians* gives us is the reverse proposition: that it was due to Athens' democratic values that she survived and triumphed, and that the same values will ensure her future success.[6] Whether either causative link is objective fact is, of course, open to question.[7]

The contrast between Athenian democracy and Persian monarchy that runs through the play is one, first, which casts a very different light on the character of the Queen. The common modern image of the Queen, reflected by Sancisi-Weerdenburg in the quotation above in Part I,[8] is that she maintains throughout the play an extraordinary dignity and a touching loyalty to her son. The *Persians* is a domestic tragedy and she is the heroine. 'Throughout the play', according to Taplin, 'the Queen receives misfortune with dignity and wisdom':[9] this dignity explains the Queen's absence from the final scene of the play as 'this role could not possibly be maintained in a final scene which resembles that which we have'. If at times 'she appears insensible to wider issues', for Broadhead this is due to her 'intense devotion to her son'.[10] Against the background of the portrayal of Persian women in Herodotus' *Histories* – and in other Greek sources on Persia – this view can only be described as naïve. Atossa is, in the Greeks' view at least, no ordinary woman: she held 'complete power' in Persia (7.3.4). Even if we do not choose to identify Aeschylus' Queen as Atossa, surely the very prominence of women in political contexts in Greek representations of Persia (by contrast to the invisibility of women in similar contexts in Greece) implies strongly some pejorative judgement on that prominence.[11] The prominence of Atossa needs also to be seen in the context of the general 'effeminisation' of Persia described by Edith Hall,[12] in particular of a corpus of stories in Greek sources on Persia which concern the disproportionate and pernicious influence of (especially royal) women upon their sons.[13] In short, you cannot have a domestic tragedy about the Persian royal family; in monarchies, the personal is political.[14]

Right from her first appearance, it is clear that the Queen's priorities are selfish ones (168-9): 'we have sufficient wealth, but I am afraid for the "light" of our household. For I consider a household's "light" to be the presence of its master.'[15] The personal nature of her priorities becomes clearer still in the concluding words to her dream, where she seeks to put to rest any thoughts of the Chorus that Xerxes' defeat would spell the end for his position (210-14):[16] 'for you well know that my son, if he were to succeed, would be a man to excite great admiration, but that if he fails he is not accountable to the city (*oukh hupeuthunos polei*), but that if he has survived he is nevertheless sovereign of this land.' This remark is often seen as a reference to the democratic institution of *euthunai* to which Athenian magistrates were subject at the end of their terms of office.[17] However, it might more accurately be said that the implicit reference is to the ethos *underlying* the institution of *euthunai* rather than the institution itself.[18]

Similar ideas of the unaccountability of Persian kings are commonplace in Herodotus and other Greek sources on Persia. Persian kings are notorious for the exacting standards they set for their ministers and servants, and for the punishments meted out to those who fail to live up to them:[19] so, for example, the helmsman rewarded with a garland of gold for saving the King's life but beheaded for doing so by killing the King's subjects (8.118.4), or the story of Sisamnes, killed and skinned by Cambyses for giving a corrupt verdict, with his skin then being used for a judge's throne on which his son could give his judgements in his place (5.25).[20] Ctesias includes the story of Darius' execution of forty Chaldaean priests for their failure to prevent his aged parents from falling off a mountain (*FGrHist* 688 F 13.19). Persian kings are even in the habit of punishing rivers and horses that cross them (1.189, 7.35.2, 7.88.2). But only one story suggests that a Persian king applied the same standards to himself as to his subjects: that is the case of Pythius, who angered Xerxes by asking to have one son excused from the expedition to Greece, when all of Xerxes' children were with him (7.38-9); the son in question was subsequently cut in half and Xerxes' army marched between his remains.[21] In general, indeed, the double standards are openly flaunted. At Salamis, Xerxes is seated on a throne above the battle, recording through his secretaries the names of all those trierarchs who displayed acts of valour (8.90.4), and beheading all those like the Phoenicians who, themselves being cowardly, slandered others who were braver (8.90.3). (Likewise in the *Persians* Xerxes threatens to behead his captains, 371.) Xerxes' advisers put the contrast in the accountability of king and subject into even clearer relief. Artabanus recommends to Xerxes that he should stay behind in Persia and leave the conduct of the campaign to his generals (7.10.θ1); he and Mardonius should stake their children on the outcome of the campaign. In the aftermath of Salamis, Artemisia recapitulates this advice: if Xerxes were to leave the conduct of the campaign to Mardonius (8.102), a victory would be his – for his slaves would have achieved it – whereas in the event of a defeat 'it would be no great disaster, so long as you survive, and your own affairs are safe at home'.[22]

Artemisia's definition of the King's responsibility, like that of Mardonius before her, neatly parallels that of the Queen in the *Persians*. Artemisia, however, sidesteps the more difficult question of Xerxes' responsibility for Salamis, a defeat at which he was present. The Queen, on the other hand, is brazen. Her reaction to the news of Xerxes' survival, recalling her remark of 168-9 on the King as the light of his household – 'a great light to my household, a brilliant day out of dark night' (300-1) – has aptly been described as 'un egoismo di gioia'.[23] When the messenger then launches into a virtuoso list of all the noble commanders who were not so lucky, Atossa calls the disaster a 'cause of disgrace to the Persians' (332) and, as if in an attempt to find a clearly identifiable explanation of the defeat, asks the number of Greek ships. After the messenger's final conclusion, she actually blames the Chorus for not having treated her dream with sufficient attention (517-20):[24]

> O what misery the destruction of the army brings me! O nocturnal vision, appearing to me in dreams, how very clearly you revealed to me our tribulations! But you friends judged them to be of too little account.

'Neither in her questions nor in her comments', comments Broadhead characteristically, 'is there anything specially characteristic': 'the chorus could have taken her part equally well.'[25] An opposite point of view is adopted by Conacher: the Persian people through the Chorus sound the note of national mourning, but 'when the Queen Mother speaks, *her* concern must be personal ...'[26] The personal priorities of the Queen, however, are specifically opposed to the interests of the Persians in general: so, for example, the Chorus earlier advise the Queen to pray for a good outcome for herself, her children and all dear to her in the city (218-19); in her reply she pointedly credits the Chorus with goodwill only to her and to her house. A similar concern emerges in a number of passages in the *Histories*: Xerxes' priorities as he discloses them to Artabanus are 'to save my household and my tyranny' (7.52.2); Artemisia declares that her job is to display frankly her opinion of what is best for the King's affairs (7.68.1).[27]

The Queen heads off to her palace shortly after. In her parting lines, however, she first instructs the Chorus to provide her with trustworthy counsels, and then commands them to keep an eye over her son, and to send word to the palace the moment that he arrives, 'lest some further evil should be added to these evils' (530-2) – presumably Xerxes' death, whether at his own or others' hands – an instruction put down again by Broadhead to maternal solicitude.[28] This personal concern is in no way lessened on her return – 'without the chariot and finery she had before' (607-8)[29] – or by the presence of Darius. The Queen blames the company Xerxes kept (753-8):

> Raging Xerxes learned the idea from talking with wicked men. They said that while you had acquired great wealth for your children by your spear, his lack of manly courage made him play the warrior at home,[30] and he did not increase the prosperity left by his father at all. It was because he heard reproaches of this kind expressed frequently by wicked men that he decided to implement the campaign against Greece.

'Atossa's love for her son does not blind her to his weaknesses: she admits the bad effects of his association with evil-minded men.' So comments Broadhead, with more than a hint of special pleading.[31] He also suggests that Artabanus' remark to Xerxes, that the advice of bad men leads him astray like gusts of wind upon the sea (*anthrôpôn kakôn homiliai sphallousi*, Hdt. 7.16.α1),[32] 'may be a reminiscence of this passage of the *Persae*'.[33] More likely it is another manifestation of a common motif in the representation of monarchies: Xerxes, while he is convinced that the planned expedition against Greece was a mistake, blames his earlier decision on the advisers who never stopped urging him on (7.13.2); Artabanus, earlier still, blames Mardonius for having persuaded the King to launch the campaign (7.10.η1-2).[34] Blaming Mardonius was indeed the reaction of the people of Susa to the news of

Salamis (8.99.2). To blame the ministers whilst preserving a belief in the integrity and wisdom of the king is a common characteristic of many monarchies.[35]

Darius' priorities are not so very different from those of his widow. Certainly Xerxes has been rash and impetuous – remember Greece and Athens, Darius says; do not try to attack them (790-2, 823-6) – but Xerxes is forgiven rather in the manner of a spoilt teenager who has written off his father's car. The Chorus should try to be a restraining influence over Xerxes, to help him to keep himself from gratuitous aggression (829-31); and the Queen, the only person in fact, as Darius acknowledges, to whom his son will endure to listen, is to soothe him in his distress and find him some decent clothes, for he has torn at his clothes through anguish (834-8). The theme of Xerxes' clothing is one that the Queen takes up, even in her last lines in the play (845-51):

> O god, numerous harsh pains are afflicting me, but the misfortune which hurts me most to hear about is that my son is disgraced by his clothes on his body. I shall go and get robes from the palace and try to meet him. For I shall not fail those most dear to me in bad times.

'The last glimpse we have of Atossa shows her still as the fond and anxious mother, deeply distressed at the undignified appearance of her son.'[36] Her final speech shows, according to Alexanderson,[37] 'a mother's concern for her son', whilst at the same time she is 'aware of the claims of his royal position (cf. v. 213f.)'. Rather, in the light of the portrayals of Persian monarchs and their female relatives in Herodotus' *Histories*, the Queen emerges as selfish, superficial, and petulant. A more accurate portrayal of the Queen's last speech is that of Edith Hall:[38] it 'clearly reveals no truth whatsoever except that the Athenians *thought that* Persian queens were psychopathically heartless, status-conscious and obsessed with sartorial display'.

The characterisation of the Queen is also a statement on the Persian monarchy as a whole. However, it is in the relationship between, on the one hand, the Chorus, and on the other, the Queen, Darius and Xerxes that the play's indictment of Persian government consists.[39]

What of the Chorus? 'The Persian elders are drawn with uninterrupted dignity', according to McCall.[40] However, though the elders are constantly threatening to assert themselves, ultimately they remain perfectly supine.[41] Throughout the play, despite the various exchanges of formalities between Queen and Chorus, there is a tension between the Chorus and what one might call the 'royalist' position, represented first by the Queen and then by Xerxes. In the opening passage of the play, before Atossa's appearance, they are quite open in their forebodings about the outcome of the war (92ff.). Their talk of the 'wise and deeply-pondered counsel' they are preparing (140-3)[42] is almost immediately belied, however, by their reaction to the first appearance of the radiant Queen Mother (150-158) in language that would certainly have appeared dangerously excessive to a Greek audience, especially as it was accompanied by an act of prostration (152):[43]

> But here comes the mother of the King, my queen, like light from the eyes of gods.[44] We prostrate ourselves, and must all address her with words of salutation. O highest queen of the deep-girdled women of Persia, aged mother of Xerxes and Darius' wife, greetings. You are the spouse of the Persians' god, and a god's mother, unless some ancient deity has now somehow turned against the army.

On the Queen's arrival, there are a good deal of formalised mutual compliments. 'You are the source of all the wise advice I receive', she professes (172). Never, they reply, need she ask them twice for any word or deed; they are her loyal advisers (173-5). But after so much rather ponderous talk of wise counsel, the Elders' performance is noticeably ineffectual: even after they have been treated to a full-scale parade of Atossa's sub-conscious fears, their counsel is so equivocal as scarcely to merit the name (215-16): 'We do not want, mother, to say anything either to frighten you too much or to make you over-confident.' They advise her to pray, then conclude (225): 'In our judgement these matters will work out well for you in every way.' This is the mere semblance of counsel.

The Queen, as we have seen, later slaps the Chorus down for not taking her dream sufficiently seriously. The failure of the Persians to generate sensible advice goes deeper than just a momentary lapse, however: it is the fault of the system and a habit of mind. For the Chorus first threaten to show initiative and then relapse into their old ways.

The Chorus' finest hour comes with the departure of the Queen. They are now quite clear over Xerxes' responsibility for the army's destruction (550-2). Darius, on the other hand, is talked of in very different, at times almost democratic terms: 'why', they ask, 'was Darius, lord of the bow[45], beloved leader of Susa, so benign in the past to his citizens' (555-7)? Finally, in a passage quoted above, they question the whole future of Persian rule (584-96):

> Not for long now will the inhabitants of Asia abide under Persian rule, nor pay further tribute under compulsion to the King, nor shall they be his subjects, prostrating themselves on the ground; for the kingly power is destroyed.[46] Men will no longer curb their tongues; for people are released to talk freely when a strong yoke has been removed. And the soil of Ajax' sea-washed island, stained with gore, holds the remains of the Persians.

The Chorus, it is often said, are motivated by their fear of rebellion. They 'fear that Salamis may have put a stop to [proskynesis]', according to Edith Hall; they are 'afraid that freedom of speech will now be impossible to prevent'.[47] If this position, aligning the Chorus firmly with the 'royalist' position of the Queen, were correct, then Aeschylus would appear to mirror the tradition preserved in Herodotus: the Persian grief at the news of the defeat of Salamis was not, he says, 'so much because they were grieving about the ships as afraid about Xerxes himself. And the situation among the Persians remained the same continuously until Xerxes himself by his arrival put a stop to them' (8.99.2-100). However, other evidence in the play suggests a more ambivalent attitude to the Persian defeat.[48] Though Persian rule is ended – and though they lament the end of Persian rule (919) – it is also the 'kingly power that is destroyed' (589-90). The Queen, as we have seen, was keen to insist on Xerxes' continued kingship even in the event of his failure (210-14):[49] possibly this aside was intended not only as a sly allusion for the audience's benefit to the disparity in accountability between Persia and Athens[50] but also to stem any ideas that the Chorus might have to the contrary. It is very noticeable, moreover, that the Chorus are not slow to ascribe responsibility for the disaster of Salamis to Xerxes.

If this is true, however, the Chorus' outspokenness and independence of mind are only shortlived. They summon Darius' spirit from the dead, 'for if he knows any further cure for our problems, he alone of men could tell how to bring it to pass' (631-2). In their subsequent evocation of Darius, the Chorus expand further on Darius' virtues: 'For he never killed our men through the ruinous waste of war. He was called and was in truth a divine counsellor (*theomêstôr*), since he steered the army well' (652-5). They dare not answer Darius' enquiries because of their 'ancient dread' (694-702).[51] When Darius has found out the full facts of the matter and turns to offering his conclusions on the best course of action, the Chorus appear to hang on his every word. None of Xerxes' predecessors, he reassures them, 'would ever have been responsible for so much suffering' (785-6). 'What then, lord Darius?', reply the Chorus. 'What conclusion are your words pointing to? In the circumstances how can the Persian people do best?' (787-9). The Chorus must then, according to Darius, merely 'use sensible words of warning to admonish Xerxes to behave temperately' (829-31).

After Darius' re-descent, the Chorus re-iterate the achievements of Darius. On this occasion, however, there is noticeably no comparison made of Darius and his son. Rather, with the exception of their final lines – in which they ascribe their current reversals only to the divine (904-6) – their focus is entirely on the past. On Xerxes' return, they repeatedly allocate responsibility to him for the destruction of the expedition (e.g. 923-4, 985, 1013-18, 1029-30)[52] – in contrast to Herodotus' epitome in which blame was put upon Mardonius (8.99.2). Xerxes, by contrast, though he acknowledges that he was born an evil for his family and for his fatherland (932-4), and though he confesses reluctantly that he 'left behind' his lieutenants, unburied (962-6), also offers the excuse that his fate was totally unpredictable (910), or observes neutrally that the Persian dead 'have gone' (1002);[53] he is inclined to focus on his own misfortunes, for example his lack of an escort (1036), or his lack of clothes (1017).[54] What appears initially, however, to be almost a tug of war between the King and his subjects gradually gives way to a situation in which Xerxes almost choreographs the Chorus' lament. At lines 1008-9 Xerxes for the first time uses the first person plural, and the Chorus responds in the same way: 'a feeling of identification is established. Xerxes has passed from utter despair to a feeling of communal sorrow.'[55] From line 1038 until the end of the play Xerxes issues a series of commands, all of which are readily obeyed by the

Chorus.[56] The Chorus' reawakened respect for Darius has been transferred to his son.

This collapse of the Chorus' initiative is made worse by two other factors. The first is that Darius was not, in fact, the successful model of kingship that they present him as having been: he was responsible (albeit less directly) for the defeat at Marathon.[57] The common way of handling this contradiction is to suppose simply that Aeschylus must be exaggerating Darius' success for dramatic contrast. 'Darius serves as a foil to Xerxes. He is the wise king, Xerxes the foolish one.'[58] Parallel to this purely dramatic explanation of the contrast is a political one: Aeschylus is emphasising the naval, therefore democratic, battle of Salamis above the hoplite, therefore less democratic, Marathon – all this in support of Themistocles against Cimon, the son of Miltiades. It is certainly true, as Suzanne Saïd has pointed out, that while Herodotus presents the succession of Persian kings as forming a continuous progression – 'a repetitive machine, always compelled to affirm its power and, by doing so, to destroy it'[59] – Aeschylus' Xerxes is in general represented as marking an abrupt break from his predecessors.[60] However, Aeschylus does not maintain this impression consistently. 'Long ago', the Chorus observe at the opening of the play, 'Fate ... commanded the Persians to engage in wars which destroy walls, in the tumult of cavalry charges and in the overthrowing of cities' (101-5). The idea of Xerxes as the exception to the rule of Persian kings is also undermined by Darius' own words in his recounting of the achievements of his predecessors: he concludes by saying that none had done as much damage as Xerxes (785-6) – hardly a ringing endorsement.

Moreover, just as Aeschylus fails quite to erase Plataea completely – rather he makes Plataea into a 'mopping-up operation' in Richmond Lattimore's words, or the 'crowning disaster' in the words of Kitto[61] – so he makes no attempt to erase Marathon.[62] The Athenians manage well enough without a shepherd 'to have destroyed Darius' large and excellent army' (244; cf. 236[63]). The Queen later laments that 'the barbarians whom Marathon destroyed were not enough' for Xerxes (475). If the Chorus knew anything of Darius' Scythian campaign – knowledge of the Persian conquest of the 'Acheloian cities neighbouring the gulf of Strymon' and of the 'mouth of the Black Sea' are announced at 865-80, though these are examples of conquests made without Darius' venturing from his hearth – or if they knew anything of Cyrus' campaign against the Massagetai or of Cambyses' expedition into Ethiopia, then the improbability of Darius' distinction would have struck them still more strongly.[64] But, whether or not we judge it likely that Aeschylus' audience knew of these earlier campaigns – or rather that they knew of the *Greek versions* of these campaigns later recast by Herodotus – it is surely stretching credibility to suppose that they were ignorant of the name of the Persian ruler responsible for Marathon, still more so to imagine – even if only a proportion of that audience were aware of Darius' past history – that Aeschylus could have presented him as straightforwardly blameless.[65]

Though the Chorus then has forgotten this past history, and envisages the succession of Persian kings as having been broken by Xerxes' failure, the audience, I suggest, is intended to observe the Persians' forgetfulness and the continuity that Xerxes represents.[66] This continuity can be seen, first, in the Chorus' very dependence on Darius' advice. They are, as we have seen, possibly disillusioned with Xerxes; they have just enough strength or independence of mind to acknowledge their own slavery. For them then immediately to revert to their awestruck ways shows clearly that they are failing to address the root cause of their defeat. It is not any individual's foibles but monarchy itself that is responsible for their defeat.[67] The option of freedom indeed is perhaps quite illusory: for, just like the Persian woman in Atossa's dream who bears herself proudly under her yoke (192-7), submission is a reflex action.[68] Freedom of speech is impossible within a monarchy, a truth which emerges from a number of contexts in the *Histories*: Xerxes, for example, summons his elders together 'so as to learn their opinions and inform them all of his wishes' (7.8), or (as he remarks later) 'so that I may not seem to follow my own counsel' (*hina de mê idiobouleein humin dokeô*, 7.8.δ2); when Artabanus, alone of his advisers, dared to speak against Xerxes' planned expedition, the King was duly furious (7.10-11).[69] On another occasion, Artemisia's advice is accepted, Herodotus tells us, for the simple reason that it coincides with Xerxes' own opinion (8.103).

The continuity between Darius and Xerxes can also be seen in Darius' own behaviour. Though his manner may be more emollient, Darius' priorities are little different from those of his Queen. His actions also provide an illustration of the practical limitations of monarchy. When he has recognised, on the basis of prophecies he remembers, that the time for this catastrophe had come sooner than he had expected, he then sees the immediate future clearly: he now believes the oracles he had previously dismissed with wishful thinking.[70] Here again a political contrast is surely pointed between democratic Athens and Persia. Aeschylus alludes, of course, elsewhere to the oracle of the wooden wall (348-9). Darius' 'fountain spring of misery' (743) may possibly refer back to the 'spring of silver' (238) that constitutes the wealth of Athens, and which Themistocles famously persuaded the Athenians to use for the construction of ships (7.144). Themistocles' interpretation of the wooden wall oracle was adopted by the Athenian people in preference to that of the specialist interpreters in the course of an assembly meeting (7.142-3). The Persian King on the other hand, in this instance Darius, like Spartan kings (6.57.4; cf. 5.90.2, 5.93.2) or the Lydian Croesus, has a monopoly over oracles, with the result that the tragedy of the Persian defeat is discovered too late.[71]

The second factor underlying the collapse of the Chorus' initiative is their belief in the divinity of Persian royalty. As we have seen, there is a danger of being distracted by the question of the veracity of Aeschylus' picture of Persian religious practice or belief.[72] It should be stated at the outset that there is no evidence that the Persians believed that their kings were gods, or that the proskynesis expected by a Persian king constituted worship.[73] The Greeks, however, persisted in believing otherwise – this despite contradictions suggesting that some may have known better. Herodotus, for example, tells us that the Persians perform proskynesis to those better born than them, not only to their kings (1.134.1).[74] But he also tells the story of two Spartan ambassadors who volunteer to die at the hands of the Persians in expiation for the Spartans' killing of two Persian ambassadors (7.136.1):

> And when they were come into Susa into the King's presence and the guards ordered them to fall down and do obeisance, and went so far as to use force to compel them, they refused, and said they would never do such a thing, even were their heads thrust down to the ground; for it was not their custom to worship men, and they had not come to Persia for that purpose.[75]

For a Persian, on the other hand, proskynesis is presented as a reflex action. When Xerxes calls off the expedition to Greece, Herodotus mentions that the Persians of his court perform proskynesis out of relief (7.13.3), a passing piece of characterisation akin to the Chorus' prostration before Atossa. Similarly, Harpagus performed proskynesis in response to his being invited to dinner by his king, the Median Astyages (1.119.1), and, after a clap of thunder confirmed the choice of Darius as King, his fellow-conspirators together leapt from their horses to prostrate themselves (3.86.2). That such actions imply a belief in the divinity of the King is not, of course, made as clear here as in Herodotus' account of the Spartan ambassadors. Such reflex proskynesis, however, surely reflects a powerful Greek perception of the slavishness of the King's subjects; it also insinuates the excessive pretensions of the Persian King.[76]

A similar pattern of ideas underlies the *Persians*. The raising of Darius may find parallels in other tragedies.[77] But the evocation of Darius itself must be distinguished from the significance attached to it by the participants. The impression that the Persians believe their kings to be divine is one that is built up progressively through the play.[78] Xerxes is envisaged, before his failure has been discovered, as leading his 'divine flock against every land' (75). He is an 'equal of the gods' (*isotheos*, 80), a phrase that may be innocent in epic but which is suggestive of a dangerous self-aggrandisement in tragedy.[79] Atossa's first appearance is met by the self-abasement of the Chorus (*prospitnô*, 152);[80] she is addressed as a 'light equal to the eyes of gods' (150-1) and as the mother and wife of gods (155-8) although the condition is added: 'unless an ancient deity has now somehow turned against the army'.[81] Darius, as we have seen, is described as a divine counsellor (*theomêstôr*), a king 'equal to a daimon' (*isodaimôn basileus*, 634), the Susa-born god of the Persians (643).[82] His arrival inspires the Chorus to chant their 'dread' (*diomai*, 700-1) and 'reverence' (*sebomai*, 694-5) more fitting perhaps for gods than men; it was possibly also accompanied by an act of prostration.[83] The divinity of Darius is arguably more clearly stated than that of his wife or son. This is not necessarily, however, to be explained in terms of Aeschylus' attempt to portray the ritual honours paid to Persian kings after their deaths, as suggested by Hall.[84] Rather it is perhaps simply a reflection of Darius' perceived success: Atossa's position as the mother and wife of gods (155-8) is, as we have seen, conditional (in the Chorus' eyes) on the success of Xerxes' expedition; Darius' status as a *theomêstôr* seems also to be the result of his successful command of the army (654-5).[85] A more significant distinction is that the delusion of the divinity of Persian royalty is not one shared by royalty themselves. With one possible exception – the Queen's reference to Darius as leading his life 'like a god' (711)[86] – it is noticeable that it is only the Chorus who ascribe divinity to Darius, Xerxes or the Queen. Darius, according to the Queen, amassed his wealth 'not without the help of some god' (164). And Darius himself also seems to be quite clear on his own status: he blames Xerxes for having hoped to rule the gods and Poseidon too, although himself a mortal (744-50). The Chorus' belief, then, in the divine status of the Persian monarchy (and, correlative to this, in their own powerlessness) adds extra emphasis to the theme of their attempt at their own emancipation: the Chorus, we may remember, look forward to the end of proskynesis as one of the consequences of the Persian defeat (588). Their dread and reverence on being confronted with Darius show, however, that their slavishness of mind is too deep-rooted.

But how is the Athenian audience meant to receive this? 'The Persians' view of Darius as divine cannot', according to Taplin, 'be regarded as barbarous blasphemy or as mere oriental colour, since his audience is also obliged to accept it. The kletic hymn succeeds; and when Darius says that he is a great power in the underworld (691) there is no room to disbelieve him. All this gives his prophecies and moral judgement the requisite authority.'[87] A number of distinctions need to be drawn, however. That Darius is successfully evoked by the Chorus, or that he has status within the underworld,[88] do not constitute proof of his divinity. The audience is not then obliged to accept the divinity of Darius. Indeed, against the background of reverent language and prostration, and in the light of the evidence in other sources for the persistent Greek misunderstanding of proskynesis, it is hard to see how they could have understood the evocation of Darius as anything other than 'barbarous blasphemy'.[89] There is also no reason to suppose that the prophecies delivered by Darius are in any sense 'his prophecies'. His language rather suggests that they are oracles the significance of which he has missed (739-41):

> Alas! How swiftly oracles have been accomplished! Zeus has hurled down on my son the consummation of prophecies. I trusted, I suppose, that the gods would bring them to fulfilment in some far distant time.

Now he will know to trust in the inevitable fulfilment of the 'gods' ordinances' (*theôn thesphatoisin*, 800-2). In what sense then does Darius exude authority? Darius, it is often said, represents the voice of the poet himself. Darius is, according to Broadhead, the 'figure, more than any other in the play, [who] shows how far Aeschylus has risen above the level of narrow nationalism'. He presents 'the concentrated essence of the poet's philosophy'; 'the significant thing for our present purpose is that a Persian is made to set the calamity down *not to the superiority of the Greeks ... but to the transgression of the divine law*, transgression that would bring disaster upon any human being, be he Greek or barbarian'.[90] The question of whether the Greeks are liable to similar transgressions and, consequently, to a similar punishment, I will defer until later. Two important points need to be made here. The first is that it could hardly have been anyone else but a Persian who delivered Darius' truths: the moral, for example, that the Persians should refrain in future from making war on the Greeks (790-1), that Xerxes should not have attempted to bridge the Hellespont, or that the remaining Persian forces in Europe would be decimated at Plataea. These truths are in no way devalued by a second observation, however:[91] that regardless of the authority of certain of Darius' words, his words of wisdom are simply too late. There is no way of telling, especially in the light of the Scythian or Marathon campaigns, whether Darius would have been able to heed his own advice.

Darius' authority then is to a significant extent a false authority, one which is projected upon him by the Chorus. There is indeed only one authentic source of authority, as Darius himself reveals: Zeus is a stern assessor (*euthunos barus*, 827-8).[92] Zeus' prerogative as an unaccountable assessor of men is one that kings and tyrants habitually usurp.[93] Herodotus' story of Thrasybulus of Miletus cutting off the heads of the tallest ears of corn to illustrate to his junior 'colleague' Periander that the tyrant must kill his city's best citizens (5.92.ζ-η1) is not by accident reminiscent of Artabanus' description of the divinity who cuts down all things that grow too tall (7.10.ε). It is precisely this mistake of attempting to usurp divine power that the Persian kings, by their excessive and whimsical punishments and by their assumption of an unaccountable position (210-14), have also committed. Xerxes' subjects too have mistaken their master for a god. On finding the Strymon conveniently frozen over, 'those who previously had not taken the gods at all seriously then called on them with prayers, prostrating themselves (*proskunôn*) before Earth and Sky' (497-9).[94] The Strymon then gave way beneath their feet. The Persians on Psyttaleia involuntarily perform proskynesis through their deaths (*prospitnontes*, 461). They have learnt the proper object of their proskynesis, but too late.[95] The Chorus, on the other hand, have actually unlearnt this lesson.

Does the end of the play imply no upturn in the Persians' fortunes? The shift from the dislocation of Chorus and monarchy to a mood of communal sorrow has been explained by critics, as we have seen, as due to the dramatic device of Xerxes' new clothes; these are seen as reflecting symbolically the re-arming of Persian royal power, and a warning to the Athenians of the resurgence of the Persian threat.[96] This change of clothes, however – though it cannot be ruled out with certainty as a contributory factor – is by no means a necessary condition of this shift of tone: the Chorus' gradual reversion to its earlier ways of submission to royal authority, a reversion inspired by Darius' intervention,[97] provides a sufficient explanation of this change. For the end of the play to be marked by the resurgence of Persia would surely also be out of keeping with the recurrent emphasis on the Persians' destruction that has gone before, and indeed which persists even in these last lines: that Persia's past glories are irrecoverable is emphasised by the frequent use of the perfect tense.[98] As the empty quiver of Xerxes suggests, the remnants of the Persian elite have closed ranks only in the face of the imminent collapse of the Empire. The Chorus' violent mourning – the only example in extant tragedy of a male chorus indulging in such a lament[99] – through its implication of effeminacy, again suggests that Persia is beyond remedy. Xerxes' tattered clothing, like the change in the Queen's mode of entry that earlier prefigures it (607-8),[100] would merely have reinforced this impression. If a new set of clothes were introduced then, it would be more likely to have been as a symbol of a false resurgence against a backdrop where all has changed. The Chorus' response to Xerxes is, in their own words, 'a wretched response of wretched cries to wretched cries' (*dosin kakan kakôn kakois*, 1041). There is nothing redeeming about their communal suffering – unless it be the Athenians' joy in observing it (1034).

Part III

Conclusions

9

Themistocles and Aristides

We return finally – after a long detour – to some of the themes raised in Part I. As we have seen, the play has often served as a prop in the reconstruction of the politics of early fifth-century Athens. By alluding to Themistocles' naval victory at Salamis, by making a number of other allusions to sentiments voiced by Themistocles (or at least ascribed to him by Herodotus), Aeschylus, it is often held, was the protagonist in a propaganda battle to save Themistocles from ostracism. In the light of our thematic exploration of the play in Part II, can anything of this 'party political' stance be salvaged?

The play is markedly vague on the proper extent of Greek vengeance against Persia. Persian rule over Asia is finished (584-90). Darius is afraid that his wealth will fall prey to the first plunderers (751-2). The empire is defenceless. However, except for the Chorus' description of the conquests of Darius in the Mediterranean (by implication reconquered or due to be reconquered by the Greeks), if we exclude the omen of the hawk and the eagle as prophetic only of events in the Persian wars, the agents of Persian destruction are left unspecified. This studied vagueness could be for many reasons: it could be the result of the play's ostensibly Persian focus; it could be a concession to historical reality. Could it just possibly – together with the emphasis on the Hellespont as the natural frontier between Asia and Europe – be seen as a justification of Themistocles' act of allowing Xerxes to withdraw safely across the Hellespont (8.108-10)?[1]

Exactly what Themistocles' position on this question was is uncertain, however. Herodotus has Themistocles initially support the opposite point of view, that they should set out in pursuit of Xerxes: he only changes his stance when he realises that he is unable to persuade a majority of the Greek commanders; then famously he sends his message to the King claiming the credit for preventing the destruction of the Hellespont bridge – a precaution in case of his ever falling out of favour with the Athenians. Given Themistocles' various manoeuvrings in this account, and given especially the possibility that the story of Themistocles has been rewritten in the light of his subsequent exile, it is not possible to be certain of what in 472 a Themistoclean policy might have been deemed to be. Moreover, the line between a defensive policy of allowing Xerxes to withdraw and an offensive one of harrying him to the Hellespont is rather less clearcut in Herodotus' account: Eurybiades concludes his argument that Xerxes should be left to withdraw to Asia by saying that the battle could then be fought on Xerxes' own ground (8.108.4).

On the whole, it is better not to look to tragedy for approval or disapproval of such very specific 'policy positions'. Any direct or unmistakable stand on such a narrow issue would, as was argued above, surely have stood out uncomfortably from the rest of the play and have polarised its audience. It is perhaps possible, however, to detect a political stance to the *Persians* that runs with rather than against the grain of its main arguments.

The Persian monarchy, as we have seen, is not a success. Whereas in Athens the best advice is received from any quarter – notably in the case of the oracle of the wooden wall to which the play alludes – in Persia the Chorus is prevented from giving frank advice by a paralysing fear of royalty, rooted partly in their perception of their kings as divine. Xerxes' impulses are left unchecked: he pursues his expedition to Greece, egged on by his advisers and his sense of his father's reputation; his position remains undisputed even after the expedition's failure. Themistocles, by contrast, is never named, but only alluded to. But it is precisely the anonymity of the Greeks – by comparison with the lavishly named Persian commanders – which emphasises most clearly the submission of every Athenian to the city as a whole.[2] Unlike the Persians who must be forced to fight, the Athenians each fight for themselves. 'Every man is the lord of his oar' (378).[3] Herodotus expresses the same ideology succinctly – albeit in the context of hoplite warfare – in his judgement on the change in the Athenians' military fortunes after their liberation from tyranny: 'This makes clear that while they were in subjection they were lazy in so far as they were working for a master, but as soon as they were freed each man worked for himself' (5.78).[4]

It is precisely through Themistocles' submission to this ideal, *precisely through his anonymity*, that the best case for Themistocles can be made out.[5] Themistocles is not, of course, the only prominent Athenian to be trumpeted – albeit in a muted fashion – in the play. Other commanders, most notably Cimon, were responsible for the 'liberation' of Darius' acquisitions (852-907). Most clearly, Aristides receives an equivalent fanfare in Aeschylus' account of the destruction of the Persian infantry on Psyttaleia.[6] The attention given to Psyttaleia in the play, as has been observed by a number of critics, seems indeed disproportionate to its military significance, at least to judge by Herodotus' account.[7] Psyttaleia is presented in fact as a counterweight to Salamis (435-40):[8]

> M: You can be sure that they [the Persians' catastrophes] are not yet half-narrated. Such was the suffering which happened then that it outweighed these by at least twice.
>
> Q: And what misfortune could be even more hateful than this? Tell me, what other disaster happened to our force to swing the balance even further down?

This surprising emphasis on Psyttaleia has been interpreted as evidence of Aeschylus' support for Aristides;[9] this in turn has led other critics to despair of any particular political message behind the play.[10] But there are other possible explanations for the prominence of Psyttaleia in the *Persians*. Psyttaleia may serve, for example, as a means of giving credit to the Athens' infantry as well as its navy, and so of making her victory total, both by land and sea.[11] Aeschylus' emphasis has also been explained as due to the distinction of the Persian victims,[12] or as a means of emphasising the ignominious nature of the Persians' defeat.[13] It is also possible that the balance between Psyttaleia and Salamis is connected to the theme of individual submission to the collective.

Aristides, in Herodotus' account, was a bitter enemy of Themistocles (8.79.2), but before the battle of Salamis, he came to his old rival and made the suggestion that their rivalry from then on should be rivalry for the good of their fatherland (8.79.3). The truth of this story of

Aristides' and Themistocles' competition for the good of Athens has been doubted.[14] There is no question that the story has been elaborated further by Plutarch;[15] it seems to have attained the status of a national myth by the time of Herodotus. Aeschylus' *Persians*, however, is the best evidence that this was not merely a retrospective piece of myth-making, that the idea of their competition for the good of Athens was current in 472.[16] 'Themistocle et Aristide s'effacent derrière Athènes.'[17] The play's themes, according to Pelling, were 'themes which all Athenians would thrill to, not the stuff of partisan ideology'.[18] If the *Persians* was indeed interpreted as a message of support for Themistocles, however, it was a message that had power only by *harnessing* the play's patriotism to a partisan end, by disguising that partisan stance behind themes that all could rally to, to which none could object.

Ultimately, of course, the question of whether or not the play was intended, interpreted, or effective as a political message of support for Themistocles or Aristides is – like the question of their attendance at the *Persians'* original performance 'qui leur absence eût rendue incomplète, où tous les regards les cherchaient, où toutes les voix les nommaient'[19] – quite incapable of proof. The *Persians*, however, tells us about much more than just this narrow question: more important than Aeschylus' political stance – for or against Themistocles – are the terms in which either argument could have been made out. Aeschylus' play gives us a snapshot in the development of Athenian democratic discourse.

A common view holds that the question of how the Athenian state should be governed was not yet a live issue in the 470s; only in the following decade did the democratic Argos of the *Suppliants* reflect a 'sympathetic interest in the view that the *demos* ought to be sovereign'.[20] The early years of the Pentakontaetia are, of course, even more scantily equipped with evidence than later decades. In the account of the *Athenaion Politeia*, the period between the Persian wars and 462 is a history written in reverse, termed the 'Areopagite constitution' in deference to the reforms which deprived the Areopagites of their powers. Our other sources concentrate largely on Athens' imperial expansion. Arguably, however, this political vacuum is one that – on the basis of likelihood – should be filled by extrapolation. It has recently been argued by R.G. Lewis, for example, that the *Athenaion Politeia*'s story of Themistocles' association with Ephialtes in a series of legal assaults on the Areopagus might in fact have been historical (25.4): though it has been presumed that they must immediately have preceded the reforms, there is nothing in the account of the *Athenaion Politeia* to suggest that these legal stunts were not staged over a longer period of time.[21] It is possible also to extrapolate from preceding events. The pejorative association of Persia with tyranny – implying surely a mirroring democratic ideal – was almost certainly well-established by the time of the Ionian Revolt.[22] Brian Lavelle has sketched a process of the gradual Athenian demonisation of the sixth-century tyranny, and of tyranny in general, in parallel to the Persian wars.[23] The first victims of ostracism, in the decade between Marathon and Salamis, were (surely not coincidentally) relatives and friends of the expelled Athenian tyrant Hippias (22.4-7), Hippias who had accompanied the Persian expedition to Marathon in 490. It was in the immediate aftermath of the Ionian Revolt, in 493/2, that Miltiades was prosecuted in Athens for the tyranny he had exercised in the Chersonese (6.104.2). Some tyrannical associations seem to hang over his prosecution for deceit after Marathon (6.136.1): Miltiades had requested seventy ships from the Athenians, an army and money, but without telling them the object of his expedition except that they would become rich (6.132). In the event he returned from his expedition to Paros having acquired neither the island nor money, but with his tail between his legs (6.135.1). If the *Persians* represents a democratic defence of Themistocles (as sketched above), it is easy to imagine how *criticism* of Themistocles might equally have been clothed in the language of accountability and democracy. Indeed a trace of such criticism may survive in the tradition of Themistocles' profiteering activities after Salamis: Herodotus reports, for example, how the Parians 'propitiated' (*hilasamenoi*) Themistocles with money and so escaped the fate of being beseiged (8.112.3).

The *Persians* – with its repeated emphasis on the differences in government between Athens and Persia – is a central piece of evidence for the political complexion of the 470s, for the proposition that ideological issues underlay the competition of personalities. Everything in Aeschylus' play tends to the impression of Athenian unity, Athenian singleness of purpose. If Themistocles is praised it is in the guise of an ideology that sees all Athenians as resolved to compete for the good of Athens. If Athens is glorified above other cities, it is beneath a veil of

Panhellenism; she is glorified for her having saved Greece through her sacrifice of her land.

But – with a risk, undoubtedly, of over-ingenuity – we may attempt some guesses at underlying ideological tensions. The pairing of Aristides and Themistocles as competing for the good of Athens tells us nothing of their actual relationship; we might suppose, however, that this ideological slogan disguised at least some current animosity or ideological differences between the two men. That Aeschylus pays nearly equivalent attention to both the land engagement of Psyttaleia and the naval battle of Salamis suggests equally that two constituencies – whether they were political, social or both – demanded some acknowledgement. Aeschylus' nods to the part of Sparta in the war – his reference in particular to the Dorian lance of Plataea (817) – suggest again a certain self-consciousness, a sense that relations with Sparta were a matter of dispute in contemporary Athens.

No tidy alignment of political interests is possible, however: we cannot assume that pro-Laconism coincided necessarily with an antipathy to increased democracy and *vice versa*. Indeed, if (as I think we may) we take Aeschylus' play – by virtue of its large popular audience – as indicative of a consensus of values that the vast majority of Athenians could have subscribed to, we must acknowledge not only those fissures in Athenian political life such as that over her relationship with Sparta or over the extension of popular sovereignty but also, and equally importantly, the fragile notion of a dual hegemony of Sparta and Athens, and of a democratic ideology that gave space to the achievements of men of different, more traditionally aristocratic, persuasions.

It is not only, finally, for its value as a source for contemporary *political* ideology that the play has been used. The picture of two political camps, one Cimonian and one Themistoclean, that has been constructed around the evidence of Aeschylus' political sympathies has in many readings also a broader, religious-philosophical dimension. Herington, for example, has appointed Anaxagoras an honorary member of the Themistoclean camp:

> Just how far Anaxagoras' thinking penetrated into Athenian society during his residence we cannot tell, but it had certainly reached Pericles and, presumably, Pericles' circle; there at the core

> and center of the new democratic movement, the new philosophic-scientific learning was quietly at work. Was Aeschylus aware of this thinking, the direct antithesis of the ancient mythic-religious thinking with which he had grown up? Certainly he must have known Pericles, since ... the two were associated in the production of the *Persians*. ... In almost every area of human experience – religious, artistic, social, economic, and political – the immemorially old was being abruptly confronted by the utterly new.[24]

A great deal hinges apparently on the question of Aeschylus' political sympathies. It would be easy to dismiss such cosmic excesses too glibly, however. For one thing, such grand historical progressions as that sketched by Herington are becoming no less frequent. Christian Meier, for example, has painted a picture of the fifth century in which events became 'to a probably unprecedented degree ... commensurable with human action'.[25] Moreover, the ideas stated explicitly by Herington can be found implicitly to underpin even much of the more traditional material on this period. Herington's position is not a million miles away from the powerfully attractive model of progressive demystification developed by George Forrest, for example,[26] or his idea of a Cimon whose 'world was also Pindar's world'.[27] The idea of a transition from an archaic reliogiosity in which 'religious power' is mobilised as easily as toy soldiers on a tablecloth to a period in which, armed with the tools of democracy, men had no need to fall back upon their old gods is – perhaps to understate the position – a tenacious one.[28]

The examination of any single, sustained text from this period provides a salutary caution against such a deterministic model. Who can say whether the indictment of Persian monarchy in Aeschylus' play – with its implicit comparison of Darius' and Themistocles' interpretation of oracles, with its emphasis on the false 'divinity' of Persian kings as a factor keeping their subjects in slavery – is one delivered primarily in religious or political terms?[29] Given the interconnectedness of religious and political issues in the play, who is to say that the world of Cimon and Pindar was not perfectly compatible with that of Pericles and Anaxagoras? As has been emphasised recently, 'the traditional religious framework' was, in fact, a 'loose and accommodating structure within which certain forms of doubt, criticism, and revision were, in fact, traditional'.[30] We cannot presume that Ephialtes was embarked on a programme of the secularisation of Athenian politics, still less that he succeeded in such a programme.

It is also questionable to what extent it is reasonable to talk of religious 'themes', consciously deployed by Aeschylus. Simon Goldhill has remarked, for example (in the context of a discussion of Aeschylus' genealogy of the Persian kings), that the playwright 'is concerned ... to place the historical and genealogical narrative within a theological and moral framework'.[31] It is not mere sophistry to object that it is unlikely that Aeschylus saw his own task in such terms. We need arguably to discover new ways of talking that reflect the fact that many of the 'themes' employed by Aeschylus, the theme of hybris for example, are cultural commonplaces, that the religious argument of a play such as the *Persians* is one embedded in its other arguments.[32] Nor do we need to choose between a 'theological and moral framework' and a patriotic purpose. Religion may both reflect and reinforce patriotism. As Parker has observed of the many cults founded or reorganised in Athens in the fifth century, it is striking to what extent they reflect 'its great historical centrepiece, the struggle against Persia .... In this perspective Greek religion does not appear as a mechanism for controlling the world; it is rather a celebration of achievement – that achievement in the face of Persian hordes which for the Greeks was almost heroic in the literal sense – an affirmation of value.'[33]

10

Athens and Persia

'It would ... be wrong to say that Aeschylus sought to make of this play a Greek paean on the one hand, a Persian dirge on the other.' So judges Broadhead.[1] As we have seen, however, the *Persians* again and again focusses on the Greek victory and its causes, contrasting Persian vices with Greek virtues.[2] The position criticised here by Broadhead seems in fact an accurate description of the play.

Is there no sympathy, however, implicit in the play for the Persian victims? A number of critics have tried to reconcile a degree of sympathy or even empathy for the Persians with its patriotic or militaristic aspect. Some accept that there will be a necessary trade-off between sympathy and patriotism. Others, however, resist this zero-sum game. Their formulations tend, as a result, to be markedly vague. The tragedy, according to duBois, 'threatens to dissolve their opposition in a moment of shared lamentation'.[3] Gagarin sees a 'basic tension or irony throughout the play' between its tragic and celebratory elements; at the same time 'we can see how Aeschylus has blended the two perspectives in *Persae* so that each supports the other in an important synthesis'.[4] Prickard simply saw two threads of interest running through the play, the 'patriotic interest' and the 'dramatic or ideal interest', without attempting to reconcile them'.[5] Pelling excels all in elasticity. 'The polarity' between Self and Other 'is simultaneously challenged and asserted'.[6] Pelling argues for an Athenian audience ready and waiting to have their prejudices challenged:[7]

> If the audience, or some of them, are brought to feel pity, should we regard that as a shattering surprise to them? If so, that would go with a view that tragedy was a deeply disquieting genre, and also with an assumption that their initial prejudices were crude

> ones … I argue that the audience, or some of them, might find such pity less of a surprise, and the tragedy therefore less disconcerting: on that view, the initial prejudices would be richer-textured, with a cultural expectation of empathy towards a vanquished foe as well as vindictiveness.

But how can *empathy* be compatible with *vindictiveness*? There must surely be limits to the conflicting emotions that tragedy can inspire.[8] Pelling suggests – perhaps half-jokingly? – that 'paradoxically, those spectators whose emotions crossed the Greek-barbarian divide most completely could simultaneously feel themselves as most completely fulfilling a national stereotype: for was not pity a distinctively Athenian virtue?'[9] Athenian claims of virtue, however, can hardly be taken as evidence of virtue.[10] More plausible perhaps would be to ask whether the Athenians – from the vantage-point of victory – could not have afforded to feel a pity for the Persians, a pity predicated precisely on the Persians' powerlessness. But that, of course, though it might be consonant with what one might call the official posture of the play – that of the utter destruction of the Persians – would not so easily be compatible with the historical reality that lurks only a little beneath the surface.[11]

Two more ingenious methods of reconciling the opposition between these two elements of the play deserve attention. For Macleod, the purpose of the praise of Athens in the play is to increase the 'bewilderment and gloom' of the Persians on stage:[12] all is subordinated to the dramatic reconstruction of Persia; the political is subordinated to the 'tragic'. Hall falls back on a psychological explanation:[13]

> Despite their own construction in the play as fearless and invincible killing machines, the unique psychological process offered by the theatre allows them, through watching fellow-citizens 'playing the other', vicariously to work through the difficult emotions which they had themselves experienced. Yet the displacement of those emotions onto the enemy (a process psychoanalysts call 'projection') simultaneously permits them to retain the comfortable identity of unemotional Greeks so scrupulously maintained by the text. They could simultaneously enjoy profound patriotic pride, a sense of ethnic superiority, confirmation of their own

> masculine self-image, the thrill of victory, *and* the covert exorcism of their own psychological pain.

Hall avoids the word pity here; but in order for the process of psychological projection to operate, some form at least of identification is surely necessary. The repeated emphasis of the play on the differences between Athens and Persia surely militates against any such identification.

Other critics have accepted that any sympathy for the Persians detracts from, or mitigates, the patriotic element of the play. A 'sense of common mortality mitigated the patriotism that the audience no doubt also feel', according to Euben.[14] For Michelini, 'the piquancy of foreign names' in Aeschylus' battle narrative – names 'which ... appear bizarre and repellent' – 'is *played off against* the equally great potential of the Persians' tragedy to arouse compassion'.[15] Criticism of the *Persians* becomes then the task of marking the spot on a scale that runs between 'outright xenophobia' (or 'mere jingoism') on the one hand and 'extraordinary compassion' on the other,[16] of measuring the degree of sympathy or empathy expected by Aeschylus of his audience.

One particularly full and forthright assault on the 'jingoistic and heavily moralistic reading' (associated with Edith Hall) deserves to be singled out. While simultaneously 'a disreputable challenge to, or negation of, democratic norms', the Persian monarchy, Mark Griffith has argued,[17] also represented 'a desirable and irresistible object of admiration and fascination, even of comfort ...'.[18] Not all Athenians, he acknowledges, but *some* 'might have looked on Kyros and Dareios and other Asian potentates as unequivocally impressive and admirable models of leadership and achievement ... especially those who were most familiar with aristocratic lifestyle, military command, athletic competition, and property ownership, and those who were not entirely content with democracy'.[19] After all, the Athenians (or at least some of them) believed it possible that one of their leading families, the Alcmeonids, had been responsible for raising a shield at Marathon as a signal to the Persian forces (6.121-4).[20] The oriental tyrant, moreover, may not have seemed such a contemptible 'other' as has been supposed. Tyranny in the archaic period was not only the object of disapproval but also of aristocratic competition.[21] It was only recently, according to Thucydides, that the Athenians abandoned a softer, more luxurious lifestyle, and their rich old men ceased to wear linen tunics and fasten their hair with gold grasshoppers, as the Ionians learnt to do from them (1.6.3).[22] Xenophon's *Cyropaedia* in the fourth century employs the Persia of Cyrus as the exemplar of the just monarchy.[23] Against this backdrop, Griffith suggests, Xerxes seems not so very 'unGreek'.[24] Aeschylus' rather jarring emphasis on the Dorian dress of one of the women of Atossa's dream may be intended to emphasise the 'similarity or identity of Persian and Ionian women's dress in the early fifth century'.[25] Finally, though extravagant laments such as that which closes the play may have been forbidden in Athens, tragedy is not real life: the Athenian audience may have felt distaste for the Chorus' lamentations, but they may also have experienced a 'half-guilty surrender to tears and pity', pleasure and excitement in 'hearing and seeing such forbidden (unAthenian, undemocratic) sights and sounds'.[26] Griffith observes that it is with 'unmixed delight' that Dionysus in Aristophanes' *Frogs* recalls the chorus' 'exotic cries' (*Ran.* 1028-9 tr. Sommerstein):[27]

> I certainly enjoyed it when [they listened to] the dead Darius and straight away the chorus clapped its hands together, like this, and went 'iaow-oy'.

There are a number of problems with Griffith's assault, however. To take Aristophanes' Dionysus first, 'unmixed delight' is not the reaction one would expect of an audience who had been moved to (even guilty) tears of sympathy. More persuasive for Griffith's case would be a reaction akin to that recorded by Herodotus to Phrynichus' *Capture of Miletus*: the whole theatre is said to have burst into tears – out of guilt, according to modern opinion, at their failure to help their Milesian allies[28] – and the people fined the playwright one thousand drachmae for reminding them of their own misfortunes (6.21.2). Dionysus' delight, on the other hand, emphasises precisely the foreignness of the Persians. As for the similarity between Persian and Ionian dress, as Leslie Kurke and others have shown,[29] it was precisely at the beginning of the fifth century – in parallel then to the demonisation of Persian (and Athenian) tyranny, and to the development of a democratic ideology sketched above – that the change in clothing described by Thucydides occurred. The democratic ethos underpinning the rejection of luxury is reflected indeed in Thucydides' account of this change: the Spartans, he says, first turned to a simpler style, so that their first citizens should seem to have exactly the same lifestyle (*isodiaitoi*, 1.6.4) as the majority. The Dorian garb of the lady of Atossa's dream may then actually have served to *avoid* the similarity of Ionian and Persian dress, to emphasise the simplicity of Greek lifestyle by comparison: Herodotus interestingly is the source of an alternative tradition that the dress that was in his day called 'Dorian' was, in fact, the original uniform of all Greeks, but that (in an unspecified, distant past) Athenian women were condemned to wear Ionian clothes in punishment for murdering the messenger who had told them of their husbands' deaths (5.87.3).

Of course, there must have been many who did not conform to this ideal of egalitarian simplicity. The denunciations of aristocratic luxury in Old Comedy, or the reference in a scholiast to Aristophanes' *Knights* (580)[30] to the proposal of a law that young men should not wear their hair long or be *habrodiaitoi* (soft in lifestyle) in the old manner, must reflect an aristocratic counter-culture in Athens – at least later in the century.[31] As for aristocratic attitudes towards Persia, though to use the fourth-century *Cyropaedia* as evidence may seem to ignore the playful, even whimsical, tone of that text (and its concluding condemnation of Persian luxury[32]), clearly it is not inconceivable – as the cases of the Alcmeonids or of Hippias reveal – that an aristocratic family should have harboured feelings of sympathy towards Persia, or at least have thought to use Persian power for domestic ends as the lesser of two evils. After the evacuation and destruction of Attica and the victory at Salamis, the Spartans – if we may believe Herodotus – seriously feared that the Athenians might join forces with the Persians (8.141). However, what these examples also show is that any such accommodation with the Persians was regarded as nothing less than treasonous. Like the Alcmeonids, the Athenians – in one of the most often quoted passages of the *Histories* – denied that they were contemplating such 'medism' fiercely, appealing to the common blood, the common language and shrines of the Greeks, and swearing that while one Athenian lived, they would never come to terms with the King (8.144). The unfortunate Athenian Lycidas, who proposed (perfectly properly perhaps) to his fellow-councillors that a Persian peace proposal should be put before the people, was stoned to death by his colleagues, his wife and children similarly lynched by the women of Athens (9.5). All these passages may, of course, to varying degrees represent a retrospective re-writing of the Persian wars[33] – but they are no less valuable for that. If we accept the (surely reasonable) proposition that anti-Persian feeling was stronger in the aftermath of the conflict than, say, at the time of Aristophanes' *Frogs*,[34] these stories provide *some* measure of the pitch of feeling at the time of the *Persians'* production.[35] Such Athenian aristocrats as yearned nostalgically for a Persian-sponsored oligarchy in Athens are likely, in other words, to have kept such private fantasies to themselves as they sat uncomfortably through the *Persians*.

Is there no level, it might be objected, at which the Athenians and Greeks are imagined potentially to be liable to the same fall as their Persian enemies? Is not the triumphalism of the *Persians* tempered by (even a cosmetic) humility? As Parker has commented on another play dealing with the destruction of the Greeks' enemies, Euripides' *Trojan Women*, 'the city which the love of the gods failed to defend was not Athens, but the spectator would have been complacent indeed who did not feel that it might have been'.[36] The *Persians* too has frequently been seen as representing a warning – more or less muted – to the Athenians of the dangers of their burgeoning empire.[37]

There are ostensibly some grounds for this position. The Persians' crime, in the Herodotean schema, was to exceed the limits of Asia in their quest for empire, to attempt to join Asia and Europe together. For Xerxes to have imagined it possible to rule both Asia and Europe was, of course, according to the 'well-known Themistoclean sentiment' recorded by Herodotus (8.109.3) one of the crimes for which he was punished by the gods.[38] The Persian dream of uniting Asia and Europe is a recurrent image in the *Histories*. Cyrus, for example, had a dream presaging, apparently, the Persian conquest of Europe, albeit by another man: he dreamt that Hystaspes' eldest son Darius grew wings which covered Asia and Europe (1.209.1),[39] wings that may show a distant familiarity with Persian iconography.[40] Atossa's dream of her son's ill-fated attempt to yoke together Asia and Europe clearly needs to be read against the background of this tradition. Why, however, if the *Persians* implies the imminent Greek destruction of the Persian empire, would Athenian-led aggression in Asia be any different? Would the Athenians not be subject to similar retribution?

The question is not one which the play directly confronts; indeed it is one which is very clearly sidestepped. Except for the conquests of

Darius in the Aegean and Thrace, conquests later reversed by the Athenians (880-902), and (as said before) if we exclude the omen of hawk and the eagle that appears to the Queen as prophetic only of the events of the Persian wars themselves, the Greeks significantly do not feature in the Persians' forebodings. Persia lies open to plunderers (751-2), but the precise identity of the plunderers is not specified. 'Not for long now will the inhabitants of Asia abide under Persian rule, nor pay tribute under compulsion to the King ...' (584-7), but how this revolution, set in motion by Salamis, will be accomplished is again a mystery.[41] This vagueness may, as suggested above, be the result of the play's ostensibly Persian focus: ongoing Greek assaults on the western fringes of the empire might just – with a little goodwill and some wishful thinking for the future – constitute the plundering feared by Darius. This vagueness may also be a concession to historical reality – or, to put it another way, a justification of the Athenians' inability (by 472 at least) to topple Persia completely – but it also has another result: it neatly avoids identifying the Athenians as subject to the same tendency of imperial expansion as Persia. The Queen's vision of Asia and Europe as two sisters may indeed reflect an ideal of two continents left to their own devices, free of mutual interference.[42] One implication of Darius' outrage at his son's crossing of the Hellespont is surely that the Athenians would know better than to try to tame the mighty Bosphorus, to turn sea into land. One moral implicit in the Queen's vision of two women is that the Greeks, unlike the Persians, the slaves of the King (241-2), are free (188-96). And as the watery deaths of the Persians as they crossed the frozen Strymon makes clear, the Greeks, unlike their enemies, take proper consideration for the gods (495-506):[43] after the Strymon froze, 'those who previously had not taken the gods at all seriously then called on them with prayers, prostrating themselves before Earth and Sky'. The first to cross, before the rising of the sun, crossed safely; the remainder drowned. Democracy and piety then together – whether these be naturally acquired, a reflection of virtue, or somehow both – immunise the Athenians from the dangers of Persian imperialism.[44]

As to the question of whether the play represents a warning against Athenian expansion in the area of the Aegean, a less equivocal answer is possible. The Chorus' list of Darius' conquests – unless we are to believe that there is no connection between these and those areas 'recovered' by Athens in the early years of her empire – elevates the expansion of Athens' influence in the Greek world into a Panhellenic mission of liberation. Such an implication is straightforwardly incompatible with a warning against imperialism, whether muted or not. The *Persians* then represents a very different point of view from that which is revealed in later fifth-century sources. The conclusion to Herodotus' *Histories*, as many critics have discussed, reveals – with the Persian Artaÿctes' barbaric execution overlooking the Hellespont, by order of Pericles' father Xanthippus – a cynical sense that the Athenians have taken on the mantle of empire from the Persians.[45] Thucydides' account of the Athenian expedition to Sicily similarly equates the Athenian and Persian empires and – in keeping with his idea of Athens as a tyrant – the Athenian people with the Persian King.[46] If this difference between the *Persians* and later writers reflects a chronological shift – rather than being simply the result of Aeschylus' more popular audience – this progression runs neatly parallel to the increased problematisation and refraction of the Greek-barbarian distinction that can be traced in the plays of Euripides or Aristophanes.[47] The *Persians* would represent then the high-water mark of Athens' conviction in her imperial project.

It is necessary finally to ask why the ideas of the play as sympathetic to Persia or as critical of Athens have persisted.

The first explanation is that it is the result of a common assumption regarding the nature of tragedy: that is, that in a tragedy sympathy is demanded for the protagonists. This, as we have seen, is explicitly stated by those such as Broadhead who suppose that for the *Persians* to constitute a 'genuine tragedy' it must be free of patriotic bias and contain imaginative insight into the Persian situation.[48] But the same idea pervades the work even of those who acknowledge the focus of the play on the polarity between Greek and Barbarian. 'If', says Simon Goldhill uncertainly, 'sympathy for others is part of the "tragic experience", it is none the less part of … Aeschylus' boldness in this play to place an audience in the position of discovering tragic sympathy for such an "other" as the Persian invaders.'[49]

This question is far too great to be discussed fully here, but some possible approaches can be raised. The authority for this view of tragedy is, of course, Aristotle's *Poetics*. But as Pelling has admitted,[50] Aristotle's criteria for tragic pity hardly fit Xerxes or the Persians at all comfortably. Pity is increased, according to Aristotle's *Rhetoric* (1386a25-6), when the sufferer is close to his observer in 'age, character, dispositional traits, status, or family'. Pity is restricted to those who suffer undeservedly (*Rhet.* 2.8, esp. 1385b13, 1386b6; cf. *Poet.* 1453a4-5). 'The victims are all guilty!', exclaims Winnington-Ingram.[51] It is 'evidently true', Pelling concedes, 'that deserved suffering is less pitiable, and thus Xerxes' claim for pity is much weakened'; Pelling then falls back on the idea that the audience could not have responded monolithically:

> Some would put more weight on the human suffering, some on the degree to which it was deserved; some would be more moved by the shared vulnerability to universally active gods, some would find their bitterness and vindictiveness too great. In some minds relish would defeat pity, in some it would not.

Some variety of audience response is, of course, inevitable – some of the audience *might* have found the figure of the Queen's smothering maternal love both disgusting and 'seductively appealing', as Griffith suggests[52] – though there must be some limits to the variety of audience response. But this obscures a more basic point. The *Persians* – even on a sympathetic reading – fits this Aristotelian mould of tragedy so badly that we have to ask if it is the right mould. Is Aristotle's model authoritative? After all, as Hall has recently pointed out, even the *polis* is absent from the *Poetics*[53] – a fact which sits uncomfortably with recent scholarship on Greek tragedy which envisages it as a fundamentally civic genre. Nor is the Persians unique in fitting the Aristotelian model so poorly. I hope it can safely be said that the sympathy demanded of Medea or of Antigone is at least not uncomplicated. To measure the authenticity or the quality of a tragedy by the degree of sympathy elicited by the suffering of its protagonists is simply a random and futile exercise.

My second explanation for the sympathy seen in the *Persians* is that it is the product of wishful thinking, a projection of modern values onto the Greeks, and a prejudice that art, especially great art, must be free from any trace of nationalism.[54] Even if we rule out the idea that the play constitutes a warning against Athenian imperialism, it surely remains true that the play could be more patriotic? Kitto attempts to prove this by substituting a passage of his own invention:[55]

> O Athens, Athens! city powerful beyond our expectation, brave and daring beyond our conception, resolute and clear-sighted beyond our belief! With thy multitude of ships and the valour of our citizens, how has thou brought us low in deadly disaster and bloodshed – though indeed with inconsiderable and reluctant aid from the Peloponnesians.

There are two ways of answering this kind of point. The first would be to point out again the more bloodthirsty or vengeful episodes of the play: the death of the Persians at Salamis, struck at by oars and broken fragments of wreckage like tunny fish, while 'groaning and shrieking filled the sea' (424-7),[56] or the description of the butchery of those Persians stranded on Psyttaleia (459-64):

> They were struck repeatedly by stones thrown from Greek hands, and arrows shot from the bow-string fell on them and destroyed them. In the end the Greeks, rushing at a single cry against them, struck them, butchered the poor men's limbs until they had all been deprived of life.

Such passages may, of course, again, like the barbaric punishment of Artaÿctes at the hands of Xanthippus at the close of Herodotus' *Histories*, constitute a note of warning of the excesses that follow upon victory. Such a clear and brutal shock, however, would curiously jar with the triumphalism evidenced elsewhere in the play. Quite possibly we have missed a more obvious, though less palatable, possibility: that such passages reflect a relish in the details of the slaughter of the Persians.

But merely to fight over example and counter-example – as if the patriotism of the play could be measured on a simple scale – obscures a more important point. Rather than demonstrating that the play could have been more patriotic, Kitto shows only that it could have been more crudely, more ostensibly patriotic. The conviction that patriotism need be crude lies at the heart of modern criticism of the play.[57] There seems often indeed to be an inverse relationship imagined between art and patriotism, an idea that the further nationality is somehow transcended the nearer one reaches to a pure art. In his view that patriotism does not make for good literature, however, Gilbert Murray was perhaps something of a pioneer.[58] Many critics from the early part of the twentieth century identified themselves almost defiantly with the Greek victors:[59]

> In the Persians there is much that is flattering to Athenian pride .... But who will say that the praise was undeserved and that the pride of the Athenian audience was not legitimate? Who will assert that the theme used at this time was inappropriate and that the motives of the dramatist, who himself was a veteran of the victorious war of defence, were unworthy?

'If the Persian war had shown nothing else', wrote J.L. Myres, 'it had shown the superior efficacy of an army which was mutually intelligible ... and even more forcibly it had impressed the belief that what mattered was not equipment, nor language, but breed'.[60]

Such sentiments have lingered on in some circles. In Peter Green's perennially popular work, *The Year of Salamis*, for example, the struggle of Greece and Persia is throughout that of free men against slaves; the Greeks' victory is a victory of the human spirit, one which 'continues to irradiate and quicken our whole western heritage, now and for ever'.[61] Persia 'perpetuated a fundamentally static culture, geared to the maintenance of a theocratic *status quo*, and hostile ... to original creativity in any form'; Persian culture is 'almost as alien to us as that of the Aztecs'.[62] Such ideas, it should be remembered, until very recently underpinned the study of Achaemenid art – through the scholarly dogma that it owed all to Greek influence and even Greek craftsmen; the study of Persian history has only recently begun to rid itself of clichés of oriental decadence inherited from Greek sources.[63]

In general, however, we might suppose that such views are now in the minority, that the battle has been won. As Josiah Ober has recently remarked, in seeking (in awe-struck tones) to explain why ancient political debates continue to hold our fascination, 'essentialist fantasies about the "Greek miracle" ' are now seen as embarrassing. However, as Ober's work itself demonstrates, these old claims have simply adapted and reconfigured themselves in order to survive in a new environment.[64] In place of such fantasies Ober suggests – in language suggestive of Chester Starr – that 'we think about the productive capacities of a complex culture that existed for a very long time in a state of dynamic social tension ...'.[65] We seek now to give substance to the 'Greek miracle'. To return to the *Persians*, it was Gilbert Murray again who first 'drew attention' to the shaming gulf between ancient and modern values: 'to read the *Persae* during the Great War did indeed fill one with shame at the contrast between ancient Hellas and modern Europe.'[66] Such ideas have proved remarkably tenacious. After acknowledging the possibility that the Athenians might – 'a crowd, after all, is a crowd' – have appreciated a propaganda play, Kitto goes on: 'We may have our own opinions about this; we might reflect on what more than one archaeologist has said, that really vulgar objects are rarely found in Attica, or indeed in Greece.'[67] More recently, the pity felt by the Athenians for their Persian enemies – revealed both in the *Persians* and in that conveniently adaptable play, Phrynichus' *Capture of Miletus* – has been seen by Sarah Morris as characteristic of 'the Greek mind':[68]

> What remains extraordinary about the Greek mind is how different it became from the Orient in ways like this, perhaps precisely because of their historical conflict. No other ancient nation was curious as well as compassionate enough to experience victory from the vanquished side, whether in composing laments for the enemy or in reacting to drama in sympathy so extreme that its source was censored (as the Athenians did to Phrynikhos' *Capture of Miletus*).

The motivation for these implicit claims of Greek superiority is, of course, very different from that of Gilbert Murray or other earlier critics: no longer imperial justification or (in Murray's case) the cause of world peace, but now the validation of Classics as a discipline. New concerns have taken the place of Murray's World War anxieties. Increasingly Athens or Greece are seen now as the source and example of *liberal* values. We imagine Aristophanes a feminist or Aeschylus or Herodotus pacifists;[69] we see tragedy as a profoundly questioning genre, the *Persians* as a play which 'seeks to raise questions about a response to the victory'.[70] The assumption of cultural superiority behind such modern programmes is arguably, however, no less potent.

We must, finally, confront directly the assumption of patriotism as crude, and accept that the strength of the *Persians* as a play consists in the manner with which it puts forward its patriotic – often aggressively patriotic – agenda. 'Much of the appeal of the play', in Griffith's paraphrase of the 'jingoistic reading', 'derives from the complacent contemplation of the defeat of Xerxes ... and from the accompanying reinforcement (both implicit and explicit) of "our" democratic ideology'.[71] This underestimates, however, the subtlety with which Aeschylus achieves his patriotic effect. The focus on Susa and the Persians, in particular, far from being the function of a sympathy for Persia's plight or of a strangely displaced historical sensibility, provides an ingenious means of throwing Greek qualities into greater relief: a comparison of Aeschylus' suggestive *stichomythia* with Kitto's substitute encomium of Athens leaves no doubt, I suspect, as to which would have been more effective. The Persian focus also arguably allows Aeschylus to revel in the destruction of the Persians in a way that would have been impossible if the play had, to adapt the phrase of J.D. Craig, been written in direct speech:[72] the grisly details of the butchery of the Persians might have seemed more appropriate in the mouths of Persian mourners than of a Greek messenger or Chorus.[73] The play may seem, superficially, to be lacking in action, with only the gradual revelation of the Persians' defeat – and the substantiation of that defeat in the return of Xerxes – providing a structure to the play. However, that is to ignore another plot that runs in parallel to it: the play's gradual striptease of Athenian virtues and achievements.

The *Persians* then is not a work with which we can, or should, identify too readily. It is not a play that could be performed – to a liberal audience, at least – without blatant anachronism or a chilling detachment. It would be wrong, however, as Edward Said has observed of Jane Austen's *Mansfield Park* or Conrad's *Heart of Darkness* – both 'in complex ways part of the imperialist undertaking' – to indict such works wholesale, or to suggest that they are as a result 'less interesting as art'.[74] Though the glorification of Athens may provide a more ostensible focus to Aeschylus' play than imperialism to *Mansfield Park*, this is no less true of the *Persians*. To observe the centrality of patriotism to the play is not to mark out Aeschylus and the Athenians as uniquely chauvinistic – but only as unexceptional.[75]

Notes

Introduction

1. See further Broadhead 1960: lv-lx, Moreau 1993b, Hall 1996a: 10-11: Phineus, a famous seer, may possibly have uttered prophecies spoken of as fulfilled by Darius in the course of the *Persians* (739-40, 800-2); the play may also have foreshadowed the *Persians'* emphasis on the opposition of Asia and Europe; Glaucus has associations with Boeotia, leading some to suppose that the play alluded to Plataea; any further speculation is largely fruitless. The extant fragments are collected as *TGrF* Aeschylus F 36-42, 204a-7a, 258-60.

2. See below, chs. 1-2.

3. See esp. Hall 1989, 1996a, Goldhill 1988.

4. For a fuller survey of the sources, see D.M. Lewis 1992.

5. For the barbarian in tragedy, see esp. Hall 1989, Saïd 1984; for Aristophanes and Persia, see Daumas 1985, Long 1986, Pretagostini 1998. For a full survey of 'the place of Persia in Athenian literature', see Tuplin 1996: ch. 3.

6. See esp. Bovon 1963, Miller 1995, 1997.

7. See e.g. Armayor 1978, D.M. Lewis 1985 (concerned with historical veracity); for the barbarian, see e.g. Laurot 1981, Redfield 1985, Hartog 1988.

8. Drews 1973; for relative datings, see now R.L. Fowler 1996.

9. D.M. Lewis 1992: 14.

10. Rhodes 1992: 65.

11. (London, 1968) 171.

12. J.A.K. Thomson 1927: 77; cf. the summary of the play's action by Lucas 1950: 59.

13. 1924: 72, 75. See Holtsmark 1970 for a survey of earlier negative views of the play, or Winnington-Ingram's judgement, 1983a: 15 ('In conclusion, *Persae* is not the greatest of the surviving plays of Aeschylus; it may well be the least great').

14. Lattimore 1958: 38-9; cf. the anonymous reviewer 'Ignotus' cited by Kitto, 1966: 75: 'Take away the poetry from *The Persians* ... and what is left? Anti-historical rhodomontade, propaganda, ill-directed emotionalism.'

15. Hickman 1938: 30.

16. Taplin 1977: 106.

17. Cf. Conacher's description of the account of Salamis as a 'series of brilliant pictures', 1974: 156. Contrast the comments of Winnington-Ingram, 1983a: 2: 'We are of course free to say that Aeschylus, observing that his play lacked action, decided to expand it with a characteristic exhibition of what ancient critics called *to teratôdes* – "the portentous", "the sensational". We can even regard Darius as a rather uneconomical device for introducing the battle of Plataea. Such explanations are, however, best kept in reserve to be brought forward if no reason more creditable to the dramatic skill of the poet can be found.'

18. Against this deterministic picture of the progression of tragedy, and the 'arbitrary picking out of features assumed to be primitive', see Michelini 1974: 6: a study of the *Persians* 'in its literary-historical context must ... begin with the heterogeneity of tragedy as a basic given'. Though Michelini does not see this as symptomatic of the date of the play, she nonetheless judges the *Persians* the 'weakest in dramatic illusion and the most static in form' of Aeschylus' surviving works. Cf. Taplin 1977: 61, Wardman 1959: 51: 'The *Agamemnon* is seen as the high peak of the dramatist's achievement, and for this reason other plays have been turned into minor summits, parts of the same chain, but without the perfect structure of the last play .... This type of criticism has acquiesced in "detecting" flaws in the *Persae*, thereby demonstrating that the dramatist would still have something to learn by the time he arrived at the *Oresteia*.'

19. Meier 1993: 64. Cf. Patin 1877: I.218: 'Ce que Phrynichus n'a pu faire vivre au delà d'un jour, Eschyle l'a rendu immortel.'

20. Cf. the argument of Thalmann, 1980: 260, against the idea of the play as 'primitive pageantry' that Aeschylus could hardly have developed from primitive pageantry to high artistry in the fourteen years that separated the *Persians* from the *Oresteia*; an argument for the quality of one play that hinges on the *self-evident* quality of another work will never carry great conviction.

21. Conacher 1974: 146.

22. 1962: 72. Cf. B.H. Fowler 1967. Contrast also the innocence of Patin, 1877: I.212: 'Est-il besoin de montrer des heureux effets qui devaient résulter de la conception d'Eschyle?'

23. As conceded by Anderson 1972: 166

24. Sidgwick 1903: viii; cf. Kitto's judgement, 1950: 35, on Phrynichus' *Capture of Miletus* as not a drama but a 'lyrical lamentation'.

25. Cited by Broadhead, 1960: xv.

26. Murray 1940a: 115.

27. The view of an anonymous reviewer cited by Anderson 1972: 166-7, Jacobs cited by Craig 1924: 101, and Conacher 1974: 148. See also Duchemin 1974, esp. 133-42, J. Jones 1962: 71 on the *Oresteia*, Herington 1986: 39-40 ('the elaborate audio-visual fabric that is an Aeschylean tragedy') and Adams 1983: 34-41, esp. 34: 'It is a composition in three movements marked off from each other by concluding choral lyrics and followed by a kind of scherzo, the whole being knit together by recurrent themes and by a single governing design.' By contrast, the author of a book on the musical design of Aeschylus, Scott 1984: xi, opens his work with the acknowledgement that Aeschylus was 'interested primarily in giving form to ideas'. Cf. the architectural analogy of duBois 1982: 80: 'the *Persae* are structured on the same principles as the metopes of the temples of the early fifth century.'

28. Michelini, 1982: 74; cf. her comment (p. 76 n. 1), that 'the themes of the *Persians* have been listed quite comprehensively in the recent book of Petrounias' (cf. p. 81 n. 17).

29. See also against the over-intellectualisation of tragedy, Heath 1987: 71-80, preferring an idea of an '*ordered* emotional experience' (p. 80 n. 69, his italics).

30. Cf. Winnington-Ingram 1983a: 15: 'Perhaps *Persae* demonstrates the superiority of myth over history as a theme for tragedy.'

31. Broadhead 1960: xvi.

32. Broadhead 1960: xxiii.

33. 1940: 123; cf. Kakridis 1975: 154.

34. 1989: 73.

35. 1989: 100. Contrast her statement, 1996a: 3, that 'Giving the Persians a sympathetic hearing was probably not Aeschylus' priority: his own brother had died a particularly bloody death at Marathon ...'

1. Aeschylus the historian?

1. A. Bowie 1997: 42. Cf. the similarly difficult idea of the 'political play', advanced by Zuntz 1955 of *Heraclidae* and *Suppliant Women*, and by Forrest of Aeschylus' *Supplices*, 1960: 239, for which see below, chs. 2, 9.

2. A similar definition of historical tragedy is implicit in the suggestion of Gregory, 1991: 15 n. 22, that the 'experiment [of historical tragedy] was evidently soon abandoned as too harrowing for the audience'. (The remark is clearly founded on the story of Phrynichus' *Capture of Miletus*, 6.21.2; however, this would clearly be difficult to reconcile with a reading of the *Phoenician Women* or the *Persians* as primarily concerned with patriotic stimulation.)

3. Cf. Podlecki 1966: 8 ('it is the only surviving example of a *genre* which can never have been large, historical tragedy'), Pelling 1997a: 1-2.

4. See above, Introduction, n. 1.

5. For the Greek distinction of myth and history, see esp. Brillante 1990, Nickau 1990, Cartledge 1993: ch. 2, T. Harrison 2000a: ch. 7; for myth and history in the *Persians*, see Petre 1978: 327, or the curious comments of Mitsis 1988.

6. E.g. 266-7, 341 (cf. 246), on which see Lattimore 1958: 32 n. 5, Hall 1996a: 130 (on 266); as Hall points out, such assurances of autopsy are common to other tragedies, e.g. A. *Sept.* 40-1, *Suppl.* 930-2.

7. Salanitro 1965: 216, Tourraix 1984: 123 ('tragédie historique, les *Perses* véhiculent une image de la monarchie achéménide'), or more uncompromisingly Tourraix 1993: 99-100. See, however, the remarks of Delcourt 1934: 247 ('Eschyle traite les faits avec la même liberté qu'il apporte à traiter un mythe'), Martin 1952: 9 (cf. p. 4) on the 'serene indifference' of tragic poets towards historical truth, explicitly including the *Persians*, and of Kitto 1966: 79-81.

8. Murray 1940a: 111, 115. Cf. Smyth 1924: 84 ('the most authentic description of a battle scene ever written by a poet').

9. de Romilly 1974: 10. Cf. the comments of Puech 1932: 757: 'Eschyle n'est pas seulement un contemporain: il a pris part à l'action. Un combattant, il est vrai, ne voit guère que des épisodes. Mais par son rang social, par son talent déjà connu, Eschyle était bien placé pour obtenir ensuite les informations les plus sûres. Il a pu s'intruire auprès de bons témoins sur les préparatifs du combat et sur ses péripéties. Il écrit huit ans plus tard; le délai n'est pas tel qu'il implique un trop grand péril de confusion dans les "souvenirs".' For Nenci, 1950: 218, Aeschylus' historical duty derives from his participation at Salamis.

10. A motive suggested by Lattimore, 1943: 91, for the concentration on Salamis at the expense of Marathon or Plataea. See, however, Easterling's observation, 1993: 14, that ' "dramatic effectiveness" is not a particularly useful criterion if no meaning is attached to the dramatic effects beyond the immediate excitement they offer the audience'.

11. de Romilly 1974: 11. It is apparently in this spirit of confidence that Plutarch cited Aeschylus for the number of the Persian ships, Plut. *Them*. 14.1.

12. Macan 1908: II: 290 (appendix 6).

13. Podlecki 1966: 25, Stoessl 1952: 133 n. 34, the strictures of Zuntz 1955: 4 or ch. 3 (esp. 58-63), and now the survey of Saïd 1998: 279. Identifications of mythical and historical characters are drawn by, e.g., Davison 1949, Post 1950: 49ff., Davison 1966. For ancient anecdotes of audiences seeing references to individuals in tragedy, e.g. Plut. *Arist*. 3.4, see below, ch. 2. See also, against such direct 'references' to contemporary events and individuals, Gregory 1991: 6 and n. 20 (pp. 14-15); Gregory does, however, argue for a role of 'instruction' for tragedy. A near consensus is suggested by Pelling's 1997 collection on *Greek Tragedy and the Historian*, with Easterling (p. 28) insisting on the futility of looking for 'univocal messages' in tragedy, Pelling (pp. 216-17) on the vague nature of references to contemporary events ('we may ... find the historical Cleopatra shimmering behind Virgil's Dido without implying that the two characters collapse into one another'), and Angus Bowie (pp. 61-2) searching not for any 'particular line' but for similarities in the 'structures of the events and the myths' (cf. A. Bowie 1993: 10-11). The most extraordinary substitution of a historical figure for a dramatic character is Konishi's suggestion, 1979, that Xerxes stands for Cimon; Konishi also sees Cimon behind the other plays of the Persian tetralogy.

14. As Hammond points out, 1956: 39, the attention paid to the differences of Aeschylus and Herodotus is the result of the assumption of a comprehensiveness on Aeschylus' part; compare also the line of Gomme, 1954: ch. 5. Aeschylus' messenger, of course, explicitly draws attention to his own selectiveness, 513-14.

15. Fornara 1966: 51.

16. This is on the assumption that the play was written for an Athenian and not for a Sicilian audience, as was maintained by Wilamowitz 1898, on the grounds, e.g., that the play was not suitably Dionysiac, and that the details of the numbers of combatants would have been well-known to the Athenians. For this and the question of a separate Sicilian text, see Broadhead 1960: lff.

17. Kitto 1966: 74-5; see also e.g. Lattimore 1943: 87 ('we have no right to assume that the Athenians would award first prize to a tragic poet for dealing wildly with known facts in a contemporary theme'), Ehrenberg 1954: 17 (though compare his judgement, p.16, that 'it cannot be assumed that [Phrynichus] dealt with historical events for the sake of, and in agreement with, their historical character'), Podlecki 1966: 8-9, Conacher 1974: 143-4, Lazenby 1988: 185.

18. Conacher 1974: 144, Pelling 1997a: 1; this is possibly also the point made by Kitto 1966: 74, though it is unclear to me ('How intelligent were the Athenians?', Kitto's subheading asks; 'not very', he replies).

19. For Salamis see e.g. D'Amico 1931, Hammond 1956: 32-54, Pritchett 1959, Broadhead 1960: App. 6 (pp. 322-9), Podlecki 1966: 131-41, Wallace 1969, Roux 1974, Kakridis 1975, Lazenby 1988 (attempting to vindicate both Aeschylus and Herodotus), Pelling 1997a: 1-9.

20. See esp. Saïd 1981, but also, e.g., Delcourt 1934: 245, Kitto 1966: 74, Belloni 1982: 192-3, Euben 1986: 363, Rosenbloom 1993: 190 (envisaging this as the 'central distortion' of the play). Aeschylus may also arguably have represented the Persians as considering their kings as gods in full knowledge that this was not the case: Richardson 1952: 63. See further below, ch. 8.

21. Lattimore 1943: 84-8; see also Broadhead 1960: App. 5 (pp. 318-21), Péron 1982: 9, and esp. Schmitt 1978.

22. Cf. Kitto 1966: 74; Walters 1981 makes the obvious point that the Athenian claim that the Athenians fought alone at Marathon was not true.

23. Broadhead 1960: 322 (appendix 6); cf. p. xxxii. For the Strymon, see also Rose 1957: 161 (the 'strangeness of the whole affair ... a strong reason for supposing that it is true'), Conacher 1974: 147 n. 8, Horsfall 1974 (for the suggestion that the Strymon episode is intended to balance the Hellespont). Prickard, 1879: 87 on 472-514, suggested that 'while it seems highly probable that Aeschylus had no historical foundation for the story, he may have received some geographical information about the Strymon and its frosts (possibly from Hecataeus ...) of which he availed himself to construct the striking incident here recorded'.

24. By Tarn 1908: 226, Fornara 1966, followed by, e.g., Loraux 1981: 162-3. Cf. the observations of Émile Cahen, 1924: 297-8 on the difficulty of using a literary source for the reconstruction of precise tactical manoeuvres, and the remarks of Péron 1982: 19: 'par ailleurs, l'évènement est moins saisi en lui-même qu'appréhendé (par le choeur dans la parodos), entrevu (par Atossa dans sa rêve), justifié (par Darius dans la scène de nécromancie), déploré (par Xerxès et le choeur dans l'exodos), Eschyle ayant en somme subordonné l'évocation de la réalité à une étude des causes et des conséquences les plus lointaines, et sacrifié le présent au passé et à l'avenir.'

25. 1974: 143-4.

26. 1960: xvii. For Péron similarly, 1982: 3-4, while Aeschylus could not escape the 'tyranny of reality', this historical duty exists as a pretext for Aeschylus developing his ethical or religious conception.

27. Avery 1964: 173.

28. Contrast Petre 1978: 331.

29. Richardson 1952: 61.

30. There is a clear analogy with visual representations: cf. Bovon 1963: 600 ('Pour l'Athénien qui achète un tel vase, la représentation peut évoquer un souvenir précis; mais elle se réfèrera aussi, spontanément, à des images que l'art l'a habitué à considérer comme typiques et symboliques').

31. Hall 1996a: 6; see also, for echoes of Achaemenid ideology, Tourraix 1984, and now more broadly Tuplin 1996: 133-4, arguing for a 'quite limited' amount of 'distinctively, ethnographically Persian material' implied by the play. Criticism of the *Persians* often takes place in terms of its veracity by comparison with art and archaeology, apparently on the assumption of some form of historical duty: see esp. Gow 1928, though even Hall seems often to be drawn back to the discussion of Aeschylus' sources or of his Persians' costumes, to questions of the play's veracity, that are distinct from her main theme of the ideological construction of the barbarian (e.g. 1989: 77-8: 'the problem of the veracity of Aeschylus' account of the barbarian leaders will ... probably never be solved'). The distinction of historical reality and a distorted Greek representation is perhaps maintained most clearly by Bovon 1963.

32. 1997a: 9.

33. Kebric 1983: 6. The idea was first suggested in print (to my knowledge) by Gow 1928: 154-5; cf. Craig 1924: 101 ('the raison d'être of this enumeration is given in lines 904-6. The Persians have been robbed of them by the defeat at Salamis'), Broadhead 1960: 213 on 852-908, Tozzi 1980, Tourraix 1993: 106 (according to whom the play offers a justification for Athens' contemporary enterprises). See, however, for Cyprus, Meritt et al. 1950: 207-9 (cf. Meiggs 1972: 56-8): 'The cities of Kypros enter the list because they show how far the Greek offence *had* reached in one direction' (my italics); they concede that if Cyprus had been included in the Delian League, it would have made 'a powerful scene indeed'.

34. Contrast Meiggs 1972: 55-6 ('Aeschylus includes Cnidus and Rhodes in the Greek cities that threw off the Persian yoke after Salamis'); one might conclude from Meiggs' remark that Aeschylus had made the dramatic irony of 857-906 explicit. Another possibility is that some of the cities were known to Aeschylus' audience to have been reconquered and that others were known to be earmarked for reconquest: this would preserve the dramatic irony of the passage, whilst lending it an aggressive implication that the reversal of Darius' conquests was unfinished business.

35. 1966: 9.

2. Politics and partisanship

1. Schmid-Stählin 1934: II.174-6, Salanitro 1965; cf. the comments of Thomson 1973: 279 on Aeschylus' *choregos* Pericles as a 'moderate democrat' and supporter of Cimon.

2. As Gomme observes, 1945: 401, Aeschylus was capable of reproaching his fellow citizens after the event (though he admits that it is more likely that Themistocles had not yet been ostracised). For the date of Themistocles' ostracism, see also Cary 1922: 161-2 (arguing for a date of 470 on the grounds of the *Persians* and of Diod. Sic. 11.54), Ure 1923: 64 (arguing against Cary that the 'ostracism suggested the panegyric'), Lenardon 1959: 23-48, Forrest 1960: 221, Lang 1967, Cawkwell 1970: 47.

3. Rhodes 1992: 67.

4. Podlecki 1966: ch. 2, influenced by Forrest 1960: 236. That the *Persians* was written in part as a statement of support for Themistocles has been stated or implied recently by, e.g., duBois 1982: 55-6, Cartledge 1997: 25, though contrast duBois 1982: 90, Goldhill 1997: 344, A. Bowie 1997: 43, Pelling 1997a: 8-13. Other plays allegedly pro-Themistoclean are the *Supplices* (for which see, on the basis of a different dating, Cavaignac 1921) and the *Telephus* (Séchan 1967: 123-7).

5. An allusion accepted in surprisingly straightforward terms by Goldhill 1988: 191: 'the text hints at the income – and its distribution – which made such a victory possible'.

6. A comparable allusion to a contemporary oracle is the reference to the Syrian chariot in the preceding Delphian prophecy to Athens, 7.140.2, at line 84: see Hauvette 1894: 126 and n. 6, Hall 1996a: 115 (ad loc.).

7. See further Hall 1996a: 7, Taplin 1972: 68 n. 36.

8. See Barron's judgement on the *Phoenician Women*, 1988: 618, that 'it was a story the mere telling of which could not but glorify Themistocles'. Podlecki goes even further in suggesting, 1966: 14 and n. 18-19 (p. 158), that it was 'highly probable that Themistocles inspired and encouraged the dramatist' in his production of the *Capture of Miletus* 'perhaps as part of a program of support of the Ionian revolt against reactionary, isolationist forces at home'. The only evidence for this is that the play was probably produced in the year of Themistocles' archonship; cf. Stoessl 1952: 117, Freymouth 1953, Roisman 1988 (for the meaning of the Herodotean expression *oikeia kaka*, 6.21.2, and the question of the relationship between Phrynichus' plays) and now the exhaustive survey of Rosenbloom 1993 (arguing against such political camps behind the production of tragedy).

9. See Rhodes' summary, 1992: 67-8.

10. Podlecki 1966: 42-62, Rhodes 1992: 68.

11. On the political stance of the *Eumenides*, see Dover 1957, Dodds 1960, Podlecki 1966: 63-100, Beer 1981, Macleod 1982, Heath 1987: 68-9, Bearzot 1992, Rhodes 1992: 74, Schaps 1993.

12. Lacedaimonius, moreover, was so named in the 470s: see Davies 1971: 305-6.

13. A suspicion perhaps prompted by news of Ephialtes' reforms: see Rhodes' summary, 1992: 68-9.

14. See above, n. 11.

15. For Theseus' increased prominence in fifth-century Athens, see e.g. Connor 1971a, Boardman 1972, Calame 1996: ch. 6, Mills 1997. The ascription of this increased prominence to a single factor is, of course, unlikely.

16. Cf. Plut. *Them.* 3.4-5 for Themistocles' silence after Marathon, *Them.* 5.4 for the rivalry of Cimon and Themistocles at Olympia.

17. See further Podlecki 1971; for the relationship of stories of the life of Theseus with the actions of Cimon, see Mills 1997: 12-13, 35-6.

18. See Barron 1980: 6-7 n. 23, Davies 1971: 293-312, Thomas 1989: 162-9, Mills 1997: 36 n. 155.

19. Podlecki 1966: 14.

20. Podlecki 1966: 12. See further (and for the afterlife of this 'battle of the battles' in the fourth century) Loraux 1973, 1981: 157-73, Petre 1978, Saïd 1993, Mills 1997: ch. 2.

21. Podlecki 1966: 13.

22. This pattern-making is made explicit by Ste Croix, 1972: 183-5, and by Forrest, 1960: 236: 'Themistokles is directly praised in the *Persae*; Themistokles was the refugee of 470; Themistokles' successor, Perikles, who had already been *choregos* for the *Persae*, shared with Ephialtes the responsibility for the measures of 462 and for the alliance with Argos, both of which Aeschylus certainly favours in the play.' Davison, 1966: 102, appears to presume the existence of such an axis: 'Besides, it may well appear from the line which his later plays appear to recommend that [Aeschylus] was on the Themistoclean-Ephialtean side of the political argument, and opposed to Cimon and Aristeides neither of whom comes to light in Aeschylus' account of the Persian defeat.' He goes on to say that it 'may not be entirely an accident' that Pericles was *choregos* for the *Persians*. Cf. also Stoessl 1952 (fixated with opposition between Themistocles and Cimon), Mazzarino 1960 (emphasising the role of Pericles), Delvoye 1975 (an overtidy picture of 'Cimonian propaganda'), den Boer 1962 (for a more complex pattern of sources surrounding Themistocles).

23. Rhodes 1981: 283-4. See, however, the compelling argument of R.G. Lewis, 1997 (discussed further below, ch. 9), that Themistocles helped Ephialtes in early attacks on the Areopagus before his ostracism. See the speculative suggestion of Robinson, 1946, that a Themistoclean reform of the archonship in 487/6 became confused with the reforms of 462/1; this presupposes, however, that the reform of 487/6 marked the beginning of an attack on aristocratic power (see Robinson 1939), and that a causal connection between the two reforms would have been evident at the time: contrast Badian's doubts, 1971, as to whether the reform was intended to weaken the 'executive'.

24. Pelling 1997a: 10.

25. Pelling 1997a: 10. Cf. the view of Meier, 1993: 63, that Marathon was simply 'too insignificant for treatment' in a tragedy, extraordinary given Marathon's prominence in later Athenian self-representations.

26. Podlecki 1966: 13. Similarly, in introducing Themistocles as *choregos* for the *Persians*, he comments that 'the parallelism between the productions of 476 and 472 is not yet complete', 1966: 15 (with n. 20, p. 158 for refs.).

27. For a number of uncanny parallels between the careers of Solon and Peisistratus, see Podlecki 1987, recommending complete scepticism.

28. For Archestratus, see Davies 1971: 346, Hornblower on Thuc. 1.45.2.

For the dangers of exaggerating Pericles' early career, in particular his alleged association with Ephialtes, see Hignett 1952: 197, Sealey 1967: 69; for Plutarch's focus on Pericles, see Gomme 1945: 70 n. 2. See, however, Connor 1971b: 58-64 on the alliance of Pericles and Cimon. See also the comments of Sartori, 1969/70: 793, on the assumption of static political parties.

29. As suggested by Balcer in the course of his 1979 reconstruction of politics in the decade between Marathon and Salamis; for political parties, see esp. Connor 1971b.

30. See above, n. 28.

31. For a reconstruction of the murals, see Barron 1972. For a 'similarity of spirit' between tragedy and monumental painting, see Stansbury-O'Donnell 1989: 213-14, Méautis 1937.

32. See, in general and for further bibliography, Castriota 1992: 76-89, and more reliably Mills 1997: 40-1 n. 174. See also Pelling 1997a: 12 for the argument that the absence of Salamis from the Stoa was for artistic reasons. For the identification of the building, see Meritt 1970 (Cimonian propaganda: pp. 256-7). For the identification of the scene of the battle of Oenoe (a battle in the so-called First Peloponnesian War, a mythological subject, or part of the build-up to the battle of Marathon?), see Jeffery 1965, Andrewes 1975, Francis and Vickers 1985a, 1985b, Francis 1990: 86-90. For the theory that the paintings were arranged alongside the Simonidean epigram (e.g. to emphasise the claim of Athens to be the 'bulwark of Greece'), see Francis and Vickers 1985c.

An interesting irony is the detail, e.g. in Pliny *NH* 35.57 and Aelian *de nat. animalium* 7.38, that Aeschylus' brother Cynegirus, fighting by the Persian ships at Marathon, featured prominently in the Marathon painting: for full testimonies, see E.B. Harrison 1972b: 359-60. (Miltiades and Cynegirus are omitted, however, from Harrison's reconstruction of the Nike south frieze of Marathon, Harrison 1972a: 355, though the scene of fighting at the ships also allegedly features in Brescia sarcophagus: Vanderpool 1966: 105 and n. 26 (Pl. 35).)

33. Miller 1997: 32 and n. 13 for further refs.

34. For reconstructions, see Stansbury-O'Donnell 1989 (*Iliupersis*), 1990 (*Nekyia*). For the Cnidian Lesche as built in (favourable) response to the Athenian victory at Eurymedon and in support of the Delian League, see esp. Kebric 1983; contrast Dugas' construction, 1938, of the *Iliupersis* as pro-Dorian, or Stansbury-O'Donnell, 1990: 230-1, arguing against a pro-Athenian or pro-Dorian view, but rather for a more 'even-handed argument for the necessity of Greek unity and cooperation', and for a Greek triumphalism undercut by a sense of danger in the internal affairs of Greeks (p. 231). See also Castriota 1992: 89-95 for an implicit reference to Eion on the Strymon in Eioneus (Paus. 10.27.1), and a reference to Cimon's half-brother Metiochus in the Trojan captive Metioche (Paus. 10.26.2); more generally, he claims, 'these characters show that the Troy painting of the Lesche referred more generally to Kimon and his victories in the later 470s and 460s'; other mythic characters, e.g. Iaseus (10.30.4), 'provided a genealogical prefiguration of the League and social or cultural bonds that held it together' (p. 93).

35. See Barron 1980; cf. Francis 1990: 53-62 (envisaging the poem as a 'manifesto for the Delian League', p. 62).

36. See Amandry's suggestion, 1960, that the second epigram for Marathon was inscribed after that for Salamis during the period of Cimon's political ascendancy, accepted, e.g., by Petre 1978, Loraux 1981: 58. For reviews of the arguments, see the commentaries to ML 26 and now *IG* I^3 503/4, conclusively removing the Marathon epigrams from the 'battle of the battles'. For rival traditions over the evacuation of Attica, see Rhodes 1981: 288-9.

37. See Donnay 1964, arguing, e.g., for a Cimonian context for frs. 76-7, and that fr. 74 refers to Cimonian embellishments of the agora (Athens' 'famous and highly-adorned marketplace').

38. 1971: 143.

39. See also the interesting anecdote preserved by a thirteenth-century Byzantine essayist, that Themistocles' exile was due to the enmity of a Lycomedes: Connor 1972, Podlecki 1975: 21 ('this seems to me likelier to be a retrojection into the mythical past of an account in which it was not Themistocles but his allegorical prototype Theseus who came under fire from aristocratic opponents').

40. For the persification of Midas in the mid-fifth century: Miller 1988, 1997: 201. Minos: Castriota 1992: 61. Other examples of such 'unconscious' assimilation would be that of the Amazon invasion of Attica (as described at A. *Eum*. 685-90) to the Persian attack on the Acropolis (8.52-3), for which see E.B. Harrison 1966: 128, duBois 1982, Castriota 1992: 61, and Mills 1997: 30-3 (showing a sensible caution, e.g. at p. 33: 'the reality of the Persian wars shapes it only in part: both wars are defensive, but no more detailed analogy is ever worked out'). For the assimilation of Persians and centaurs, see Castriota 1992: 34-43, Woodford 1974 (Castriota's paraphrase of Woodford sees the assimilation of centauromachies with the Persian wars as a much more conscious process, e.g. when commenting (pp. 40-1) that the 'new conception of the battle was intended to mirror the rape and impiety of the Persians during their invasion of Greece', in particular the story of a Persian embassy to Macedonia, 5.18-20).

41. 1990: 48-9.

42. Barron 1980: 4.

43. Barron 1980: 4; for further refs. see his n. 55 or Castriota 1992: 44 n. 19 (p. 250).

44. Equally we might wonder as to why Metiochus, Cimon's half-brother, should be presented as a Trojan woman captive, Metioche (cf. Castriota, n. 34 above, on the Cnidian Lesche), except for his having been captured by the Phoenicians, 6.41.

45. For which see E.B. Harrison 1966: 108-9, Mills 1997: 104.

46. Cf. Davies 1971: 303 ('there is no good reason for disbelieving the story of her association with Polygnotus').

47. E.g. Francis 1990: 63 (by 'characterising Theseus as the founder of democratic institutions he himself sought both to serve and control, Cimon had outwitted Themistocles in political strategy'), Castriota 1992: 7 ('Kimon and his aristocratic supporters were well attuned to the enormous political value of manipulating mythic analogues in this fashion').

48. The expression is Roy Gibson's, intended originally to describe the unthinking combination of new themes (or methods) and texts (e.g. closure in the *Aeneid*).

49. The site allegedly of the (unknown) Polygnotan painting on which the Argonaut Krater of the Niobid painter was based: Simon 1963: 51; a nice additional touch is a 'young man departing in full armor' who 'seems to stand for the Athenian cleruchs sent to Skyros'. See also Harrison's interpretation, 1972b, of the same evidence as a description of the preparations for Marathon, a visit to Amphitrite as a salute to the 'seapower that Athens was acquiring through his [Cimon's] own naval victories' (p. 401) and Ajax and Heracles 'mourning the necessary death of the Polemarch' [Callimachus] (p. 394). A more temperate view of the 'Cimonian building program' is provided by Robertson 1975: 242-5.

50. E.g. Matheson 1995: 215 ('Amazons readily symbolised Persians'), Walker 1995: 58 ('the Amazons and the Centaurs often stand for Persians').

51. Tyrrell 1984: 67 in explanation of the origins of Amazon sacrifice on the eve of the festival of Theseus. A fuller quotation reveals more interesting assumptions: 'One reason comes to mind immediately: Cimon wanted to join his father's defense of Athens (and his own policy of ridding the eastern Aegean of Persians) with a precedent from the city's formative past. Bringing in the Amazons wherever possible had propagandistic value, but more was needed than a general's whim to expand the sacred calendar.'

52. Francis 1990: 48: 'In 476 Themistocles' *choregia* of Phrynichus' *Phoenician Women* evidently brought Themistocles renewed acclaim and Cimon responded with Eion and Scyros, for by liberating the Aegean from the threat of piracy he countered any claim to naval leadership which Themistocles might continue to promote.'

53. Boersma 1970: 50: 'Here, as at Phlya, he wanted to impress his fellow citizens. Not the least reason for doing so may have been that his political influence had begun to wane after 478 BC.'

54. Metzler 1966: 10.

55. Boersma 1970: 52, citing Plut. *Cim.* 8.7. Cf. even more sweepingly Merck 1978: 104: 'the result was the eclipse and eventual ostracism of Themistocles, the rise of his rival and the consolidation of Theseus' place in the city's devotion.' The story is continued by Podlecki, 1975: 17-20, according to whom Themistocles responded by refurbishing the Oscophoria, an occasion marked by Simonides. Podlecki shows an extraordinary willingness to reconstruct Themistocles' motivation on the basis of Plutarch, e.g. 1975: 2 ('we can detect ... the disappointment, even the disbelief, of the hero of Salamis when he found his popularity on the wane'). For a similar overview of the propaganda battle, complete with psychological reconstruction, see Walker 1995: 55-6; contrast Frost's caution towards all sources subsequent to Aristotle, 1968.

56. Cf. Loraux's blithe ascription of activity to hazy groups such as 'les amis de Cimon' or 'Cimon et son entourage', 1981: 210, 162; cf. Gomme 1948: 7 (in the context of the Eion epigram).

57. The expression used by Vickers 1990: 257; cf. the 'Cimonian Age' of Wade-Gery 1933. For justifiable scepticism over the integrity of the comparable 'Scipionic circle', see Erskine 1997.

58. Kebric 1983: 33; see also Mattingly 1977 for Timocreon and Ion of Chios, Podlecki 1968 on the friendship of Simonides and Themistocles (though for the panhellenic tone of Simonides' Plataea elegy, see the surveys of Boedeker 1995, 1996 and Rutherford 1996); for poets and patrons in general, see also Bremer 1991: esp. 47-8. Timocreon's hostility to Themistocles (not in itself evidence of support for Cimon) is noticeably direct and personalised by comparison with the subtle propaganda through myth discussed above: *PMG* 727-30.

59. Cf. Mills 1997: 40 on the Stoa Poikile ('the subjects of the murals have a general, public significance for all those who had experienced the attack of the Persians and the Athenian triumph'). Contrast, however, the opposition established by Pelling 1997a: 12 ('both Marathon and Salamis became Panathenian themes, themes which all Athenians would thrill to, not the stuff of partisan ideology'); it is *precisely because* these were Panathenian themes that they could usefully be harnessed to partisan ends.

60. A conclusion hinted at by Walker 1995: 58 in his remarks on the Athenian disapproval of self-glorification; cf. more surprisingly his assertion (p. 60) that 'in no case does [Cimon] try to manipulate the myth to his own advantage'.

61. van Wees 1995: 158-9: 'Since the episode serves no dramatic purpose but the glorification of Athens, Aeschylus would have every opportunity to mention the navy, had he felt that it had been instrumental in bringing Athens victory. Evidently he thought otherwise: Athens' success had been due to its crack army and its wealth in silver.' A 'naval ideology' is expressed elsewhere in the play, however (e.g. 378).

62. Cf. Saïd 1993: 65; Konishi, by contrast, asserts that his anti-Cimonian 'message may have been unmistakable to the audience when the tetralogy was presented as a whole', 1979: 164.

63. Something that should, he continues, 'excite suspicion': Heath 1987: 66.

64. Podlecki 1966: 18.

65. It also assumes, of course, that the sentiments reported by Herodotus are Themistoclean rather than Herodotean: Macan 1908: I.2.530, Perdrizet 1912: 360. There are degrees of reference, however: the mention of sacrilege in the *Persians* would hardly have helped Themistocles' cause unless it reminded the audience specifically of him; passages such as the description of the Greek destruction of the temples of Troy, A. *Ag.* 527-8, may well have been less directly coloured for playwright and audience by the experiences of the Persian wars.

66. Stories such as that recorded by Plutarch of the Athenian audience looking to Aristides at the mention of Amphiaraus as just in Aeschylus' *Seven against Thebes* (Plut. *Arist.* 3.4) are most likely the product of a later tradition which hunted for coded references to individuals, and so provide no parallel for references to Themistocles. For other political allusions, esp. from scholia, see

Heath 1987: 66 n. 56, A. Bowie 1997: 44-5. As Heath comments, 1987: 70, 'To be sure, if we knew on independent grounds that contemporary audiences came to the theatre disposed to ferret out covert allusions and to discern partisan meanings, then these interpretations would warrant more indulgent treatment'. Cf. Plut. *Philopoem.* 11 (the audience at the Nemean Games turn to Philopoemen at the first line of Timotheus' *Persians* – 'Glorious the crown of freedom which he fashions for Greece').

67. Cf. Salanitro's isolation of 'passages containing political allusion': 1965: 194. Stoessl, 1952: 121, at least asserts that Aeschylus 'based his [political] ideas upon general philosophical, historical and political views', even if he does not in detail show how. Beer 1981 attempts to show how the 'political aspects of the *Eumenides* are in a very real way connected with the dramatic issues' of the trilogy as a whole; however, the 'message' he sees in the play is a narrowly political one (e.g. p. 65: 'Having shown in the *Ag.* and the *Cho.* the consequences of an ineffective *boulê*, Aeschylus, through the mouth of Athena ..., pleads passionately on behalf of the *boulê* on the Areopagus, since it is the only institution with sufficient authority to prevent the dangers which, as Aeschylus sees it, are confronting Athens'). An exemplary exception to this pattern is Macleod's 1982 study of the *Eumenides*: Macleod begins by observing (p. 124) that the play's 'account of Athens and the Areopagus seems to many readers inspired more by patriotism (of whatever partisan tinge) than a sense of dramatic unity', but his subsequent reading of the play illustrates beautifully how such a partisan message may run with the grain of the argument of the play rather than against it.

68. Easterling 1985: 6. Contrast also Easterling 1997 on 'heroic vagueness' and, for the problem of allusions to myth, Stinton 1990.

69. Forrest 1960: 236. Cf., however, Mills 1997: 92 on the dramatically inappropriate praise of Athens at E. *Tro.* 207, 218.

70. A point acnowledged, strangely, by Post, one of the advocates of the identification of mythical characters with historical figures, 1950: 52: 'the reference to Pericles was not so plain to obtrude itself. The play is nicely designed to produce a favourable atmosphere without arousing opposition.' Contrast Mills' criteria for judging the validity of contemporary references in the context of her discussion of Euripides' *Suppliants*, 1997: 93: 'If there is meant to be a more explicit link between the play and history, we might expect to find details in it which can only be explained as references to contemporary events, rather than those which straddle the dramatic and the contemporary'; see also Burian 1985.

3. Aeschylus, Atossa and Athenian ideology

1. Conacher 1974: 156 n. 26; cf. Pelling 1997a: 8, Rosenbloom 1995: 95, Saïd 1998: 280.

2. 1957: 230.

3. Conacher 1974: 158.

4. Cf. Wilson 1986: 52, arguably ascribing too great a degree of deliberate intention to Aeschylus: ' "the polis of the Persians" a curious phrase perhaps designed to match the opposing polis of the Athenians.' Tourraix, 1993: 109, emphasises the characteristically Greek social conditions of Aeschylus' Susa.

5. It is possible, however, that Aeschylus believed that of the cities named in the play only Susa was in Persia itself: if so, then Susa might have been emblematic of Persia, Ecbatana of Media and so on. Herodotus, 5.49.7, has Kissia as the name of the province in which Susa was situated: see further Hall 1996a: 108 on lines 16-18. The question of Aeschylus' and the Greeks' knowledge of Persepolis is more complex: see now Tuplin 1996: 140, Miller 1997: 117 (p. 114 on the expression *eis Persas* at e.g. Xen. *Cyrop.* 8.7.1, for which see more fully Cameron 1973: 55-6, Francis 1980: 73 n. 108, and the dispute of Jacobsthal 1938: 210 n. 28 and Robertson 1939). The apparent pun on Persepolis at line 65 may suggest some knowledge of Persepolis on Aeschylus' and his audience's part: see Root 1980: 6, Francis 1980: 73 n. 108, Tourraix 1993: 112-13. The expression 'city of the Persians' (511-12) seems to Root 'contextually to describe Susa', though contrast again Francis 1980: 73 n. 108 (cf. also Olmstead 1960: 173). Broadhead thought that Aeschylus mistakenly believed Darius' tomb near Susa rather than Persepolis, 1960: xlv, just as he may have mistaken the province of Kissia for a distinct city. Hickman, 1938: 22, assumes that Aeschylus knew that Darius' grave was at Persepolis but that 'since the Persian elders, the royal messenger, and Xerxes himself would not naturally resort to that place, Aeschylus transferred the dead monarch's tomb to Susa'.

6. I do not mean to deny the difficulties of distinguishing this ideological background. See e.g. E. Said's charming discussion, 1978: 93-4, of how the 'appearance of success' reinforces what he calls the 'textual attitude'.

7. Hall 1989; cf. Hall 1993, 1996a. Contrast the focus of Hall's predecessor Helen Bacon, 1961: 1 ('what follows is mainly an attempt to establish facts').

8. Hall 1989: 99; for this and other such structural polarities as characteristic of Greek thought, see esp. Cartledge 1993.

9. Hall 1989: 70. Cf. Cartledge 1993: 39 (the *Persians* as 'an early version of the specific form of derogatory stereotyping now known as "orientalism" '), or E. Said's description of the Orient, 1978: 1, as 'one of [Europe's] deepest and most recurring images of the Other'; he also, however, talks glibly (p. 78) of how to be a European means to belong 'to a part of the earth with a definite history of involvement in the Orient almost since the time of Homer' (cf. his comments on the distinction of Orient and the West in Homer, pp. 20, 56; contrast Hall's compelling survey of the Homeric evidence, 1989: ch. 1). See also Griffith's observations on the discontinuities in the history of 'orientalism': 1998: 52 n. 107.

10. E. Said 1993: xxviii, 60.

11. E. Said 1978: 7; for the history of the idea of Europe, see the introductory survey of Hay 1957, and now Hartog 1996 and the collection of Sordi 1986.

12. 1953: 7. Cf. his comments of p. 53 ('For many centuries Europe was supreme among the organized societies of the world ...') or his description (p. 58) of America: 'Yet we know that there is waiting across the Atlantic a greater Rome which may at the best establish a true world Peace, and will at the worst maintain in an ocean of barbarism a large and enduring island of true Hellenic life.' Cf. the remark of a character in Disraeli's 1834 *The Rise of Iskander*, cited by Vickers 1990: 253: 'we must do something more than read the Persae, we must act it.'

13. Hall 1989: 71-2.

14. 1989: 99; cf. p. 97 ('The political contrast is not just a "picturesque tableau" but sets up an antithesis between east and west predicated on differences in political psychology').

15. 1996a: 20.

16. Cf. Podlecki 1983: 23 for the Queen as the 'backbone' of the play, who 'serves to bind together its various scenes'.

17. 1996a: 16-19.

18. Edward Said noticeably allows for a far less conscious and so more subtle construction of the barbarian Other; he sees, for example the possibility that the conception of the Orient as an Other may coincide with increasing familiarisation, 1978: 12. 'Therefore Orientalism is not a mere political subject matter or field that is reflected passively by culture, scholarship, or institutions; nor is it a large and diffuse collection of texts about the orient; nor is it representative and expressive of some nefarious "Western" plot to hold down the "Oriental" world. It is rather a *distribution* of geopolitical awareness into aesthetic, scholarly, economic, sociological, historical, and philological texts; it is an *elaboration* not only of a basic geographical distinction ... but also of a whole series of "interests" which, by such means as scholarly discovery, philological reconstruction, psychological analysis, landscape and sociological description, it not only creates but also maintains; it *is*, rather than expresses, a certain *will* or *intention* to understand, in some cases to control, manipulate, even to incorporate, what is a manifestly different (or alternative, or novel) world; it is, above all, a discourse that is by no means in direct, corresponding relationship with political power in the raw, but rather is produced and exists in an uneven exchange with various kinds of power ....' Said suggests this more complex pattern specifically of the *Persians* at p. 21. For the the Greek familiarisation (or appropriation?) of Persians through mythology, see Braun 1982: 29-31, Hall 1989: 36, Georges 1994: 66-71, R.L. Fowler 1996: 73 and n. 82.

19. Hall 1989: 57 and n. 3, 1996a: 140 (ad loc.). Cf. Saïd 1984: 52 (the *Persians* represents 'la défense et illustration la plus parfaite de cette vision dichotomique du monde'), duBois 1982: esp. 17, 89-90: 'The form of the Persae involves an almost compulsive separation between the Greeks and Persians, one which paradoxically threatens to dissolve into identity, yet which finally keeps the barbarian at a distance, polarised spatially in his difference from the Hellene.' For the development of the concept of the barbarian, see also Lévy 1984.

20. 1989: 70.

21. Cf. Hall 1996a: 5: 'if the goal is the appreciation and understanding of the play, the important point is surely not its historical veracity in terms of detail, but its interest as a document of the Athenian collective *imagination*.'

22. 1989: 2, 86.

23. 1989: 86-93, 1996a: 15-16.

24. The attempt to distinguish Greek cultural prejudices from Persian reality has, of course, been central to recent studies of Achaemenid Persia: see e.g. Sancisi-Weerdenburg 1985, 1989a, Briant 1989b, Gammie 1986, and the essays collected in the second volume of *Achaemenid History*, e.g. Kuhrt and Sherwin-White 1987. For the portrayal of Persian women, see Brosius 1996, and the comments of Wiesehöfer 1996: 79-88, Briant 1996: 533-4.

25. See the comments of E. Said 1978: 21 (cf. p. 71): 'The dramatic immediacy of representation in *The Persians* obscures the fact that the audience is watching a highly artificial enactment of what a non-Oriental has made into a symbol for the whole Orient. My analysis of the Orientalist text therefore places emphasis on the evidence ... for such representations *as representations*, not as "natural" depictions of the Orient .... The things to look at are style, figures of speech, setting, narrative devices, historical and social circumstances, *not* the correctness of the representation nor its fidelity to some great original.'

26. 1983a: 7; cf. Lattimore's observation, 1943: 92-3 (and n. 29) that 'there are often close resemblances in thought and language', though contrast the remarks of Pelling, 1997a: 2, that 'Herodotus can help a little, but only a little' (admittedly in the context of the account of Salamis, though Herodotus also features little in his discussion of 'ideology and national stereotypes'. For the ideological affinities (and contrasts) between Aeschylus and Herodotus, see esp. Patin 1877: I.243-4, Delcourt 1934, Saïd 1981, Hall 1989. Wardman 1959 sees affinities in treatment of tactics and weapons (e.g. the theme of the bow vs. the lance), due to a pro-Athenian tradition and a 'shared interest' in tactics.

27. For the problems of Xerxes' succession, see Root 1979: 83-95, Briant 1996: 534-8. Knowledge of these problems may possibly be reflected at l. 716. See also Martorelli 1977: 123-4 for the claim that Herodotus' account echoes (indirectly) the 'official version' of Persian inscriptions.

28. For whom see Griffiths 1987.

29. Cf. the desire of Alexander and Amasis for Greek wives: 1.3.1, 2.181.1.

30. The affinity in presentation of Atossa is noted by Delcourt 1934: 244-5, and by Tourraix 1984: 124. Contrast, however, Brosius 1996: 109 ('the originally unnamed Persian queen in Aeschylus' *Persae* is by no means depicted as either a powerful or an influential queen'), or Tuplin 1996: 166 (noting that the prominence of Atossa is 'in the context of Greek tragedy hardly "odd" in any ways which could be thought to reflect a special perception of Achaemenid women').

31. For this timidity, see below, ch. 8.

32. Sancisi-Weerdenburg 1983: 24. The identification of the Queen as Atossa is one regularly taken for granted by e.g. Craig 1924, Ghezzo 1938/9, Wardman 1959, Meier 1993, van Wees 1995. Cf. the discussion of Vogt 1972: 136.

33. Sancisi-Weerdenburg 1983: 24; cf. Broadhead 1960: xxvi, xxxi, Tourraix 1984: 124, D.M. Lewis 1985: 111. See also Podlecki's cautious designation of the Queen simply as 'the Queen' in his edition of the play, 1991: 63 (assuming, however, that Aeschylus knew the name of the Queen even if his audience did not).

34. 'In a complicatedly symbiotic relationship': Tuplin 1996: 166. The conflation of Atossa and Semiramis is observed by Photius of Conon (see Conon *FGrHist* 26 F 1.IX) but perhaps also lies behind Hellanicus' description of Atossa, *FGrHist* 4 F 178a (= 687 a F 7), as the first to wear the tiara and trousers, establish the service of eunuchs, and begin giving judgements in writing. Correspondence justice is a classic hallmark of the oriental tyrant – the innovation of written judgements is ascribed by Herodotus to the first Median king (and archetypal tyrant) Deioces, 1.100: Hellanicus' description may imply a similar status for Atossa as the originator of tyranny.

35. See e.g. the parallelisms between the succession of Xerxes and the failed succession of Cyrus: Ctesias *FGrHist* 688 F 17.

36. See now esp. Miller 1997, arguing (p. 1) that 'Persians were not so little known to Athens as is claimed, for all that they were (deliberately?) misunderstood and misinterpreted', and Tuplin 1996: ch. 3 for a survey of references to Persia and Persians in Athenian literature (for Old Comedy, see also Schmitt 1984, Daumas 1985; for Herodotus, see Hegyi 1973, Armayor 1978, and the balanced discussion of D.M. Lewis 1985). Cf. Tucker 1935: 6: 'If we imagine a similar play produced at Moscow after the retreat of Napoleon, there would be no surprise in our finding the Russians acquainted with the names and functions of numerous French marshals and generals.'

37. *FGrHist* 4 F 178a (= 687 a F 7). See further above, n. 34.

38. For reminiscences of Aeschylus in Herodotus' text, see Jouanna 1981: 7-11, but esp. Hauvette 1894: 125-7: though there are some precise verbal reminiscences of Aeschylus that can only be explained on the basis that Herodotus followed Aeschylus (or that he held the text of the *Persians* 'sous les yeux ou dans la mémoire'), e.g. l. 50 and 7.8.γ, 728 and 8.68.γ, some such similarities can be explained in reverse terms ('Inversement, il paraît légitime de reconnaître dans Eschyle des allusions à des anecdotes déjà répandues en Grèce de son temps, et rapportées ensuite par Hérodote'). Hauvette is also careful to point out omissions (e.g. the Strymon episode) and Herodotus' use of other sources.

39. Cf. E. Said's comments, 1993: 79, on Conrad's Africans as deriving 'from a huge library of *Africanism*'.

40. Cf. Tuplin 1996: 165 (though contrast p. 166, quoted above, n. 29). The effect of personal priorities on monarchical government is signalled clearly at the beginning of the *Histories* by the story of Candaules (including the telling detail that Gyges was accustomed to go the Queen whenever she called); the intrigue of Candaules' court is mirrored at the close of the *Histories* by the story of Amestris' robe, 9.108-114.1, for which parallelism see Griffiths 1999. This implicitly moralising portrayal of monarchy is arguably not restricted to Oriental monarchies: see Osborne 1996: 334-5 on the 'marital irregularities' of the kings of archaic Sparta. Ctesias, of course, reports similar stories of cruel Persian women such as Parysatis: for a summary see Sancisi-Weerdenburg 1987a: 40.

41. Sancisi-Weerdenburg 1983: 27-31. Her statement, however (p. 31), that 'there are no connections between the defeats in Greece and these partly romantic, partly tragic, tales' must be qualified: there is surely an *imagined* causal affinity between the Persians' defeat and the decadence implied by such stories. Cf. the model of oral transmission developed by Sancisi-Weerdenburg, e.g. 1985, 1994: she reveals perhaps a slight tendency to over-categorise in her discussion of Greek sources as e.g. in her distinction, 1987: 34, between 'literature that was meant to add something to the knowledge about Persia and writings that use the already available knowledge for other purposes'. Contrast the more subtle model of Murray 1987. For possible written sources of Herodotus, see Drews 1973: 22-32, Balcer 1987: 22-5 and now, for the relative dating of these fragmentary historians, the important work of R.L. Fowler, 1996: 62-9. For an Athenian culture of story-telling see Trenkner 1957: 14-22, Thomas 1989, S. Lewis 1995, 1996.

42. See Bianchi 1978 (in the course of his demonstration of affinities between Persian inscriptions and Aeschylus, especially concerning the presentation of Darius), di Benedetto 1993; see also for the Achaemenid genealogy, Balcer 1987: 38-42, M. Waters 1996. For contacts between Greece and Persia, see esp. D.M. Lewis 1977, and now Miller 1997, esp. chs. 3-4, arguing for a personal contact with the 'peoples of the Persian empire' for a 'comparatively large population' (p. 3). The means by which Miller envisages such contact taking place are often, however, very speculative, e.g. through slaves who 'must have retained to some extent the habits if not the clothing of their country of origin' (p. 81) or through military experience on the Athenian expedition to Egypt ('Every squadron must have taken back to Greece their share of booty and stories', p. 18). For widespread epigraphic evidence of a Persian presence in the Aegean (not just Asia Minor), see Baslez 1985; for aristocratic contacts between Greeks and Persians in Asia Minor, see now Mitchell 1997: ch. 6 and the ingenious argument of Whitby 1998.

43. Cf. Drews 1973: 33 and nn. 53-4.

44. Hall, 1996a: 121 on l. 155, makes the suggestion that Aeschylus may be implying that 'Persian royalty did not permit such easy familiarity'. Atossa is named neither in the Old Persian royal inscriptions nor in the published Fortification texts: Brosius 1996: 14, 48, Sancisi-Weerdenburg 1983: 22, D.M. Lewis 1985: 111-12; it would not, I suppose, be thought likely that her name was not popularly known in Persepolis. See also Brosius' explanation, 1996: 14, for the absence of Atossa's name in Persian records as due to the 'rather unusual circumstances of Darius' accession'. Brosius does, unlike Sancisi-Weerdenburg, appear to entertain the possibility that Aeschylus and his audience knew the name of Atossa: she suggests (pp. 16-17), that the play expresses a Greek attitude that Persian women should not be named. She also suggests, despite her blanket statement that the *Persians* is 'not a historical source', that Aeschylus probably chose Atossa as the only female character 'primarily because [as the King's mother] she held the most important position at the female court'.

45. See esp. Cornford 1907: chs. 12-13, Macleod 1983, Connor 1984 (for refs., see Harrison 2000b), Ober 1996: 78-9, Rood 1999. For Thucydides' knowledge of Herodotus, see the excellent comments of Hornblower, ii. 24-38, 122-45.

46. 1907: 201. Cf. Kitto 1950 45: 'Anyone who cares to read Thucydides VI and VII with attention and awareness will find it an interesting companion-piece to the *Persae*.'

47. T. Harrison 2000b.

48. Though, depending on one's view of the date of Herodotus' publication, Aristophanes may have expected a significant portion (though not entire: Johnson 1995: 243-4) of his popular audience to be familiar with *vignettes* from Herodotus' *Histories*: see e.g. Riemann 1967: 9-10, Fornara 1971b, Cobet 1977, Sansone 1985, Hartog 1988: 275.

4. The use and abuse of Persia

1. This consensus is observed e.g. by McCall 1986: 44; see also the sketch of two camps by Hall, 1989: 70-2, though cf. Paduano 1978: 15-16, Griffith 1998: 43, for a 'celebratory' *communis opinio*. Against jingoism and in favour of a common humanity: Ghezzo 1938/9: 428 ('Non esiste nella tragedia alcuna intenzione di celebrare i Greci o di denigrare i Persiani'), Jaeger 1939: I.254-5 ('not a cheaply patriotic melodrama written in the flush of victory ... His entire interest is the effect of destiny upon the soul'), Lattimore 1943: 82, Kitto 1939: 33-45 ('what patriotic celebration there is – and there is obviously some – is incidental'), 1966: 74-106, Broadhead 1960: xviii-xix, Lesky 1965: 61 ('what informs [the messenger's speech] is not triumphant chauvinism but a deep faith in the divine powers'), Vogt 1972, Conacher 1974: 146, Duchemin 1974: 132, Thalmann 1980: 281 ('in the whole Aeschylus transcends the boundaries of nationality and of enmity with sympathy and humanity, to show the effects of the disaster through Persian eyes'), Péron 1982: 30, Belloni 1982: 187, duBois 1982: 89, Meier 1993: esp. 71, Moreau 1993b: 133, Segal 1996: 165 (the *Persians* 'recreates ... the tearful and pitiful suffering of their recently defeated enemies' and 'foreshadows the reaching out to the defeated and degraded hero, some fifty years later, in the endings of Sophocles' *Oedipus Tyrannus* or Euripides' *Heracles*'), Pelling 1997a: 12-13. Drews 1973: 32 is particularly outspoken in criticism of the suggestion of Aeschylus 'savouring [his] enemy's anguish': 'the only ground for such an interpretation is a disbelief that an Athenian veteran of Marathon, writing for Athenian veterans of Salamis, could have looked at the battle through Persian eyes long enough to appreciate what a tragedy for Xerxes Salamis must have been'. A more subtle view is taken e.g. by Macleod 1982: 131: 'For Aeschylus' Persians represent human delusion, fear and suffering; and if there is praise of Athens in that play, it is designed to intensify the bewilderment and gloom of the characters on the stage.'

2. Podlecki 1966: 8.

3. Murray 1940a: 127-8; see also Forrest 1963: 6 on Murray's similar comparison of the *Acharnians* with the 1914-18 war.

4. Exceptions to the consensus include Craig 1924: e.g. p. 99 ('Is it likely that the Athenians were going to look as neutrals and extend to the Persians that measure of sympathy which would lead to that tragic *katharsis* of pity and terror in view of their sufferings?'), Lavagnini 1927: 295, Tucker, 1935: 5

('motive of the piece may be put down as patriotic stimulation'), Wardman 1959: 60, Forrest 1986 (conceding, p. 229, 'a touch of the Falklands about it'), Georges 1994: 82-3. For patriotic Athenocentrism in general in tragedy, see Heath 1987: 64-71 (seeing the excitement of patriotic feeling as an 'ancillary pleasure', pp. 67-8), Hall 1996b: 299-300.

5. Cf. Gagarin 1976: 30.

6. According to Ion of Chios in his *Epidemiai*: see Aeschylus *TGrF* Test. 1.10-12, 11-15. The remark at Ar. *Ran*. 1296-7 that Aeschylus picked up some Persian at Marathon may also imply that his presence at Marathon was well-known (or that it could be assumed of any Athenian of his generation?). Cf. Aeschylus' epitaph (to which his part in Marathon is central), *TGrF* Test. 162.

7. And which was also studded with spoils of the Persian war: see Thompson 1956 and now Miller 1997: 37-8 (Hellespontine cables, 9.115, 121), 44 (the corslet and bridle of Masistius, 9.20, 22.2, Paus. 1.27.1), 47 (golden *akinakes* of Mardonius). The effect of this backdrop of Persian devastation is stressed by Cartledge 1997b: 19 ('a no less potent political message than the astonishing plenitude of civic and imperial architecture of fifty years later'). For the suggestion that the tent of Xerxes may also have formed the original skene of the theatre, see also Broneer 1944, Francis 1980: 81-2. Miller 1997: 35-6, 49-53, ch. 9, esp. 235ff. (further refs. at n. 114). For the influence of Persian dress on tragic costume, see Alföldi 1955, though cf. Pickard-Cambridge 1988: 201-2, and for the influence of Persian dress in general Miller 1997: 163-5.

8. Allen 1941: 176 ('To this end, I suggest, Themistocles salvaged the timbers of the Persian ships and used them for the erection of new ikria, and later, under Pericles, these were removed and used, so far as they were still sound, as the roofbeams of the Music Hall'), O'Neill 1942: 425-7 ('he can feel under him the solid memorial of that hidden sea'); see also the amusing reconstructions of the thoughts of a member of the original audience by Balcer 1983: 258-9, Ridley 1922: 15-19 ('You are sitting on hard wooden boards, and though you have a cushion it does not seem either so thick or so soft as at the beginning of the day').

9. For Cynegirus, see Hdt. 6.114 with Kirchner *PA* s.v. Aeschylus son of Euphorion, and *TGrF* Test. 16-48. See on this point Craig 1924: 101 ('we have only to remember Cynaegirus and Aminias'), Georges 1994: 84 ('the playwright takes poetic vengeance for his brother Cynegirus'). For Ameinias at Salamis, see *TGrF* Test. 49-50. Perdrizet, 1921: 79, adds the extra biographical consideration that Aeschylus would 'without doubt, on returning to his home at Eleusis have discovered the burial place of his family ravaged' (for Aeschylus' Eleusinian background, see *TGrF* Test. 8).

10. Ar. *Ran*. 1026-7. Cf. Craig 1924: 101, Gagarin 1976: 31. Alternative readings of the passage seem implausible, though contrast Martyn 1964, Franco 1986. Aeschylus' enthusiasm for Salamis may perhaps be reflected also at Ar. *Ran*. 1463-5. though Dover, ad loc., appears to see the lines as a reflection only of the Periclean defensive strategy. For the detection of appeals to patriotic sentiment in scholia, see Heath 1987: 64 and n. 49; for the reflection of the patriotic function of tragedy in fourth-century oratory, see Hall 1996b: 299-300.

11. McCall 1986 (cf. the association of Aristophanes and the purportedly pro-peace Dicaeopolis, for which see E.L. Bowie 1988); cf. Podlecki 1991: 14 ('it must be admitted that Aeschylus took a serious risk. For if his audience had not been able to make this projection onto some universal plane where national boundaries dissolved and only common human values remained, this would have been not tragedy but travesty'), Pelling 1997a: 19 ('a pointed community of suffering with one's greatest enemy doubtless retained its challenging aspect').

12. Conacher 1974: 147.

13. Cf. Broadhead 1960: xxiii, xxix, Richardson 1952: 61; Kitto sees the view of the play as propaganda as the result of a false belief in a historical duty, in that inaccuracies are explained by an intention to deceive, 1966: 79-81.

14. Broadhead, 1960: xx, reacting against the suggestion of Sidgwick (on l. 847). Cf. Péron 1982: 6-8, for whom proskynesis, the stress on Xerxes' clothing, or the characterisation of the Queen are (though Péron acknowledges that l. 213 would have been shocking to an Athenian) primarily dictated by realism.

15. Cahen 1924: 306.

16. Broadhead 1960: xviii-xix (the description of the battle 'is remarkable for its restraint as well as for its brevity'). Balcer, 1983: 258-9, suggests that the passage may echo political songs honouring the tyrannicides, *PMG* 893-6, Green, 1996: 186, that it echoes Themistocles' speech before Salamis.

17. Podlecki 1966: 156-7 n. 4, Péron 1982: 15.

18. Cf. the Syrian chariot at l. 84.

19. The absence of the Strymon episode from Herodotus is for Conacher, 1974: 147 n. 8, evidence that it was an Aeschylean invention. See also above, ch. 1.

20. See below, ch. 8.

21. Cf. the observation of Broadhead, 1960: xlvii, that 'to a modern reader it appears little short of ludicrous that Xerxes should arrive wearing the same garments as he had rent in his despair at Salamis'. Alexanderson, 1967: 7-8, explains the concern for Xerxes' clothing at 845-51 as an attempt to make less absurd the idea of 'Xerxes tearing his robes at Salamis and then hurrying through the whole of Asia in the same rags'. A further parallel for Xerxes' failure to change is the oath of Histiaeus, 5.106.6, not to change his clothes until he had made Sardinia pay tribute to the king.

22. Cf. Kitto's comment on the comparison of Aeschylus and Herodotus, 1966: 85-6, that it would not have been surprising had Aeschylus introduced a first message (cf. Kitto 1950: 35-6).

23. A description adapted famously by the US post office: 'Neither snow nor rain nor heat nor gloom of night stays these couriers from the swift completion of their appointed rounds.' Cf. Timotheus fr. 791.40-2 *PMG* where a barbarian dying at Salamis is described as coming 'from the land of couriers who run across it in a day'.

24. For other evidence of the Persian courier service, see Briant 1996: 382-4; see also the comments of S. Lewis 1996: 60.

25. See *P. Oxy* II.221 (1899) col. III.1-16 (=*TGrF* 3 Phrynichus F 10a) with Marx 1928; cf. Stoessl 1945, Salanitro 1965: 222-5. Such synchronisms could perhaps be the product of dramatised retellings of the Persian Wars. For the synchronism of Himera and Thermopylae, see 7.166 with Thebert 1980: 95-6, Asheri 1988: 78, Dench 1995: 11, 51, connecting the story to P. *Pyth.* 1.72 ff. ('it is a small step from the synchronization of battles to a sense of a "common cause", and, indeed, of a common enemy'); it is possible indeed that the synchronism may be the product of the idea of common cause. Bremer, 1991: 41, suggests that Hiero's desire to equate Salamis and Himera lay behind the commission to Aeschylus to stage the *Persians* in Syracuse (*TGrF* Test. 1.68-9, 56a); see, however, the detailed analysis of Gauthier 1966. Aristotle, *Poet.* 1459 a 25, famously uses the synchronism as evidence of two events contributing to no common purpose.

26. See Rosenbloom 1993: 193, but esp. Tracy 1986; cf. Dover 1977: 63-6 for an implicit allusion to Pausanias in the *Agamemnon*.

27. Cf. Briant 1996: 547 on the return of Xerxes ('Hérodote la doit probablement à Eschyle').

28. Broadhead assumes, 1960: 118 on l. 348, that the Queen's ignorance was intended by Aeschylus ('Aesch. has chosen to represent her as ignorant of this, as of other facts'), rather than simply that he had not heard of the Herodotean variant.

29. Other common themes of the Persian Wars include the cost of providing for the King's dinners, 7.118-20 (for which see D.M. Lewis 1987, Briant 1989b, 1996: 297-306), or the enormous fortunes made up by non-Persians from the scraps of Persian wealth: e.g. Ameinocles, 7.188, Sataspes' eunuch, 4.43.7, Kallias, Plut. *Arist.* 5.7-8 (see Davies 1971: 260, Miller 1997: 30-1).

30. For references to the Persian wars even in other tragedies: Soph. *Aj.* 596-8 (Salamis), *Trach.* 633-42 (Thermopylae), E. *Ion* (tapestries of barbarian and Greek ships in battle and mythical scenes in the style of the Stoa Poikile). Cf. eulogies of Athens at Soph. *OC* 668-739 ('oh land most of all others eulogised with praise'), E. *Ion* (praise of Athens' blood), E. *Heracl.* 191-204 (praise of Athens as refuge for suppliants), E. *El.* 1319-20, though cf. dramatised suspicion of false flattery of Athens, Soph. *OC* 1003-4, and the injunction not to overpraise at E. *Heracl.* 191-204.

31. See below, ch. 8.

32. Craig 1924: 99.

33. Kelley 1978: 215.

34. Cf. Nenci 1950: 219; cf. the non-committal Pelling, 1997a: 13-14. The same emphasis on Persian mourning can be seen in Simonides' Cyprus epigram, 46 Campbell.

35. For which see especially Konstan 1987: 61-2.

36. Cf. the conversation of Hecataeus and Artaphernes at Diod. Sic. 10.25.1 in which Artaphernes comes out surprisingly well.

37. See Jouanna 1981: 9 for the comparison of 8.101-4 and 230-45.

38. Broadhead 1960: xix-xx; cf. Kitto's emphasis on Aeschylus' restraint, 1939: 41, 1966: 76-7. Contrast Craig 1924: 99 ('what deep chords must have vibrated to these lines'), Richardson 1952: 59-60, Podlecki 1966: 9 ('How could the audience not have thrilled to these words?'), Gagarin 1976: 33, Hall 1996a: 126-7.

39. Cf. Taplin, 1977: 127 n. 1, complimenting Kitto on his rebuttal of the argument of the *Persians* as 'mere jingoism dressed up as poetry', Macleod's assertion, 1982: 131 n. 37, that Kitto 'demolishes the notion that the *Persians* is a merely patriotic play', or the remark of Goldhill, 1988: 190, that the exchange 'does not arise merely out of "jingoism" '.

40. A similar experience was had by Podlecki in the Odeion of Herodes Atticus, 1986: 78, and is hypothesised by Griffith 1998. See Hall 1996a: 1-3, for a fascinating survey of modern performances of the play: in general, performances seem to have taken place in the context of war, or after victory ('at moments of patriotic fervour'), though since the war the play has been used to protest against war.

41. Kitto 1966: 87.

5. Where is Athens?

1. See Hall 1996a: 127.

2. 1903: ix-x.

3. Patin 1877: I.223. Cf. Flickinger 1918: 219-20 ('from a dramatic standpoint these questions are out of place, since Atossa's ignorance is *improbable* and is shown to be feigned by vss. 348 and 474f. ... Aeschylus valued dramatic verisimilitude less highly than the fervent response that each of these couplets would evoke in every Athenian breast'), Kitto 1939: 41 ('Aeschylus was mentioning facts which tend to strengthen the fear of the stage-audience').

4. These similarities are partially observed by Hauvette 1894: 126 and n. 5, Craig 1924: 100, Gow 1928: 153, Broadhead 1960: 101-2, Podlecki 1966: 156-7 n. 4, Saïd 1981: 32, Belloni 1988: 74. Ironically Manganaro, 1960: 114, describes 5.105 as a 'scene worthy of a tragedian'.

5. D.M. Lewis 1977: 62: 'whether or not they had really sent a message to this effect to Cyrus the Great before 540, they will certainly have believed it in Herodotus' day.'

6. A contrast between Greeks and Asians forgotten at 1.37.2 where Atys asks Croesus how his confinement will make him look as he goes back and forth to the agora.

7. Cf. also Darius' curiosity concerning the Paeonians, 5.13.1-2 ('who are these Paeonians, from what land do they come, and desirous of what do they come to Sardis?'), or Xerxes' laughing response to the Spartan request for justice, 8.114. For the *topos* of the laughing tyrant in Herodotus, see Lateiner 1977.

8. For the actual symbolism of earth and water, see Orlin 1976: 265-6, Kuhrt 1988.

9. Broadhead, 1960: 101 on 284-5, comments that 'These words, like *memnêsth' Athênôn* (824), could hardly fail to remind the audience of *despota, memneo tôn Athênaiôn* (Hdt. 5.105)'; we cannot say for sure, however, that Aeschylus was referring to a story later recorded by Herodotus, only that there is an affinity between the stories which suggests a larger common pool of such anecdotes. Cf. also Vickers 1990: 254 (for whom the 'point Herodotus was clearly trying to make was the immense contrast between Athens' comparatively insignificant position within living memory and the city's present power and influence'), Root 1985: 117 ('Herodotus' pointed suggestion (5.73 and 105) that Darius had never heard of Athens in 507 needs to be evaluated as something other than pure fact. It was perhaps a moralistically barbed way of reminding the Greeks that to the Persians Athens was hardly the focal point of their interest and destiny, but just one small part in the scheme of things'). Orlin, 1976: 255, sees these stories as literary devices of Herodotus: on 5.73 he comments that it has the 'quality of a cliché'; 'Herodotus does but repeat a motif which he finds useful elsewhere for dramatic purposes.'

10. For the theme of memory, see the comments of Hall 1996a: 1. Cf. Euben 1986: 365: 'the point of the play is not that Persia should remember Athens but that Athens should remember Persia for both its political dissimilarities and its human similarities.' For (alleged) warnings to Athens implicit in the play, see below, ch. 10.

11. Cf. Delcourt 1934: 247, Saïd 1981: 32, Péron 1982: 17.

12. Cf. D.M. Lewis 1958 on the Phoenician fleet of 411, 1977: 133-4. Cf. also the evaporation of Darius' anger against the Eretrians, 6.119.1-2: the truth may have been rather more dull, that Darius was never sufficiently furious to allow of such dramatic abatement. A rare acknowledgement that a Persian king had other, greater concerns than the Greeks is 1.153.3.

13. This is not to deny the King's (almost certainly historical) interest in foreign curiosities, including entertainers (see e.g. Martin 1965 on exploration, or the emphasis in Persian epigraphy, e.g. the Susa Foundation Charter (= Kent 1953: DSf), on the collection of luxuries representative of various subject peoples), only that Greece was a particular focus of that interest; cf. Darius II's fascination in the strong man Polydamas, Paus. 6.5.7 (pointed out to me by Amélie Kuhrt).

14. A similar idea of Persian dependence on Greek culture survived until comparatively recently in the scholarly idea that Achaemenid sculpture was created by Greeks, even the named Greeks Telephanes of Phocaea and Theodorus of Samos: see, redressing this, esp. Nylander 1970, Root 1979: 5-42, 1980: 9-11, and Root 1991 for a greater influence of Persian art forms on the western empire, and for a redefinition of 'Persian' and 'Greek'. Balcer, 1983: 262, can still speak of the 'Hellenisation of the Achaemenid empire'. For the relationship of the Parthenon and the Apadana reliefs at Persepolis (a relationship in which the Greeks are the imitators), see Lawrence 1951, Root 1985, and for imperial tribute, Wallinga 1989, Miller 1997: ch. 9, less compellingly Vickers 1985.

15. Cf. the desire of Alexander and Amasis for Greek wives, 1.3.1, 2.181.1.

16. See Martin 1965.

17. For the Aristophanic *parabasis*, see esp. Goldhill 1991: 188-222.

6. Athens and Greece

1. As Hall comments, 1996a: 127, 'there is no clearer evidence of the play's Athenocentrism'; cf. Paduano 1978: 26, Goldhill 1988: 190 ('Athens holds the key to Greece'). A similar implicit logic can be seen at E. *Suppl.* 163-4 (the lord of Athens is the strongest person in Greece).

2. See further the excellent discussion in Mills 1997: ch. 2 of the 'Athenian image of Athens'.

3. See Podlecki 1968, W.C. West 1970, Barron 1988: 621.

4. For the political context of the First Pythian, see Gauthier 1966: esp. 9-11.

5. Cf. D.M. Lewis 1977: 148: 'we should not, I think be in any doubt that, despite Herodotus' praises of Athens, it is Sparta which for him was Persia's principal antagonist'. See also the over-simplistic summary of explanations for the Greek victory of Starr 1962, e.g. pp. 322-4 on Herodotus: there are many more currents within Herodotus' account than Starr allows for. See the excellent remarks of Oswyn Murray, 1987: 102, on the bias of Herodotean anecdotes: 'Words like bias, *Tendenz*, or prejudice have the wrong connotations; we need a more neutral word, covering both conscious and unconscious self-interested distortion, as they operate over time within a tradition. The word I would offer is "deformation".'

6. Salamis: Podlecki 1966: 9-12, Gagarin 1976: 34, Bordaux 1993: 74. As Gagarin illustrates, 1976: 34, Athens is mentioned at a number of crucial moments in the play (285, 286, 355, 474, 716, 975-6).

7. See especially Fornara 1971a.

8. E.g. line 771 (in the context of Cyrus' conquest of Ionia); cf. 7.51 (all of Ionia except Athens subdued by Cyrus).

9. A usage that dates back to Solon: fr. 4a.2 West. Cf. also Hdt. 7.51 for Cyrus' conquest of all of Ionia save Athens, Plut. *Sol.* 10.6 for Salamis as Ionia and Plut. *Thes.* 25.4 for Isthmus epigrams marking the boundary between the Peloponnese and Ionia (thus perhaps bringing all of Greece north of the Isthmus under Athenian leadership). For the reflection of Athens' territorial ambitions in the myths of Theseus, see Calame 1996: 421-4. Lattimore asserts, 1943: 92, presumably on the basis of 1.143 that 'Herodotus ... would not so have used the term' Ionian to describe Athenians; cf., however, Mardonius' agreement with Xerxes, 7.9.1, that they should not allow the 'Ionians in Europe' to laugh at the Persians.

10. This usage has been interpreted by Edith Hall, 1996a: 123 on l. 178, as carrying with it 'no implication whatsoever that it means Ionians as opposed to Dorians'; she suggests rather that it reflects the Persian usage, known to the Greeks, whereby all Greeks were Ionians. It is unclear whether she means to exclude an emphasis on the common Ionianism (as distinct from the Dorians, if not as opposed to them) of the Ionians of Asia Minor and of Attica; there is, at any rate, no reason to my mind to suppose that these readings are incompatible.

11. See further above, ch. 1. It has been suggested by Gow, 1928: 154, that

Aeschylus' list mirrors the tribute districts of the Delian League, though cf. Bacon 1961: 47 n. 40. See also Stadter 1992: 185-95 for the suggestion of similar echoes in Herodotus' *Histories*. The Ionian touches to the Greek of the *Persians*, though they may have been a shorthand for the oriental, may also have been a nod to this political Ionianism: cf. Broadhead 1960: xxx, Hall 1989: 79, 1996a: 23.

12. The descent of Dorus and Achaeus from Creusa and Xuthus neatly makes the Dorians and Achaeans subordinate to the Ionian Athenians. For the 'Ionian propaganda' of the Delian League, see esp. Barron 1964 on the Samian *horoi*, suggesting a 'series of common League cults set up voluntarily at the suggestion of members ...', and the sensible remarks of Parker 1996: ch. 8, esp. 144-5.

13. Contrast e.g. Podlecki 1966: 18, emphasising Aeschylus' absolving of the Ionians of responsibility, Péron 1982: 10, underlining the 'community of race' and identifying the Greek and Ionian causes, or Broadhead's innocent reading, 1960: 221 on ll. 897-900 where the Ionians are referred to as Greeks: 'the fact that they are called *Hellanôn* may be taken to imply that the cause of the Ionian colonists of Asia Minor was regarded by the poet as identical with that of the mainland Greeks.'

14. See, on this story, S. West 1985: 285-7, Pritchett 1993: 159-60.

15. Broadhead 1960: 44, Podlecki 1966: 17, Gagarin 1976: 36, Péron 1982: 10. This blurring of the Ionians' part in the Persian wars undermines Prickard's interpretation of the two sisters of Atossa's dream as representing '(1) the Ionian colonies who had submitted to Persian dress and manners, (2) the western Greeks generally'.

16. Hall offers two explanations for this, 1996a: 135 on l. 347: either that it is part of an attempt to make Salamis Panhellenic or that it is the result of the masculinisation of the Athenians. For the effeminisation of Asians, see Hall 1993. Cf. also Winnington-Ingram 1983a: 2-3 ('Athena would be too patriotic, too local'); Konishi, 1979: 164, exasperatingly explains Athena's absence as due to an alleged association of the goddess with Cimon.

17. Hall 1996a: 12. Cf. Pelling 1997a: 10: 'the presence of the Ionians on the Persian side would be an uncomfortable blurring' of the contrast between free and slave; that contrast does not, however, exist in isolation.

18. Some might also like to read significance into the Dorian dress of the woman who breaks free from Xerxes' yoke in the course of the Queen's dream (183), but the Doric dress was in early times, according to Herodotus, 5.88.1, worn by women throughout Greece. R. di Virgilio, 1973, finds any number of references to a Dorian-Ionian antithesis (e.g. pp. 25-7 on Doric dress, for which see below, ch. 10).

19. Lattimore 1943: 91.

20. See Perlman 1976 for a survey of the 'Panhellenic ideal' (beginning essentially from Pericles). His conclusion (p. 5) that 'the *Panhellenic* ideal' serves as a tool of propaganda for the hegemonial or imperial role of a *polis*' underestimates, if anything, the extent to which members of an expansionist *polis* such as Athens might have believed sincerely in Panhellenic ideals and in the blessings offered by their *polis* to the Greek world. Cf. Payen 1997: 187: 'L'argument du panhellénisme alimente la propagande athénienne.'

7. The emptiness of Asia

1. Stressed esp. by Michelini 1982: 86ff., though see below, n. 24. It is hardly necessary to say that I am not concerned with the issue of the actual Persian numbers, for which see Young 1980.

2. For such repetition, see Kelley 1978, esp. 214-15, Assaël 1993: *anandria* is also used in a different sense of Xerxes (755) but, as Kelley points out (p. 215), the word 'brings to mind also the result of its taunt'.

3. An image picked up upon by later writers other than Herodotus: e.g. Pind. *Isthm.* 5.49-50 (*en poluphthorôi Salamis Dios ombrôi / anarithmôn andrôn Khalazaenti phonôi*), E. *Tro.* 748 (Andromache wishes her son had been tyrant of *Asiados polusporou*), Hipp. *AWP* 12 (everything in Asia grows to greater size), Lys. 2.20-21, 27-28, 36; cf. Herodotus' curious comment, 1.58, that the Pelasgian race, 'being barbarian, in no way increased greatly'.

4. Though it is also a characteristic shared by Croesus who blames his initial defeat by Cyrus on the numbers (*to plêthos*) of his army, 1.77.1.

5. For Xerxes as viewer, see the interesting observations of Konstan 1987; for Thucydidean echoes, see T. Harrison 2000b. His review of his troops is later ironically inverted in a review of the dead after Thermopylae (8.24-5): the men of his fleet rushed eagerly to witness the battlefield, which Xerxes had doctored by burying the evidence of the numbers of the Persian dead; he was not entirely successful, however, and his trick was exposed as 'laughable'. Such reviews of the number of troops (and the concern for numbers generally) may reflect Greek knowledge of Persian royal self-representation: see below, n. 43.

6. The passage reflects the grandiose manner of the Persian king as reflected, for example, in Thucydides' version of Xerxes' letter to Pausanias, 1.129.3.

7. Michelini, 1982: 95, stresses that '7.49 evidently owes a good deal to Aeschylus'. Cf. Thucydides' possible echo, 6.68.3.

8. Cf. Lys. 2.41 (a few free men are better than many enslaved).

9. For these natural miracles, see T. Harrison 2000a: ch. 3.

10. Cf. lines 74-80, 102-14, 719-20, 953-4. Cf. the gratuitous reference (in Artabanus' mouth) to a land-sea duality at 7.10.α3, that the Persians are planning a campaign against a people much braver than the Scythians both by land and by sea. Such phrases, of course, predate the Athenian empire, e.g. Hes. *Erg.* 101 (sea and land free of evils). See Pelling 1997a: 6-7, stressing the differences in the two authors' presentation of the land-and-sea theme, and Mills 1997: 139 on E. *Her.* 851-2 and Thuc. 2.41.4.

11. Cf. the stranglehold on others resulting from the Athenian control of the sea, as described by the Xenophontic *Athenaion Politeia*.

12. For the reversal of Pylos, 'a truly tragic, not merely a casual, irony', see esp. Macleod 1983: 142-3, but now also Flory 1993, using it as evidence, however, that Thucydides abandoned his work after the recovery of Athens' naval strength.

13. Compare, however, Achaemenes' advice to Xerxes to ignore what his enemies are doing and the size of their numbers (7.236.3): this should be put in the context, however, of his concrete advice not to split the Persian fleet into two (as Demaratus advised so as to occupy Cythera), thus allowing the Greeks to face them on equal terms (7.236.2). Contrast also Xerxes' reply to Demaratus that, even with equal numbers of Greeks and Persians, the Greeks would have difficulties (7.103.4).

14. An idea echoed by Aristophanes, *Vesp.* 1084.

15. Cf. Pelling 1997a: 7-8, stressing the differences between Aeschylus and Herodotus (a stress on 'Persian maritime clumsiness in Aeschylus, hostility of terrain in Herodotus'): in Aeschylus, Pelling argues, the cramping is 'largely a result' of the Persian ships' fouling one another; proof of this is that the Greek ships 'have room to cruise around the outside' (417-18); there is no sign of the Greeks' backing water to draw the Persians into the narrows, something which is in keeping with 'Aeschylus' stress on the inspirational fight for freedom' as opposed to the picture of 'wily Themistoclean deceit' intended by Herodotus. Certainly, a description of the Greeks' backing water would have sat oddly with Aeschylus' contrast between flight and rushing into battle (esp. 384-94), but Pelling's contrast is too emphatic: his reliance on 417-18 seems inappropriately legalistic given Aeschylus' stress on Xerxes' intention to entrap the Greeks (370); the contrast between flight and fighting is one that originates in a stress on Greek deceit (albeit Themistocles is not mentioned by name, 353-63); Aeschylus at 413 makes an unequivocal statment that the narrows gave rise to the Persians' maritime clumsiness, a theme present perhaps implicitly in Herodotus' account, in the story of Artemisia (8.87-8).

16. For the theme of drowning in the play, and the contrast in the presentation of the Persians' watery deaths between Aeschylus and Timotheus, see Hall 1994: 66-8.

17. Cf. Broadhead 1960: 135 on ll. 482-5.

18. Cf. Saïd 1988: 330. Similarly the expression 'a spring of woes' (*kakôn … pêgê*, 743) picks up on the 'spring of silver' (*argurou pêgê*, 238) that is the Athenians' alternative to a royal treasury.

19. Cf. A. *Sept.* 1082-3 (*allodapôi / kumati phôtôn*).

20. Cf. Wilson 1986: 52 on ll. 89-90: 'the irresistible momentum of the vast Persian force is compared, ironically it turns out, to the action of the sea itself.' Cf. Saïd 1988: 329, emphasising the extent to which the theme transforms the Persians into 'une masse indistincte'.

21. Cf. Ghezzo 1938/9: 435, Holtsmark 1970: 17-18, Conacher 1974: 150.

22. At Pylos, the argument that numbers do not necessarily constitute strength is employed by Demosthenes, 4.10.4-5; cf. also the Melians' knowledge (a reminder to the Athenians of the Persian wars?) that in war numbers are not everything, 5.102, or the reverse formulation by Cnemus and Brasidas at 2.87.6 that numbers and equipment generally ensure success.

23. The trick by which Themistocles kept the Persians at Salamis is paralleled also by the Syracusan Hermocrates' message to Nicias, 7.73, delaying the Athenians' retreat by land till daytime.

24. For the theme of emptiness and the consequent effeminisation of Persia, cf. Bacon 1961: 3, Anderson 1972: 169-70, Francis 1980: 72-3 n. 106, Belloni 1988: xxvii-xxviii, Bordaux 1993: 75, Hall 1993: 117-18, Hall 1996a: 13. Cf. Plato's observation, *Leg.* 694e, on the consequences of the upbringing of Persian children in a 'desert of men'.

25. Though Artabanus himself is noticeably absent in Aeschylus, as noted by Tourraix 1984: 125.

26. Cf. Thébert 1980: 99.

27. Cf. the Athenian claim to give refuge to *apoleis andres*, Soph. *OC* 1357, or the description of the *polis* of Troy as *apolin*, A. *Eum.* 457.

28. It is perhaps impossible to say with certainty, as Podlecki suggests, 1966: 16, that Aeschylus was here alluding to a phrase actually used by Themistocles; only that it was a common Athenian slogan that derived from the circumstances of the evacuation, and which was later imagined to have originated in an expression of Themistocles.

29. The expression could also be read as a warning against the rebuilding of the walls, Salanitro 1965: 231-2, Saïd 1993: 65, for ideas of the play as a warning to Athens against excessive imperialism, see below, ch. 10. The same sentiment is expressed by Sophocles, *OT* 54-7; cf. Soph. *Ant.* 739 (Haemon to Creon: *kalôs erêmês g'an su gês arkhois monos*), Soph. *OC* 917-8 (*kai moi polin kenandron ê doulên tina edoxas einai*), A. *Suppl.* 913 (Pelasgus asks herald if he imagines he has arrived in a city of women). The idea of what a city consists in is taken in a different direction by Ion of Chios, *TGrF* 19 Ion F 63: *ou gar logois Lakaina purgoutai polis*. The theme also predated the Persian wars: cf. Alcaeus E.1.10 Lobel-Page; the idea that a city should preserve its men is also present in the poety of Solon, for example 36.25 West. By terming l. 349 'something of a commonplace', Brock, 1991: 168, underestimates its force.

30. An irony noted by Rosenbloom 1993: 191.

31. Cf. 4.123.1 on the evacuation of the city of the Budini.

32. Cf. Ober 1996: 84, suggesting that the desire to defend one's land is represented in Thucydides as 'an unworthy, even slavish, impulse'. For Athens' island ideology, see also Payen 1997: ch. 8 (La résistance insulaire).

33. For the continuity of strategy between the Persian and Peloponnesian wars, see Rood 1999; for the affinity between the Periclean defensive strategy and that of the Scythians in face of Darius, see Hartog 1988: 51, 203.

34. Avery 1964: 176, Saïd 1988: 330.

35. As Avery observes, 1964: 178, as 'each disaster is announced we are told that it is total (*pas*) and absolute (the perfects), only to hear later in the play that there were other disasters'.

36. Cf. Ghezzo 1938/9: 433, Avery 1964: 173-9, Hall 1996a: 24-5. The exaggerated idea of the whole barbarian army being involved in Xerxes' campaign need not lead one to suppose that such references are spurious or that they were introduced from a Sicilian version, as suggested by Wilamowitz 1898: 382-98, on the grounds e.g. that they would have been unbelievable to an Athenian: see Broadhead 1960: 199-200 on ll. 798-9.

37. This line, as Hall observes, 1996a: 140 (ad loc.), implies an 'absolute polarisation of "Hellene" and "barbarian", which here means "not-Greek" rather than just Persian': cf. Soph. fr. 857 (*philarguron men pan to barbaron genos*), and further parallels in Hall 1989: 161, 1996a: 140.

38. Cf. the Cyprus epigram of Simonides, epig. XLV Campbell.

39. Cf. Simonides' epitaph for the Corinthians, epig. XI Campbell = ML 24 ('now Salamis, the island of Ajax holds us').

40. Cf. also 670, 677-8, 714 ('the affairs of the Persians are destroyed'), 718 ('Xerxes has emptied the whole continent'), 729, 730, 925-7, 1016.

41. Cf. Conacher 1974: 150 ('Splendid processional to match the final grim recessional'), Péron 1982: 10 (and n. 1 for references), Loraux 1973, stressing (in the context of Lys. 2) that two contradictory propositions are put forward: ' "Les ennemis sont grands. Athènes a vaincu les ennemis. Athènes est grande." "Les ennemis sont médiocres. Athènes a vaincu les médiocres. Athènes est grande." '

42. A similar piling up of the stakes occurs in the case of Darius' Scythian expedition: Darius led every people under his rule, 4.87.1. Cf. also the story of the Hellespontine man who, on watching Xerxes leading his forces across the Hellespont observed: 'Zeus, why, taking the form of a Persian man, and adopting the name Xerxes instead of Zeus, do you wish to subvert Greece, bringing all mankind with you' (*agôn pantas anthrôpous*, 7.56.2).

43. See Kent 1953: DB 1.12-17, DNa 15-30, DSf 30-55, XPa 11-17, XPh 13-28. Cf. Hegyi 1973, Armayor 1978, Tourraix 1984. Cf. 9.27.5: the Athenians claim to have conquered 46 peoples at Marathon, a figure equal (as How and Wells observe, ad loc.) to the number of those who served on foot in Xerxes' army, 7.61-80 ('the assumption that they all fought at Marathon is purely gratuitous'). For the Achaemenid lists of subject peoples and the ideology underlying them, see Briant 1996: 184-94.

44. Cf. Connor 1984: 176-80 for a convincing attempt to connect the digression to its context.

45. Though contrast Nicias' estimate of the consequences of failure in Sicily: that Athens' enemies will sail against Athens, and that the residue of Athenian forces will be unable to repel them (7.64.1).

46. See Winnington-Ingram 1983b: 199, Kelley 1978: 213-14; cf. Sidgwick (1903) on l. 9 (*polukhruson* 'suggests the pride of the Chorus in their army, but also the contempt of the poet for the empty splendour of the Persians').

47. Sheppard 1911: 55, but esp. Taplin 1977: 127.

48. See Hall 1996a: 148.

49. For clothes as a symbol of monarchy, see further Saïd 1981: 22 (cf. Saïd 1988: 336 for clothes as emphasising reversal), Belloni 1982: 190; for 7.11.3-16α as reflecting a substitution rite, see Germain 1956, Bottéro 1978.

50. See Gow 1928: 138-9, Tuplin 1996: 144, 152 (arguing that knowledge of the Persian royal eagle may be revealed by Aristophanes and Epicrates). Xen.

Cyr. 7.1.4 and Xen. *Anab.* 1.10.12 (eagle on long spears of Persians) may be confirmed by the symbol on the Persian standard in the Alexander mosaic: see Nylander 1983. The same idea of the Persians or Persian king as represented by an eagle may be reflected in Themistocles' dream, Plut. *Them.* 26.3, of rescue by an eagle.

51. Cf. Moreau 1993a: 44-6.

52. See further Moreau 1993a: 46-7, Hall 1996a: 125 on ll. 205-6.

53. Avery 1964: 179. Cf. Bordaux 1993: 78: 'Sans doute Eschyle et son public connaissaient-ils la révolte de Babylone ... et pouvaient-ils y voir, comme dans la sécession des îles et villes du littoral d'Asie Mineure, les prémices de la dislocation de l'empire, consécutive à Salamine. Sans doute même l'espèraient-ils.' The difference between hope and reality seems to me to be potentially a great one.

54. Avery 1964: 173.

55. 1964: 182-3.

56. For this awkwardness, see Macleod 1983: 141, Hornblower 1987: 148-50; contrast Connor 1984: 210 for book 8 as 'another example of a familiar pattern in the *Histories*, reopening after apparent closure'.

57. Cf. the more cautious view of Lysias 2.56: the King no longer desired Athens' land, but gave away some of his own and feared for the rest.

58. The premise behind Croesus' advice to Cyrus to fight Tomyris and the Massagetai on their own territory is likewise that defeat on their own ground would result in the loss of Cyrus' whole kingdom, 1.207.3. Cf. 1.130.3 (by conquering Croesus, Cyrus so 'ruled the whole of Asia' (*houtô pasês tês Asiês êrxe*), and the Persian claim to rule the whole of Asia, 1.4.4, 9.116.3.

59. Aristagoras' advice to the Spartan king Cleomenes, in the context of the Ionian Revolt, that he could easily rule the whole of Asia is surely, by its context, intended to appear ridiculous, 5.49.8.

8. Democracy and tyranny

1. See esp. Goldhill 1988; cf. Sartori 1969/70: 790.

2. See Missiou 1993, Briant 1996: 335-7 on the term *bandaka* rendered into Greek as *doulos* (ML 12).

3. See e.g. duBois 1982: 85-6; cf. Hall 1996a: 127 on 237.

4. See esp. Goldhill 1988; more bombastically, Ehrenberg asserts, 1954: 16, that 'the struggle between Asia and Europe is depicted as the eternal conflict between despotism and freedom'. For the political contrast between Greeks and Barbarians in general, see de Romilly 1993.

5. A.H.M. Jones 1957: 41 (misleadingly paraphrased by Ober 1998: 30); cf. Brock 1991, collecting earlier fifth-century traces of democratic ideology.

6. Cf. Euben 1986: 360 ('the victory at Salamis was won by men because of their political culture'), or his deterministic judgement (p. 380) that 'the victory at Salamis made political theory possible and necessary'. Cf. Podlecki 1986: 78 ('It is also an analysis of how political groups function vis-à-vis different kinds of leaders').

7. Though see the important article of van Wees 1995, challenging the assumption of the democracy as dependent on the naval empire (and so on the naval victory of Salamis) as an 'objective fact'.

8. See above, ch. 3.

9. 1977: 120.

10. Broadhead 1960: xxvi; cf. Patin 1877: I.233, Smyth 1924: 85-6, Ghezzo 1938/9: 429, 448 (Atossa always and only a mother), the psychoanalytic reading of Cantarella 1970: 76-81, di Virgilio 1973: 71, Podlecki 1983: 23-7, 1991: 10-12 (*Persians* as 'domestic tragedy'). Contrast Paduano 1978: 18 (Atossa concerned not only as a mother) and, confusingly, Georges 1994: 83.

11. See Brosius 1996: 105 ('the fact that women could obtain and exercise such power ... reflected the despotism of a monarch while at the same time that [sic] it proved the weakness of his rule. How could an empire be "well-ruled", if women were influential and even exercised power over over the king himself?'); see also T. Harrison 1997a: 185-7, 193. The evidence for the Greek negative stereotype of the politically active woman is enormous: see e.g. Schaps 1977, arguing for the proposition that women's names are mentioned in forensic oratory only in order to shame them, Halliwell 1997: 129-34 for the perversion of rhetoric by Clytemnestra in the *Agamemnon*. The idea that respectable Greek women should not speak or play a part in politics is made variously explicit, e.g. in the story of Pheretime, 4.165-7, 200-5, or at Soph. fr. 64 Radt, Soph. *Ant.* 525 (*emou de zôntos ouk arxei gunê*), 677-80 (better not to be vanquished by a woman) (cf. 746, 756), Soph. *El.* 302 (characterisation of Aegisthus as one who 'fights his battles with women'), Soph. *El.* 616-21 (Electra's consciousness that her behaviour, forced upon her, is unseemly), E. *Suppl.* 40-1 (wise women should act in all matters through men), E. *And.* 364-5 (limits to extent of women's speech).

12. Hall 1993; cf. E. Said 1978: 57 ('Aeschylus *represents* Asia, makes her speak in the person of the aged Persian queen, Xerxes' mother'). Another way in which ideas of gender may have infiltrated the Greek construction of Persia was in the adoption by Greek women of items of Persian male dress: the possible ideological significance of this is largely missed by Miller 1997: 170, 257-8, though cf. Tuplin 1996: 174.

13. See now Griffith 1998: 52-7, citing Pl. *Leg.* 694c.; cf. Hdt. 1.136.2, Arist. *EN* 1160b.

14. Something Herodotus establishes early through the story of Candaules' wife, mirrored at the end of his *Histories* by the story of Masistes, 9.108-114.1 (for this parallelism, see Boedeker 1988, Griffiths 1999). The point is made also in the context of Greek tyrants as much as Persian kings: Periander's stripping of all the women of Corinth to placate his murdered wife Melissa, 5.92.η1-4 (probably a distortion of a Corinthian ritual: cf. Stern 1989) is an excellent illustration of the general pattern of unaccountable monarchy as an abuse of power for personal ends established by Otanes at 3.80; cf. Osborne 1996: 334-5 on the intrigues of the Spartan court, Hartog 1988: 152-6, Cartledge 1993: 80-2, Munson 1993 for Sparta as barbarian.

15. For the association of light with the Persian monarchy, cf. Plut. *Alex.* 30 with Belloni 1986: 82-3.

16. Cf. the Chorus' idea that Xerxes' defeat would somehow make his mother no longer the mother of a god (157-8). The parallel of these lines (and of 584-97) to 211-14 is noted by Avery 1964: 183, arguing that his interpretation of the final scene, i.e. his suggestion that the mood is changed by new clothes being brought on for Xerxes, makes the lines 'more than just a constitutional aside'.

17. See e.g. Podlecki 1986: 79 ('The Queen Mother uses a word, *hupeuthunos*, which for an Athenian audience would have pointed the contrast between Xerxes' position and that of their own elected or appointed leaders'), Paduano 1978: 101 ('ancora una parola tecnica del lessico ateniese!'), Belloni 1988: 121 (esp. for parallels), Goldhill 1988: 191, Brock 1991: 168 (citing as parallels Clytemnestra's imposition of accountability on others at A. *Cho.* 715, Zeus as an unaccountable monarch at A. *PV* 324), Hall 1996a: 126 (ad loc.). Cf. Broadhead 1960: 85 (ad loc.), suggesting that Atossa is made to speak as an Athenian without questioning how an Athenian might react to this very un-Athenian sentiment, Michelini 1982: 128, asserting that the lines are directed to us, rather than the Persians.

18. Cf. Delcourt 1934: 250 ('Illogisme qui devait révolter profondément des esprits formés par l'*euthuna* attique'), Easterling 1985: 2 on a reference to a *prutanis akritos* at A. *Suppl.* 370-5 as showing the idea of the *euthuna* 'as close to the surface'. Cf. A. *Cho.* 715 (*ainô de prassein hôs hupeuthunôi tade*). Lack of accountability is seen as a characteristic trait of monarchies (*exesti aneuthunôi poieein ta bouleutai*, 3.80.3; cf. 3.80.6), not restricted to Persians: cf. Astyages' impaling of Magi, 1.128.1, or Pheretime's treatment of the Barcaeans, 4.102.

19. And also for their equally whimsical generosity to those who, in their eyes, excel: 7.106 (Maskames excels all in bravery), 7.117.1 (Artachaies has the loudest voice), 7.107 (Boges honoured for his self-sacrifice). Darius has a particularly fine line in gratitude, expressing the opinion, when asked by Artabanus what he would like to have in as great a quantity as the seeds in a pomegranate that he would rather have as many Megabazuses as Greece subject to him, 4.143.2, and also that he would rather have Zopyrus alive and unharmed than twenty Babylons, 3.160.1. Zopyrus' self-mutilation had been part of a plan to capture Babylon that involved incidentally the sacrifice of seven thousand of his more expendable men, 3.155, 157. For the King's friends and the ideology underlying these relationships, see Briant 1996: ch. 8; for his gifts, Sancisi-Weerdenburg 1989a.

20. Other Persian examples of excessive punishment, whether threatened or fulfilled: 3.27.3, 3.35.5 (Cambyses buries alive 12 men), 3.36.6 (Cambyses kills those who had protected Croesus), 3.69.5 (Smerdis' ears), 4.43.2 (Zopyrus), 7.35.3 (Hellespont architects), 7.94.1-2 (Sandoces), 7.114 (Amestris' burying alive of children), 8.90.3 (Xerxes and Salamis slanderers), 9.112 (Amestris and Artaynte). As the examples quoted in the text above show, Cambyses, despite his alleged madness, is hardly an exceptional figure in his legalistic interpretation of Persian law. See K.H. Waters 1971: 57-85, Brosius 1996: 122, Keaveney

1996 for various attempts to explain away Persian punishments (in Brosius' case, the punishments of royal women, for which see further T. Harrison (forthcoming)): the question of whether such incidents were or were not historical is, of course, irrelevant to their importance to the Greek perception of Persia. See also Hartog 1988: 322-4 for the association of mutilation and slavery.

21. Cf. the parallel of Oeobazus who makes a similar request of Darius, with a similar result, 4.84. For near-eastern parallels to the punishment of Pythius, see Masson 1950, S. West 1987. For the identity of Pythius, see now S. Lewis 1999.

22. For Artemisia, see Weil 1976 and, for the contrast between Herodotus' characterisation and the much less sympathetic representation in Hippocratic writings, Jouanna 1984.

23. Cantarella 1970: 78 ('un egoismo di gioia che può sembrare crudele'). Cf. Dworacki 1979: 104: 'above all she wants to know the fate of her son, yet she does not ask the question directly because of her pose of dignity and restraint.'

24. This point is emphasised by a number of precise verbal reminiscences between lines 226-8 and 520-2: see Korzeniewski 1966: 585-6.

25. Broadhead 1960: xxvi.

26. Conacher 1974: 155-6.

27. Cf. the Persian prayer formula, 1.132.2, whereby a Persian prays for good fortune for himself, all Persians, and the King.

28. See Richardson 1952: 58-9, Broadhead 1960: 143 (ad loc.), for the various possible meanings of this phrase, e.g. suicide or fear of revolution. For the instructions to deliberate as motivated by the Queen's 'practical nature and maternal solicitude' (although it has no '*dramatic* significance'), see Broadhead 1960: xxxvi-vii (cf. xxvii). For the similar *aporia* of the Chorus' deliberations at 140-9, see below, this chapter.

29. This entry has been seen, Taplin 1977: 99-100, as due to her 'appreciation of the divine control over changes of fortune and prosperity'; cf. Lucas 1950: 61. However, even on her previous entrance, the Queen allowed herself a certain amount of (admittedly obscure) proverbial wisdom on the nature of wealth. Is it not rather that the shock of defeat has shattered the pretences by which the Persian monarchy is hemmed around and maintained? Does her apparent humility not confirm our suspicions (and the Chorus' predictions) of the end of the monarchy and reflect her own lack of confidence?

30. As Hall suggests, 1996a: 161 (ad loc.), this reference to advisers would have had a particular resonance for the Athenians given the role of the Peisistratids, 7.6.2-5.

31. 1960: xxviii.

32. Perhaps reminiscent of an image of (the historical) Solon's: fr. 12 West.

33. Broadhead 1960: 189 on 753-5; contrast Saïd 1981: 19, noting the more precise details in Herodotus, and (p. 21) arguing for a greater emphasis on the role of advisers in Herodotus than Aeschylus.

34. Conversely, in Greek thought, tyrants are wise by virtue of the wisdom of their advisers: Soph. fr. 14 (*sophoi turannoi tôn sophôn xunousiâi*). Cf.

Mardonius' attempt after Salamis to deflect the blame from the Persians onto the Phoenicians, Egyptians, Cypriots and Cilicians, 8.100.4.

35. See e.g. Veyne 1988: 91.

36. Broadhead 1960: xxviii; cf. Richardson 1952: 60: the passage is 'only an Athenian view of an oriental Queen Mother's preoccupation with her royal son's *Persici apparatus*, exaggerated a little perhaps for satiric effect'. For a deranged idea that Xerxes' clothes are a reference to the dress of Cimon, see Konishi 1979: 164.

37. Alexanderson 1967: 9.

38. 1996: 7; cf. Butts 1947: 25 ('she represents an aggressive type of woman').

39. This seems half to have been appreciated by Ireland 1993: 43 ('the personal interest she exhibits throughout not only contrasts with the wider political interest of the Chorus but also overshadows it').

40. 1986: 45.

41. Their ineffectual character is noted by Dworacki 1979: e.g. 104, Michelini 1982: 28, Winnington-Ingram 1983a: 5, Gredley 1996: 209; Garvie, 1969: 106, describes them as 'anonymous and colourless' by contrast to the Chorus of *Supplices*. Contrast, more savagely, Georges 1994: 89 ('Theirs is the unreasoning incompetence of ultimate slaves. Their incompetence and disobedience govern the play'), 102 ('in the *Persae* the men are women and the woman is a man').

42. The lack of any evidence has been seen as a difficult *aporia* to many modern critics, necessitating the postulation of an imperfect borrowing from Phrynichus (Stoessl 1945: 150, against which see e.g. Wardman 1959: esp. 150-1) or of a short silence of deep thought ('there is no need', writes Broadhead, 1960: 258-9, 'to postulate a "long" silence ... a very short interval would suffice to indicate that the Chorus were plunged deep in thought'); Meier asserts confidently, 1993: 64, that 'the elders wish to withdraw into the council chamber'. Contrast, however, Holtsmark 1970: 6-7, Conacher 1974: 152-3 n. 16, Georges 1994: 104 ('their resolve is plainly otiose, since they have been trying to devote careful and deeply pondered thought to these questions through the whole of their soliloquy, with no material result').

43. See Hall 1996a: 119 (ad loc.).

44. For the sense, see Broadhead 1960: 68; for the expression as resulting from an oriental concept of monarchy, see Tourraix 1984: 125.

45. For this expression as an echo of Achaemenid ideology, see Root 1979: 536.

46. The paying of tribute and the prostration seem to echo the reliefs of Persepolis: Broadhead 1960: 155-6.

47. Broadhead 1960: xxiv, Hall 1996a: 149; cf. Belloni 1982: 188, Tozzi 1980.

48. Cf. Thalmann 1980: 273.

49. Her concern with the consequences of defeat must also be reflected at 165-8, notoriously obscure lines. In the event of the death of Persian men, the masses (though who are these, given the alleged totality of Persian defeat?) would not respect the wealth of those remaining. This must surely be royal wealth, referred to elsewhere by the Queen in supposing that the Athenians would be sustained by a similar royal treasury (237), and by Darius who expresses his fear that it would be a prey to plunderers (751-2). The Queen's second fear, for the consequences of the loss of that wealth, that 'the light would not shine so radiantly on indigent people as on the powerful' is harder to fathom. The Queen's remark that she is afraid for the eye of the household, in other words Xerxes, must refer back to her fears: is the eye related to the light that shines on Persia (cf. 300-1)? If so, then the passage perhaps implies a doubt as to whether the monarchy can continue to flourish without the wealth that underpins it.

50. See e.g. Craig 1924: 100 ('so distinct is the impression of the ... present tenses, we seem to hear a Greek speaking'), Broadhead 1960: xxix ('has not the poet imported into their speech something of the outspokenness that was characteristic of democratic Athens?'), 85, Michelini 1982: 128, Bordaux 1993: 74. Contrast Broadhead's argument, 1960: 93 on 242, that 'it should not be hastily assumed that the Chorus is speaking out of character' in referring to themselves as slaves (though, he concedes, 'the effect of this line on the audience can easily be imagined'). We should always attempt to see such initially jarring passages as part of a dramatic argument before falling back on hypothesising a 'lapse' from a properly sustained and historically plausible characterisation.

51. There is no hint of any such political angle in Broadhead's reading of the play, 1960: xxv: the Chorus are 'awe-struck', and do not 'have the heart to break the terrible news'. Podlecki also misses the point, 1983: 26: 'The Queen shows herself a good match for the mighty Darius. When his former counsellors, men of his own age, are so paralysed with awe at the appearance of the Ghost of their former ruler that they can say nothing, it is she who dares to face him and explain the situation to him.'

52. Noted by Péron 1982: 16-17; Rosenbloom, 1993: 180, stresses the extent to which the allocation of blame was characteristic of the *threnos*.

53. For the double meaning of *oikhetai* as going and death at 178, see Winnington-Ingram 1983b ('Aeschylus has gradually – and deliberately – unfolded the implications of *oikhesthai*'), Belloni 1988: 74, Moreau 1993a: 39, Bordaux 1993: 74.

54. Cf. Broadhead's attempted justification of Xerxes' concern with his clothes, 1960: 239 on 1017: 'after lamenting the loss of his huge host he thinks of his tattered dress! But we have seen several times in this play the concern that is felt for the King's outward appearance by Darius and Atossa, and it is quite fitting that a man of Xerxes' temperament should be equally distressed .... To make Aesch. guilty of a contemptuous presentation of Xerxes is to ruin completely the tragic atmosphere.'

55. Avery 1964: 182; cf. Dworacki 1979: 106, Griffith 1998: 62-3 ('the sympathetic blurring of their collective vision perhaps serves to mitigate the sharpness of the imagined glare of the Dream-father').

56. The absence of the Queen from this final scene enables this reconciliation to occur without her looming presence to keep them in check: see Dworacki 1979: esp. 107. See below, however, this chapter, for the idea of Atossa's re-entry.

57. Cf. Euben 1986: 363, Rosenbloom 1993: 190, Moreau 1993a: 42ff.

58. Alexanderson 1967: 2. Darius' role is foreshadowed by the Queen in her dream in which she envisages him standing pitying Xerxes as he tears his clothes, 198 (for this reason Anderson, 1972: 174, is tempted by the idea that Darius remained on stage, a brooding presence, to point up the contrast still further). Cf. Belloni 1984 (comparing Agamemnon), Easterling 1985: 3 (seeing Xerxes and Darius as representations of the two poles of the Athenian idea of monarchs), Georges 1994: 82 for Darius as Aeschylus' necessary moral mouthpiece ('to whom could he have provided the part of moral exemplar if not to a Persian?').

59. Hartog 1988: 37.

60. See esp. Saïd 1981: 18, followed by Pelling 1997a: 15 ('there is nothing to suggest that Xerxes' behaviour fitted into a wider pattern of Persian expansionism'). The continuity between Persian kings is suggested most strongly in Herodotus, e.g. at 3.134.1, 7.8.α1,7.11.2, 7.50.3. For Persian imperial expansion as a constant given in the *Histories*, see also Verdin 1982. (The same idea of never-ending, restless expansion is, of course, applied by Thucydides to Athens, e.g. at 6.18: see further Mills 1997: ch. 2, T. Harrison 2000b). For the contrast of Aeschylus' picture of the Persian Kings and their own self-representation, see Root 1979: 310 ('we move from a realm of opposing personalities to a realm of calculated sameness ...').

61. Lattimore 1943: 91, Kitto 1939: 43; against Lattimore, see also Broadhead 1960: 204 on 817, Salanitro 1965: 229, Kitto 1966: 82-3, Petre 1978: esp. 333-6.

62. Contrast Saïd 1981: 35, arguing for Aeschylus' minimising of Marathon; on the contradiction between Aeschylus' presentation of Darius and Marathon and historical reality, see esp. Delcourt 1934: 247, Petre 1978: 333-6.

63. See, though, Quincey 1962: 183-4 for the suggestion that this line refers in fact to the burning of Sardis and to the temple of Cybebe; to specify the evils done, however, 'would have been to weaken the moral of the piece by introducing a factor which could have been construed as partial justification of Persian sacrilege'. I see no reason to attempt to define the scope of these evils too closely.

64. Saïd 1981: 34, 37-8; cf. Podlecki 1993: 59-60 ('The disapproval which Darius' ghost voices for Xerxes' pontoon pridge across the Hellespont ... seems especially disingenuous in the light of Darius' own bridging of the Thracian Bosphorus.' The point, however, is merely 'to magnify Xerxes' ignominy'.) See also Saïd 1981: 26-7 for the large number of parallels between the campaigns. Implausibly detailed knowledge of the Scythian campaign is taken for granted in Aeschylus' audience by Quincey, 1962: 185-6, in the course of his discussion of 858-60. For the relationship of the Scythian and Persian campaigns in Herodotus' account, see Hartog 1988: e.g. 7, 36.

65. Contrast Kitto 1939: 38: his allegedly analogous anecdote of a Scottish sculptor's response to a complaint that there was no likeness between a sculpture and its subject ('It's no every man ... can be like his bust') seems simply to suggest that historical inaccuracies are immaterial, however great they may be, that there are no 'margins of credibility'. Cf. Podlecki's idea, 1991:

5, that 'Darius' strictures on his son are sheer fabrication'; he offers no explanation in dramatic terms.

66. Cf. Gagarin 1976: 52: 'To the Athenian audience Darius would appear not as a model of virtue but as the representative of one traditional point of view, who maintains that point of view so as to present himself and his own reign in the most favourable light.' Contrast also now Griffith 1998: 61-2, suggesting that 'we are meant to be half-aware of this discrepancy', and relating this to the anxiety of 'youthful aristocratic endeavour'.

67. Contrast the reading of Meier, 1993:73, that 'the Persian empire is thus set apart from its monarch' (cf. p. 71: 'Atossa's account of Xerxes' irresponsibility is directed not at the system, but rather at the king's personal foibles'). Why would Aeschylus have had an interest in driving a wedge between Xerxes and the Persian monarchy or empire?

68. de Romilly 1993: 284. Contrast Thalmann, 1980: 273, supposing that 'when the woman in Doric dress shatters the yoke, the woman in Persian dress ... is also set at liberty'. This is implied retrospectively, he argues, from 594: 'Being subject to the King has given the Persians political order and prosperity, reasons for pride though bought with slavery. But if these rewards are no longer available, why should they remain in servitude?' This reading seems, however, to ignore the apparent reconciliation between the Chorus and Xerxes at the end of the play. The natural slavery of barbarians is expressed at E. *IA* 1040-1 (it is right for Greeks to rule barbarians as the one are free and the other slaves) and implied by the slide into monarchy of the Medes in Herodotus' story of Deioces, 1.96-100, or of the Egyptians, 2.147, 151-2. For modern parallels, see Balfour's argument for self-government as not natural to Orientals or Chateaubriand on the absence of an idea of liberty ('Of liberty, they know nothing; of propriety, they have none: force is their god'), quoted by E. Said 1978: 32-3, 172 (respectively).

69. For freedom of speech in Herodotus, see esp. Hohti 1974 (pp. 21-3 for Persian campaign).

70. For Darius' initial ignorance of Salamis, cf. Alexanderson 1967: 2-3. It is possible that the oracles recognised as fulfilled by Darius were referred to in the first play of the tetralogy, the *Phineus*: see Broadhead 1960: lv-lx, Hall 1996a: 10-11.

71. For oracles in Herodotus, see T. Harrison 2000a: ch. 5.

72. See above, ch. 3.

73. See e.g. Bickermann 1963, Hall 1989: 91 (or the clearer summary at 1996: 121), though (following Duchesne-Guillemin 1979, Calmeyer 1981) she leaves open the possibility of posthumous divine honours. For the actual gestures of submission employed in the Persian court, see esp. Frye 1972. For the circumstances in which the Greeks did kneel before their gods, see van Straten 1974; see also now Pulleyn 1997: 191-4.

74. See Tuplin 1996: 157-8 on Isoc. 4.150.

75. For this passage, see Cartledge 1993: 143-5; cf. Gorgias 82 B 5a DK (Xerxes the Zeus of the Persians). Sensitivities over proskynesis were also, of course, to be a prominent feature of the reign of Alexander (see esp. Badian

1981, Bosworth 1988: 278-90); this later controversy, however, may have been inspired prinarily by other factors, such as the increasing gulf between Alexander and his companions.

76. 'Dislike of the Persian monarchy crystallised round the action of *proskynesis*': Momigliano 1984: 68.

77. See esp. Hall 1989: 89-90, 1996a: 151-2, Griffith 1998: 51, following on from, e.g., Lawson 1934, and against the idea of e.g. Headlam 1902 of the evocation as distinctively oriental. See also Rose 1950: 262-5 ('neither peculiarly Greek nor peculiarly Persian'), and Jouan 1981 with a review of earlier views and bibliography.

78. The scene is unprepared, according to Taplin, 1977: 106, quoted above, Preface; contrast Belloni 1982: 188 (calling the raising of Darius 'il punto focale del dramma, gradualmente preparato degli interventi che precedono') and also Jouan 1981: 404 ('La venue sur la scène de Darius est preparée de loin').

79. Conacher 1974 151, Saïd 1988: 326-7. See e.g. Soph. *OT* 31-39, though cf. *Ant.* 836-8.

80. Griffith, 1998: 48-9, lays weight on the distinction between *prospitnô* and *proskunô*, remarking that much must depend on the character of the abasement (the term clearly *can* describe more innocent supplication). His parallels from other tragedies, S. *Phil.* 485 (Philoctetes to Neoptolemus), S. *OC* 1754 (Antigone to Theseus), E. *Her.* 79 (Heracles' children to Heracles), E. *Phoen.* 293, 924 (chorus to Polyneices, Creon to Tiresias), hardly support this innocent reading of the Persians' prostration unequivocally: much depends on the object of prostration. See further Hall 1996a: 119-20 (on l. 152).

81. Cf. the comments of Couch 1931: 316 ('The speech itself, with its massed epithets of address, suggests the invocation of a deity').

82. See Belloni 1982 for the idea that these are echoes of Achaemenid sacral kingship. Cf. Georges 1994: 108 on 630ff.: 'This farrago ignores any distinction between mortals and immortals as, in sixteen swift lines, the Elders range the entire space between deity and humanity.'

83. See Hall 1996a: 157-8 on 694-702.

84. 1989: 92-3.

85. The same idea of divinity as conditional on success or power is reflected at 709-12 (for which see Broadhead 1960: 179) or, in Herodotus, e.g. in the story of the Hellespontine man, 7.56.2.

86. The Queen also refers to Darius as a *daimon*, 620, though to describe a man or woman as a *daimon* does not (in itself) carry with it overtones of divinity: see Hall 1989: 91, citing E. *Alc.* 1003, or Broadhead 1960: 163 on 619-22.

87. Taplin 1977: 115; cf. Podlecki 1993: 56-7 ('whatever the historical truth may have been, Aeschylus is asking his audience to accept the divinity of the Persian emperor').

88. Cf. the parallels supplied by Hall 1996a: 157 (ad loc.).

89. Cf. Pelling's comments in response to Taplin, 1997a: 14-15, esp. n. 63 (' "Accept it", yes, in the sense that the invocation works, and Darius appears: the point is not one of cosmological efficacy. Thus far the audience enter into the thought-world of the court they see on stage. But they would not accept it in the sense of accepting this as a normal, comfortable, and ordered view of the boundary between human and divine'). Cf. Bacon 1961: 36 (terming proskynesis the 'Persian *salaam*'), Georges 1994: 89: ('the Elders' inability to distinguish between man and god in conceptualizing their rulers' is the fact above all others which 'defines that environment of spiritual delusion in which Xerxes sped to fulfil those *thesphata* which contained the fate ordained by Zeus for Persia ...'), Clifton 1963: 113 ('Prostration was, of course, repulsive to a Greek, and any suggestions of despotism added to the oriental tone of the play').

90. 1960: xxviii-xxix.

91. Cf. Pelling 1997a: 15: 'Thus, even while Darius by nature of his continued, posthumous, divine existence is distanced from Greek thoughts, there is a good deal in what he says which the audience can appropriate as their own'.

92. 'There is no need', Broadhead comments judiciously, 1960: 206 on 828, 'to suppose a metaphorical reference to the official who scrutinised the accounts of magistrates'. Cf. also the Chorus' reminiscence of the good days of Darius when (the text is difficult) the 'system of laws, steadfast as towers regulated everything' (*nomismata purgina pant' epeuthunon*, 858-9); this, like the scenario described by Demaratus, 7.104.4, of Greek obedience to law, is clearly meant to contrast with their more recent experience. The *nomismata purgina* may refer to laws inscribed on gates or doors by the Persian kings: Rogers 1903.

93. Cf. A. *Eum.* 273-5 (Hades a *megas ... euthunos* of mortals who *deltographôi de pant' epôpai phreni*), A. *Suppl.* 595-9 (Zeus as unaccountable), A. *PV* 77 (Zeus *hôs houpitimêtês ge tôn ergôn barus*), A. *PV* 324 (*trakhus monarkhos oud' hupeuthunos kratei*). The connection between 827-8 and 210-14 is made by e.g. Kitto 1939: 44-5, Petre 1978: 332, Moreau 1993a: 49 on 826-7.

94. For Gaia and Ouranos as Greek deities (rather than reflecting an attempt by Aeschylus to recreate Persian religion), see Hall 1989: 87-8, 1996a: 145 on 497-9 ('Presumably the irreligious were praying in thanks for what initially seemed like a benevolent divine intervention').

95. Cf. Sider 1983: 191: 'The sense seems to be that all Persia bowed before the King; now, in their desperation, they bow even before the gods.' Cf. Momigliano 1984: 69: 'Love of freedom and respect for the true gods ... coalesced.'

96. See e.g. Avery 1964: 179-84, Belloni 1982: 190. Cf. Gagarin 1976: 40, for whom the end of the play is softened by the presence on stage of the Queen as a comforting symbol of continuity ('her own strength and her presence on stage ... give the audience the feeling that although Persia's prosperity has been destroyed, its continued survival is not in danger, at least not by the end of the play'), Taplin 1977: 128 ('The procession also suggests, perhaps, the final exhaustion of the lamentation: even in defeat life at home must go on'), Mitsis 1988: 117, adding or drawing out a degree of ambiguity from Taplin's reading. For Georges, 1994: 112-13, the Queen's preparation of the clothes and the recovery of Persia are in the future. Georges also sees in the reconciliation of Chorus and King 'Aeschylus' own informed calculation of the future: his audience 'was in no mood for a peace that would destroy the raison d'être of an increasingly profitable hegemony'.

97. Cf. Belloni 1982: 191.

98. Alexiou 1974: 84.

99. See Hall 1989: 81-4, 131 and now Stears 1998: 121, though contrast Griffith 1998: 50-2 (for whom the kommos would have 'repelled and attracted in equal measure'), an argument discussed below, ch. 10. The theme of the excessive mourning of barbarians is widespread: 2.61, 2.85, 3.66.1, 4.71-3, 6.58, 8.99, 9.24; see further Harrison (forthcoming). Excessive mourning and self-mutilation were forbidden in Athens by Solon: Plut. *Sol.* 12.8, 21.6. See here Hartog 1988: 133-56.

100. See above, n. 29.

9. Themistocles and Aristides

1. Cf. Stoessl 1952: 120 for the suggestion that Aeschylus excludes Mycale from the play because the 'Greeks must not fight the Persians on the Asiatic side of the sea'. A curious feature of Forrest's argument, 1960: 237, that the *Persians* was designed to remind the Athenians of Themistocles' achievement in the Persian wars, is that the play is designed simultaneously to promote a view that might detract from that message, namely that 'to abandon interest in Persia when Persia was no longer the real danger was common sense, not Medism'.

2. Goldhill 1988: 192 ('the subsumption of the individual into the collectivity of the polis' is a 'basic factor in fifth-century Athenian democratic ideology'). For other interpretations of the Greeks' anonymity, cf. Martin 1952: 5-6 (to create a necessary distance from his characters: one could not have had Themistocles expressing himself in the style of Agamemnon without provoking ridicule; cf. Patin 1877: I.211 with comparisons with Racine), Murray 1940a: 126 ('If one Greek general had been named the play would have become modern and been exposed to all the small temporary emotions of the immediate present, the gratified vanity, the annoyance, the inevitable criticism'), Broadhead 1960: xviii-xix (a proof of his impartiality?).

3. A slogan possibly reflected at [Xen.] *Ath. Pol.* 1.19: necessity drove every man to take up an oar.

4. Compare Xerxes' confidence (7.103.3-4) that compulsion makes for a more effective fighting force than free will. Interestingly, however, in a different context but in very similar language, Herodotus does not commit himself on the question of whether monarchy or some form of freedom is more effective as a way of binding a people, albeit a barbarian people, together: the Thracians, he says, would be much the strongest of all peoples 'if they were ruled by one man or were to form a common resolve' (*ei de hup' henos arkhoito ê phroneoi kata tôuto* ..., 5.3.1). At Salamis, Herodotus goes some way to endorsing Xerxes' view in saying that the Persians fought better than at Euboea due to fear of the King, 8.86. Demaratus' idea of *despotes nomos*, 7.104.4, in one sense also accepts Xerxes' premise in so far as *nomos* is an object of fear to the Spartans, who in turn are both free and 'not entirely free'. The rises to power of Deioces (1.96-100) and of Psammetichus (2.151.2), both in the context of political vacuums, suggest monarchy as the natural form of monarchy in Media and Egypt respectively.

5. Contrast A. Bowie 1997: 43, comparing the play with Simonides at Plut. *Them.* 15: '*Persae* is not especially pro-Themistoclean: it does not even name him.'

6. Though cf. Fornara's argument, 1966, that the Psyttaleia episode was the fabrication of an anti-Themistoclean tradition. The episode may, of course, have been given a great 'hoplite twist' without having been invented *ex nihilo*.

7. See e.g. Salanitro 1965: 207-8, Wallace 1969: 293, Hall 1996a: 11, 128, 141. Kitto, 1966: 90, argues that Athenian politics were irrelevant to the Psyttaleia episode, as Aeschylus unlike Herodotus does not mention that the troops on Psyttaleia were Athenian: might Aeschylus' audience not have been able to read in this knowledge without Aeschylus' help?

8. This balance has been observed by e.g. Salanitro 1965: 210, Michelini 1982: 112, Saïd 1993: 55.

9. Most notably by Salanitro 1965.

10. See e.g. Conacher 1974: 156 n. 26, Rosenbloom 1995: 95, Pelling 1997a: 8.

11. Lattimore 1958: 30-1 n. 4; cf. van Wees 1995: 159 ('No doubt this is an exaggeration for dramatic effect, rather than a sober assessment of the damage done, but its effect is to deprive the rowers of much military credit, by implausibly suggesting that in the most famous of ancient sea-battles the heaviest blow was dealt in a marginal infantry engagement').

12. See e.g. Broadhead 1960: 331 ('partly because of the distinction of the men who perished, men of noble birth who enjoyed the confidence of the King, men in the prime of manly vigour and valiant in spirit, and partly because such excellent dramatic material was worthy of separate treatment, which would heighten the effect and deepen the impression'), Salanitro 1965: 209.

13. Saïd 1993: 68.

14. By Podlecki 1966: 24, tracing its origins 'in part to Herodotus' strong anti-Themistocles bias, probably fostered by his Alcmeonid informants at Athens'; 'the truth of the matter', he continues, 'seems to be rather that the disagreement between the two men turned simply on whether Athens was to become a naval power in the 480s, and that their rivalry was buried once and for all when Aristeides returned'.

15. See e.g. Plut. *Them.* 3.1-3 (puerile affair), 11.1 (Themistocles responsible for recall of Aristides), *Arist.* 2-3, 5.4 (they and their tribes compete in bravery at Marathon), 22.2-4 (Aristides a moral check on Themistocles).

16. Cf. Forrest 1960: 235. Timocreon fr. 727 *PMG* implies that disapproval of Themistocles leads to commendation of Aristides.

17. de Romilly 1974: 13; cf. Sartori 1969/70: 790-7, Petre 1978: 329-30.

18. Pelling 1997a: 12; cf. Heath 1987: 67. Contrast O'Neill 1942: 425-7, or Macleod 1982 or Schaps 1993 on the *Eumenides*.

19. Patin 1877: I.220.

20. Rhodes 1992: 64, 68.

21. R.G. Lewis 1997. It is possible also that the reform of the archonship in 487 – changing the method of selection of archons from election to the lot – may, regardless of whether this was an intended consequence, have slowly sapped the reputation of the Areopagus (constituted from former archons), and brought the issue of democratic accountability to the forefront of politics: see further above, ch. 2.

22. Austin 1990.

23. 1993: ch. 2.1; Lavelle's reliance on Herodotean speeches for sentiments of the Persian war period (pp. 37-8) is open to question.

24. Herington 1986: 26-7; cf. Plut. *Them.* 2.5-6 for the false account of Themistocles as a pupil of Anaxagoras. In one respect at least, according to Herington, Aeschylus still belonged to the old world (p. 47): he wrote at a time 'before grammatical analysis is thinkable, before the intellectual chasm between signifier and signified has opened up. A word, for him, seems still to be a vision.' The presumption of a naivety on the part of the author is too often an excuse for naive criticism.

25. Meier 1990: 86-7: 'For the first time in Greek history – and world history – the civic order as a whole was placed at the disposal of the citizens .... It involved a new set of attitudes deriving from the relative weakness of primary institutions. It engendered a new openness, but the corollary of this openness was a special kind of exposure. Men acquired greater scope for action but were at the same time brought face to face with the immense difficulty of decision making. Thrown upon their own resources, they became conscious of the full measure of human suffering .... And with all this went a special form of generally relevant change. To a probably unprecedented degree, events were commensurable with human action; that is, the individual acquired a greatness and importance in relation to events that was unique in world history. The Greeks occupied a specifically "political" position in the world, above all in Athens, but also, to a degree that is not easy to estimate, in other places also .... It is hard for us to appreciate the shattering nature of this experience, its existential profundity and explosiveness.' This is occasionally excelled in Meier's 1993 *The Political Art of Greek Tragedy*. Cf. Rosenbloom's grandiose attempt to put Aeschylus' presentation of freedom and domination into the context of growing Athenian power, 1994: 94-5, or Loraux's transition, 1981: 289, from an age of the Persian wars, marked by the equation of men and city, to the age of empire, marked for Thucydides and his contemporaries by the power of Athens. See also Seaford 1994 for a much more compelling analysis of the *Eumenides* as reflecting a process of the gradual subordination of reciprocal violence to judicial process (on which see my comments, T. Harrison 1997b: 114-15).

26. Forrest 1966.

27. Forrest 1960: 228. A rather different line – if equally impossible to substantiate or disprove – is taken by Brian Lavelle for whom, 1993: 49, Cimon dissolved any 'rudimentary distinction' that may have existed between myth and history by the political coup of returning the bones of Theseus to Athens, an act which confirmed Theseus 'as a real element of the democracy'.

28. See e.g. Jouanna's portrait, 1981: 3-4, of a transition during the Pentakontaetia from 'archaism' to 'rationalism' in the explanation of the causes of Persian defeat, or Loraux's argument that the need for heroes such as Theseus had evaporated by the fifth century, 1981: 66 ('La démocratie d'Ephialte et de Périclès n'avait donc aucune raison de rétourner à Thésée une mention particulière; elle avait au contraire tout intérêt à attribuer au démos les actions légendaires du héros') against which see Mills 1997: 56 n. 33. The assumption that a 'transformation from a hieratic, obscurantist world order to a new self-validating domain of secular politics' (pp. 102-3) was possible is also a fundamental weakness of the excellent study of Adshead 1986. Against the idea of progressive secularisation, see e.g. Connor 1988, Parker 1996: 124; see also the excellent remarks of Kearns, 1985: 191, on 'emancipation' from religious power.

29. Cf. Heath 1987: 65 ('patriotism in tragedy inevitably takes on a religious aspect'); contrast Goldhill 1988: 193 ('Aeschylus' *Persae* seems to suggest that the Greeks are victorious not only because of the gods, not only because of Persian *hubris*, but also because of the values of democratic *collectivity*, embodied in Athens, as opposed to barbarian tyranny').

30. Parker 1996: 210.

31. 1988: 192.

32. See e.g. Conacher 1974: 142: Aeschylus chose the Persian wars as his subject because of their 'metaphysical importance' (for the '*hybris* theme', see p. 145). Contrast Lloyd-Jones 1956: 67 ('There was nothing new in [the morality of the play], and among most Athenians there will have been little disposition to dispute it. Aeschylus probably never thought of doubting it, and to that extent his plays may certainly be said to recommend it'), Conacher 1974: 145 ('the simple historical facts of Xerxes' Greek experience, viewed in the light of Greek ethical thought, clearly suggest the theme of divine nemesis'). Cf. Kitto's response (allegedly in defence of Aeschylus' intelligence), 1966: 38-40, or Adams' curiously heavy-handed discussion, 1983: 34-5 ('even if this interpretation of Salamis was not universally seen in 480, it must by 472 have become public property. Assuredly it did not take Aeschylus eight years to see it. Nor was he the craftsman to be content with teaching in slow evolvement a lesson everyone in Athens had long since learned'). For a much more subtle view of the 'theology' of tragedy, see Parker 1997.

33. 1996: 187.

10. Athens and Persia

1. 1960: xxxiii.

2. Hall 1989: 100.

3. duBois 1982: 89

4. Gagarin 1976: 30. Cf. Gagarin's remarks, 1976: 29, on Phrynichus' *Phoenicians* ('The play must have been a lament of Xerxes' fall, and thus directly or indirectly a celebration of the Greek victory').

5. Prickard 1879: xxvii: 'there is a twofold thread of interest running through the play; there is the dramatic or ideal interest, which requires the reader to place himself at Susa, and to feel as a Persian would do; but there is also the real or patriotic interest which an Athenian could not long forget in following the turns of his city's fortunes, and which often obtrudes itself where strict art would require the first only to be present.'

6. 1997a: 17; see also his suggestion that 'Xerxes' grief' is not distanced, but the 'manner of its expression' is, 1997b: 231-2.

7. 1997b: 220.

8. Cf. Mills 1997: 89 on Euripides' *Supplices* ('it is hard to imagine an audience swinging easily between emotional feeling stirred by the intense lamentations of the suppliant women of Argos and an intellectual understanding of the causes of their plight which would diminish their sympathy for them').

9. 1997a: 17.

10. Cf. Mills 1997: e.g. 106.

11. Nor is it compatible with the reading of the play that sees Xerxes and the Persians symbolically re-armed at its close.

12. 1982: 131.

13. 1996a: 19. Cf. Griffith's discussion of identification, 1998: 43ff.

14. Euben 1990: xii; immediately before this, however, he remarks that 'for the Athenians to see their victory through the eyes of a once powerful, still noble, but now defeated enemy meant that the theatrical occasion united loss and gain in a single moment, bringing to the victors in their exultation a wisdom borne [sic] of suffering and loss.'

15. 1982: 109 (my italics).

16. Cf. Heath 1987: 82 (for whom pity for Xerxes is not incompatible with a degree of patriotic celebration) or the judicious fudge of Cartledge, 1997: 25 ('tragic pathos is achieved by requiring the audience to sympathise somewhat, if not empathise, with their former – but also very much present – Persian enemies').

17. Griffith 1998; that his interpretation is 'in opposition to, or mitigation of' a 'jingoistic' reading is made explicit at p. 44.

18. 1998: 43; a corollary of Griffith's argument is that 'this pervasive mixture of resentment and dependency is constantly mirrored and reinforced at the level of individual psychology by the deeply-ingrained habits of respect to paternal authority'.

19. 1998: 48.

20. See further esp. Thomas 1989: 247-51.

21. Cf. Drews 1972.

22. For this and similar passages (cf. Xenophanes DK 21 F 3), see Kurke 1992; cf. Lombardo 1983, Geddes 1987.

23. 1998: 47.

24. 1998: 45.

25. 1998: 47.

26. 1998: 51.

27. For Dionysus in the *Frogs*, see now above all Lada-Richards 1999.

28. See above, ch. 1.

29. See above, n. 22.

30. See further Kurke 1992: 103. Pindar may reveal a lingering sense of oriental luxury as desirable earlier in the century when he employs a Lydian headband as an image of his own song, the ultimate luxury: *Nem.* 8.13-16 with Kurke 1992: 107-8.

31. For the orientalising pretensions of this aristocratic counter-culture, see Miller 1997; Miller is too keen perhaps to see this counter-culture as challenging the prevailing ideology of opposition to Persia (e.g. in her assertion, p. 1, that this 'cultural receptivity ... disproves ... the commonplace that the Athenians hated and despised the Persians').

32. See esp. Sancisi-Weerdenburg 1987b, Briant 1989.

33. Contrast Lavelle 1993: 37-8, arguably too credulous.

34. See below, n. 46, for a shift in representations of Persia through the fifth century.

35. Contrast Griffith, 1998: 52 n. 107, claiming (in a tone reminiscent of Gilbert Murray) that the Greeks were less antagonistic towards their enemies than the participants in modern wars, and concluding jovially 'Yes, the Persians burnt our temples – but we Ionians had burnt Sardis first.' This misses an important distinction observed by Parker, 1983: 168 n. 133, of the Greeks' burning of Sardis, 5.102.1: 'one's own side burns temples by accident only whereas one's enemy does so intentionally.'

36. Parker 1997: 155.

37. See e.g. Cataudella 1926, de Romilly 1974: 16, Gagarin 1976: 53, Konishi 1979, Melchinger 1979: 35-9, Winnington-Ingram 1983a: 15, McCall 1986: 44, and most recently and perhaps most extremely Rosenbloom 1995: e.g. 93-4. Cf. also Martyn 1964: 181 n. 5 on Aristophanes' *Frogs*: 'Aeschylus' reference at 1026 may well be hinting at his strategic advice to Athens, latent in the *Persae*, namely, the danger of expansionism and over-confidence.'

38. For the transgression of boundaries, see Lateiner 1989: 127-35. Lateiner has no clear idea of the nature of the relationship between the two authors (p. 128): 'Europe and Asia were intended to be separate, a truth central also to Aeschylus' *Persai*. Herodotus certainly was familiar with the historical tragedy; the two accounts agree in many points but also differ in details.' Cf. Saïd 1981: 34 on 864-6, arguing on this basis for the Halys as the natural frontier between Greek and Persian zones.

39. Cf. also 7.8.γ2-3, 7.19.1, 7.54.2, 8.53.2.

40. Mallowan 1985: 394, Miller 1997: 106. Cyrus' dream also forms part of a tradition of Persian dreams (not necessarily a Persian tradition): cf. Astyages' dreams of Mandane's urine flooding his city and the whole of Asia, 1.107.1, and of the vine growing from her groin and covering the whole of Asia, 1.108.1. See also Tuplin 1996: 159 on, e.g., the alleged claim of the King, reported at Aeschin. 3.132, that he was master of all men from the rising to the setting sun; Tuplin concludes that such language 'does not reproduce any genuine Achaemenid phrase'.

41. These last two passages have been interpreted by Pelling, 1997a: 12, as undermining the case for the play as 'inspirational and militaristic': these 'clear hints of the recent *weakening* of the Persian empire ... would seem to minimise any threat, accentuating the decisiveness of the Greek victory eight years earlier'. I am not clear as to why the glorification of past successes should not have been 'inspirational' or 'militaristic'; the first of the two passages, moreover, takes for granted continued Greek military involvement, albeit with an allegedly moribund Persia. See also Gagarin 1976: 36 for the view that the inhabitants of Asia here are exclusively Greek (but can we have Ionians performing proskynesis?).

42. Cf. Sartori 1969/70: 780 ('un sano ordine universale che esclude ogni forma di *hubris*').

43. For the meaning of the expression *theous ... nomizôn*, distinct from 'considering gods to exist' (4.94.4), see Broadhead 1960: 138-9 on 497-9, Fahr 1969: 42ff.

44. Cf. Mills 1997: 60: 'The Athenians are never tempted into violence or over-confidence ... in spite of their obvious superiority, unlike inferior or barbarian nations: moderation ..., after all, is one of these cardinal virtues, and the hallmark of all their actions is the impartial pursuit of justice.'

45. See further e.g. Fornara 1971a: 55-6, Boedeker 1988, Stadter 1992, Moles 1996.

46. See esp. Thuc. 6.30-32, Hdt. 7.46 (cf. 8.88, 90). For Athens as a tyrant, see Connor 1977, Raaflaub 1979. For the more problematic parallels between Athenian and Achaemenid imperial ideology, Miller 1997: ch. 9, Tuplin 1996: 193 (for the manner of the delivery of tribute in Athens and Persepolis, see Isoc. 8.82 with Goldhill 1987 and Miller 1997: 241-2).

47. For Euripides, see esp. Hall 1989, Saïd 1984; see Miller 1997: 28 for a 'new mood at Athens' reflected in Old Comedy (cf. Tuplin 1996: 141ff.).

48. Broadhead 1960: e.g. xvi, xviii, xxix.

49. 1988: 193 n. 35. Lattimore is completely immune to this definition of tragedy apparently, 1958: 38: 'As for Xerxes, who cares about Xerxes? Is there anything dramatic about a man getting so exactly what he deserves? (I merely ask.) He is in danger of becoming a moral proposition rather than a man; Aeschylus can rescue him only by turning him into sheer emotion. He weeps, and that is all.'

50. 1997a: 17.

51. 1983a: 15.

52. 1998: 56 ('every boy or man would secretly wish to be able to count on such a mother').

53. Hall: 1996b; an alternative to the Aristotelian model of tragedy is Heath's equation of the relationship of poet and audience to that of the Homeric bard and his nobility: 1987: 64.

54. Cf. Hall's discussion of the playing down of the Greeks' 'arrogant and insistent chauvinism', 1989: 72-3. A parallel idea is that the patriotic fervour of the play is somehow transcended by religious fervour: see e.g. Clifton 1963, Anderson 1972: 167, Nenci 1950: 218 amongst many others.

55. 1966: 78.

56. See also Ar. *Vesp.* 1087 with Long 1986: 89 ('The Aeschylean vision of the Persians screaming as they bob helplessly in the water is one of the most brutal in Greek literature'). Herington and Lembke, 1981: 105, report an account of a round-up of tuna off Cape Santa Maria: 'The tuna were funnelled by a great barrier of nets into a kind of corral of nets and boats, within which the tuna 'swims and swims, looking for a shadowless passage. There is none. He is trapped – doomed .... Near naked men ... thrust deftly with their hooks and long gaffs among the tuna, cutting at them with swift blows, the red blood spurting thick .... Great shapely blue bodies are everywhere, with wild staring eyes, and the water is soon tinged and then stained red with the tuna's blood.'

57. And indeed at the heart of the nineteenth-century view of the play as simple ridicule and a departure from the proper dignity of tragedy: see Blomfield cited by Broadhead 1960: xv.

58. Murray 1940a: 122-3. Murray's wishful thinking was not only projected onto ancient Athens: see his extraordinary justification of the League of Nations and his optimistic faith in the possibility of the settlement of disputes by means of an international air force, 1940b.

59. van Hook 1934: 185-6; cf. Patin 1877: I.213 or, extraordinarily in the context of a detailed examination of the topography of Salamis, Pritchett 1959: 257: 'The story of the Persian Wars, including the Battle of Salamis, needs rewriting from generation to generation; it is one of the glorious episodes in human history, a story of the victory of freedom over despotism and oppression. Of one thing, I think, we can be sure – that none of the modern accounts published up to the present time which makes Agios Georgios the ancient Psyttaleia have been convincing.'

60. 1908: 137.

61. 1996: 287; cf. Griffith 1998: 23-4.

62. 1996: 5.

63. See above, ch. 3.

64. See Tanner's 1994 critique of new approach to Greek art (Goldhill and Osborne 1994), with its 'tacit claim for classical art as exemplary' (p. 653).

65. 1998: 4.

66. 1940a: 127-8.

67. 1966: 106-7. Cf. Murray 1953: 40 on Greek civilisation: 'It was a Liberal civilisation: free, tolerant and unprejudiced; highly cultured; and out of its abundance generous and helpful to the rest of mankind.' For German views of the Persian wars, see Wiesehöfer 1990.

68. 1992: 378.

69. For Herodotus' anti-war stance, see Fornara 1971a: ch. 5. For Aeschylus, cf. Meier 1993: 78: he 'certainly did not reject war on principle, or hold that it might be abolished, but he showed that such a terrible thing should not be embarked upon lightly'. The more subtle view of the *Persians* of Momigliano also reveals a desire for a lack of narrow patriotism, 1984: 70: 'The tragedy as seen by Aeschylus was the tragedy of a nation let down by its leader'; 'the Persians were the first to suffer from the transgressions of their kings'. For

Aristophanic feminism, see Harrison 1997a: 186-7, Cartledge 1996 for the absurdity of *Lysistrata*.

70. Goldhill 1988: 193. Contrast Mills' salutary emphasis on tragedy as affirming rather than questioning, 1997: 264, or the comments of Saïd 1998: 284 on Goldhill's reading of the *Persians*.

71. 1998: 43.

72. 1924: 99.

73. Michelini 1982: 115 n. 48; cf. Butts 1947: 22.

74. E. Said 1993: 225.

75. E. Said 1978: 204.

Bibliography

Adams, S.M. (1983) 'Salamis Symphony: The *Persae* of Aeschylus', in E. Segal (ed.) *Greek Tragedy: Modern Essays in Criticism* (Oxford, 1983) 34-41, originally published in M.E. White (ed.) *Studies in Honour of Gilbert Norwood* (Toronto, 1952) 46-54

Adshead, K. (1986) *The Politics of the Archaic Peloponnese* (Aldershot)

Alexanderson, B. (1967) 'Darius in the Persians', *Eranos* 65, 1-11

Alexiou, M. (1974) *The Ritual Lament in Greek Tradition* (Cambridge)

Alföldi, A. (1955) 'Gewaltherrscher und Theaterkönig', in K. Weitzmann (ed.) *Late Classical and Medieval Studies in Honour of A.M. Friend* (Princeton) 15-55

Allen, J.T. (1941) 'On the Odeum of Pericles and the Periclean reconstruction of the Theater', *UCPublClArch* 1 (1929-44) 173-8

Amandry, P. (1953) *La colonne des Naxiens et la portique des Athéniens*, Fouilles de Delphes 2.8 (Paris)

——— (1960) 'Sur les "épigrammes de Marathon" ', in F. Eckstein (ed.) *Theôria: Festschrift für W.-H. Schuchhardt* (Baden Baden) 1-8

Anderson, J.K. (1972) 'The imagery of the Persians', *G&R* 19, 166-74

Andrewes, A. (1975) 'Could there have been a battle at Oenoe?', in B. Levick (ed.) *The Ancient Historian and his Materials: Essays in Honour of C.E. Stevens on his Birthday* (Farnborough, Hants.) 9-16

Armayor, O.K. (1978) 'Herodotus' catalogue of the Persian Empire', *TAPhA* 108, 1-9

Asheri, D. (1988) 'Carthaginians and Greeks', *CAH* IV², 739-80

Assaël, J. (1993) 'La répétition comme procédé stylistique dans les *Perses* d'Eschyle', in P. Ghiron-Bistagne, A. Moreau, and J.-C. Turpin (eds.) *Les* Perses *d'Eschyle*, Cahiers du Gita no. 7 (Montpellier) 15-27

Austin, M.M. (1990) 'Greek tyrants and the Persians, 546-479 BC', *CQ* 40, 289-306

Avery, H.C. (1964) 'Dramatic devices in Aeschylus' *Persians*', *AJPh* 85, 173-84

Bacon, H.H. (1961) *Barbarians in Greek Tragedy* (New Haven)

Badian, E. (1971) 'Archons and *Strategoi*', *Antichthon* 5, 1-34

——— (1981) 'The deification of Alexander the Great', in H.J. Dell (ed.) *Ancient Macedonian Studies in Honor of Charles F. Edson* (Thessaloniki) 27-71

Balcer, J.M. (1979) 'Athenian politics: the ten years after Marathon', in T.E.

Gregory and A.J. Podlecki (eds.) *Panathenaia: Studies in Athenian Life and Thought in the Classical Age* (Lawrence, Kansas) 27-49.
——— (1983) 'The Greeks and the Persians: the processes of acculturation', *Historia* 32, 257-67
——— (1987) *Herodotus and Bisitun* (Stuttgart)
Barron, J.P. (1964) 'Religious propaganda of the Delian League', *JHS* 84, 35-48
——— (1972) 'New light on old walls: the murals of the Theseion', *JHS* 92, 20-45.
——— (1980) 'Bakchylides, Theseus and a woolly cloak', *BICS* 27, 1-8
——— (1988) 'The liberation of Greece', *CAH* 4^2, 592-622
——— (1990) 'All for Salamis', in E.M. Craik (ed.) *'Owls to Athens': Essays on Classical Subjects Presented to Sir Kenneth Dover* (Oxford) 133-41
Baslez, M.-F. (1985) 'Présence et traditions iraniennes dans les cités de l'Égée', *REA* 87, 137-55
Bearzot, C. (1992) 'Ancora sulle *Eumenidi* di Eschilo e la riforma di Efialte (in margine ad una pagina di Chr. Meier)', *Prometheus* 18, 27-35
Beck, R.H. (1975) *Aeschylus. Playwright and Educator* (The Hague)
Beer, D.G. (1981) 'Tyranny, *anarkhia*, and the problems of the *Boule* in the *Oresteia*', *Florilegium* 3, 47-71
Belloni, L. (1982) 'L'ombra di Dareio nei Persiani di Eschilo: la regalità degli Achaemenidi e il pubblico di Atene', *Orpheus* 3, 185-99
——— (1984) 'L'intemperanza di Serse e la saggezza di Agamemnone. La conoscenza e la regalità in Eschilo', *CCC* 5, 7-18
——— (1986) 'I Persiani di Eschilo tra oriente e occidente', in M. Sordi (ed.) *L'Europa nel mondo antico, Contributi dell' Istituto di Storia Antica* 12 (Milan) 68-83
——— (1988) *I Persiani* (Milan)
Benedetto, V. di (1993) 'Dario e Artaphrenes in Aesch. *Pers.* 774-780', *Rivista di Filologia* 121, 257-71
Bengston, H. et al. (1968) *The Greeks and the Persians: From the Sixth to the Fourth Centuries* (tr. J. Conway, New York)
Bianchi, U. (1978) 'Eschilo e il Sentire Etico-Religioso dei re Persiani', in E. Livrea and G.A. Privitera (eds.) *Studi in onore di A. Ardizzoni* (Rome) I.61-72
Bickermann, E.J. (1963) 'A propos d'un passage de Charès de Mytilène', *PP* 18, 241-55
Boardman, J. (1972) 'Herakles, Peisistratos and Sons', *RA*, 57-72
Boedeker, D. (1988) 'Protesilaos and the end of Herodotus' *Histories*', *CSCA* 7, 30-48
——— (1995) 'Simonides on Plataea: narrative elegy, mythodic history', *ZPE* 107, 217-29
——— (1996) 'Heroic historiography: Simonides and Herodotus on Plataea', *Arethusa* 29, 223-42
Boer, W. den (1962) 'Themistocles in fifth-century historiography', *Mnemosyne* 15, 225-37
Boersma, J.S. (1970) *Athenian Building Policy from 561/0 to 405/4 BC* (Groningen)

Bordaux, L. (1993) 'Lecture du premier Stasimon des *Perses*, v. 532-97', in P. Ghiron-Bistagne, A. Moreau and J.-C. Turpin (eds.) *Les* Perses *d'Eschyle,* Cahiers du Gita no. 7 (Montpellier) 72-80

Bosworth, A.B. (1988) *Conquest and Empire: The Reign of Alexander the Great* (Cambridge)

Bottéro, J. (1978) 'Le substitut royal et son sort en Mésopotamie ancienne', *Akkadica* 9, 2-24

Bovon, A. (1963) 'La représentation des guerriers perses et la notion de barbare dans la 1re moitié de Ve siècle', *BCH* 87, 579-602

Bowie, A. (1993) 'Religion and politics in Aeschylus' *Oresteia*', *CQ* 43, 10-31

——— (1997) 'Tragic filters for history: Euripides' *Supplices* and Sophocles' *Philoctetes*', in C. Pelling (ed.) *Greek Tragedy and the Historian* (Oxford) 39-62

Bowie, E.L. (1988) 'Who was Dicaeopolis?', *JHS* 108, 183-5

Braun, T.F.R.G. (1982) 'The Greeks in the Near East', *CAH* III^2 pt. 3, 1-31

Bremer, J.M. (1991) 'Poets and their patrons', in A. Harder and H. Hofmann (eds.) *Fragmenta Dramatica: Beiträge zur Interpretation der griechischen Tragikerfragmente und ihrer Wirkungsgeschichte* (Göttingen) 39-60

Briant, P. (1989a) 'Histoire et idéologie. Les Grecs et la décadence Perse', in M.-M. Mactoux and E. Geny (eds.) *Mélanges P. Lévêque vol. II Anthropologie et Société* (Bésançon) 33-47

——— (1989b) 'Table du roi. Tribut et rédistribution chez les Achéménides', in P. Briant and C. Herrenschmidt (eds.) *Le Tribut dans l'Empire Perse: Actes de la table ronde de Paris* (Paris) 35-44

——— (1996) *Histoire de l'empire perse de Cyrus à Alexandre* (Paris)

Brillante, C. (1990) 'Myth and history', in L. Edmunds (ed.) *Approaches to Greek Myth* (Baltimore) 91-138

Broadhead, H.D. (1960) *The* Persae *of Aeschylus* (Cambridge)

Brock, R. (1991) 'The emergence of democratic ideology', *Historia* 40, 160-9

Broneer, O. (1944) 'The Tent of Xerxes and the Greek Theater', *UCPublClArch* 1 (1929-44) 305-11

——— (1952) 'Odeion and Skene', *AJA* 56, 172

Brosius, M. (1996) *Women in Ancient Persia (559-331 BC)* (Oxford)

Burian, P. (1985) '*Logos* and *pathos*: the politics of the *Suppliant Women*', in Burian (ed.) *Directions in Euripidean Criticism: a Collection of Essays* (Durham, North Carolina) 129-55

Butts, H.R. (1947) *The Glorification of Athens in Greek Drama, Iowa Studies in Classical Philology* 2 (Vandalia, Missouri)

Cahen, E. (1924) 'Sur quelques traits du récit de Salamine dans les "Perses" d'Eschyle', *REA* 26, 297-313

Calame, C. (1996) *Thésée et l'imaginaire athénien* (2nd. ed., Lausanne)

Calmeyer, P. (1981) 'Zur bedingten Göttlichkeit des Grosskönigs', *Archaeologische Mitteilungen aus Iran* 14, 55-60

Cameron, G.G. (1973) 'The Persian satrapies and related matters', *JNES* 32, 47-56

Cantarella, R. (1970) *Scritti Minori sul Teatro Greco* (Brescia)

Cartledge, P. (1993) *The Greeks* (Oxford)
——— (1996) 'Fanfare for the Common Chorus? Tony Harrison's *Lysistrata*', in C. Xekonkoulotakis (ed.) *Ancient Greece* (London) 5-13
——— (1997) ' "Deep plays": theatre as process in Greek civic life', in P.E. Easterling (ed.) *The Cambridge Companion to Greek Tragedy* (Cambridge) 3-35
Cary, M. (1922) 'When was Themistocles ostracised?', *CR* 36, 161-2
Castriota, D. (1992) *Myth, Ethos, and Actuality. Official Art in Fifth-Century* BC *Athens* (Madison)
Cataudella, Q. (1926) 'I Persiani di Eschilo', *Athenaeum* 4, 40-7
Cavaignac, E. (1921) 'Eschyle et Thémistocle', *Rev. Phil.* 45, 102-6
Cawkwell, G. (1970) 'The fall of Themistocles', in B.F. Harris (ed.) *Auckland Classical Essays presented to E.M. Blaiklock* (Auckland) 39-58
Clifton, G. (1963) 'The mood of the *Persai* of Aischylos', *G&R* 10, 111-22
Cobet, J. (1977) 'Wann wurde Herodots Darstellung der Perserkriege publiziert?', *Hermes* 105, 2-27
Coleman, J.E. (1997) 'Ancient Greek ethnocentrism', in J.E. Coleman and C.A. Walz (eds.) *Greeks and Barbarians: Essays on the Interactions between Greeks and non-Greeks in Antiquity and the Consequences for Ethnocentrism* (Bethesda, Maryland) 175-220
Conacher, D.J. (1974) 'Aeschylus' *Persae*. A literary commentary', in J.L. Heller (ed.) *Serta Turyniana* (Urbana) 143-68, reprinted with changes in his *Aeschylus: The Earlier Plays and Related Studies* (Toronto, 1996) 3-35
Connor, W.R. (1967) 'Two notes on Cimon', *TAPhA* 98, 67-75
——— (1971a) 'Theseus in Classical Athens', in A.G. Ward (ed.) *The Quest for Theseus* (London) 143-74
——— (1971b) *The New Politicians of Fifth-Century Athens* (Princeton)
——— (1972) 'Lycomedes against Themistocles? A note on intragenos rivalry', *Historia* 21, 569-74
——— (1977) 'Tyrannis Polis', in J.H. D'Arms and J.W. Eadie (eds.) *Ancient and Modern Essays in honor of Gerald F. Else* (Ann Arbor) 95-109
——— (1984) *Thucydides* (Princeton)
——— (1988) ' "Sacred" and "secular". *Hiera kai hosia* and the classical Athenian concept of the state', *AncSoc* 19, 161-88
Cornford, F.M. (1907) *Thucydides Mythistoricus* (Cambridge)
Couch, H.N. (1931) 'Proskynesis and abasement in Aeschylus', *CPh* 26, 316-18
Craig, J.D. (1924) 'The interpretation of Aeschylus' *Persae*', *CR* 38, 98-101
D'Amico, C. (1931) 'La battaglia di Salamina in Eschilo e Erodoto', *Atene e Roma* 12, 231-42
Dandamayev, M. (1975) 'La politique religieuse des Achémenides', tr. J. Duchesne-Guillemin, *Acta Iranica* 4, 193-200
Daumas, M. (1985) 'Aristophane et les Perses', *REA* 87, 289-305
Davies, J.K. (1971) *Athenian Propertied Families, 600-300* BC (Oxford)
Davison, J.A. (1949) 'The date of the *Prometheia*', *TAPhA* 80, 66-93
——— (1966) 'Aeschylus and Athenian Politics 472-456 BC', in *Ancient Society*

and Institutions: Studies Presented to Victor Ehrenberg on his 75th Birthday (Oxford) 93-107

Delcourt, M. (1934) 'Orient et occident chez Eschyle', *Mélanges Bidez (= Annuaire de l'Institut de philologie et d'histoire orientales 2)* 233-54

Delvoye, C. (1975) 'Art et Politique à Athènes à l'époque de Cimon', in J. Bingen (ed.) *Le Monde Grec. Hommages à Claire Préaux* (Bruxelles) 801-7

Dench, E. (1995) *From Barbarians to New Men. Greek, Roman and Modern Perceptions of Peoples from the Central Apennines* (Oxford)

Dodds, E.R. (1960) 'Morals and politics in the "Oresteia" ', *PCPhS* 186, 19-31, reprinted in his *The Ancient Concept of Progress* (Oxford, 1973) 45-63

Donnay, G. (1964) 'Pindare et Cimon. Thème et contenu politique du premier dithyrambe en honneur d'Athènes', *RBPhH* 42, 205-6

Dover, K.J. (1957) 'The political aspect of Aeschylus' *Eumenides*', *JHS* 77, 230-37, reprinted in his *Greek and the Greeks* (Oxford, 1987) 161-75

——— (1977) 'I tessuti rossi dell'*Agamennone*', *Dioniso* 48, 55-69

Drews, R. (1972) 'The first tyrants in Greece', *Historia* 21, 129-44

——— (1973) *The Greek Accounts of Eastern History* (Cambridge, Mass.)

duBois, P. (1982) *Centaurs and Amazons* (Ann Arbor)

Duchemin, J. (1974) 'Du lyrisme à la tragédie: réflexions sur l'*Agamemnon* et les *Perses* d'Eschyle', in J.L Heller (ed.) *Serta Turyniana* (Urbana) 122-42

Duchesne-Guillemin, J. (1979) 'La royauté iranienne et la *xvarenah*', in G. Gnoli and A.V. Rossi (eds.) *Iranica* (Naples) 375-86

Dugas, C. (1938) 'A la lesché des Cnidiens', *REG* 51, 53-9

Dumortier, J. (1963) 'La retraite de Xerxès après Salamine (Eschyle, *Perses*, 480-514)', *REG* 76, 358-60

Dworacki, S. (1978) 'Atossa's absence in the final scene of the *Persae* of Aeschylus', in G.W. Bowersock, W. Burkert and M.C.J. Putnam (eds.) *Arktouros: Hellenic Studies presented to Bernard M.W. Knox on the occasion of his 65th birthday* (Berlin and New York) 101-8

Easterling, P.E. (1985) 'Anachronism in Greek Tragedy', *JHS* 105, 1-10

——— (1993) 'Presentation of character in Aeschylus', in I. McAuslan and P. Walcot (eds.), *Greek Tragedy,* Greece and Rome Studies 2 (Oxford) 12-28

——— (1997) 'Constructing the heroic', in C. Pelling (ed.) *Greek Tragedy and the Historian* (Oxford) 21-37

Ehrenberg, V. (1954) *Sophocles and Pericles* (Oxford)

Erskine, A. (1997) 'The Scipionic circle', *OCD*^{3}, 1369

Euben, J.P. (1986) 'The battle of Salamis and the origins of political theory', *Political Theory* 14, 359-90, reprinted in his *Corrupting Youth. Political Education, Democratic Culture, and Political Theory* (Princeton, 1997) 64-90

——— (1990) *The Tragedy of Political Theory* (Princeton)

Fahr, W. (1969) THEOUS NOMIZEIN, *Spudasmata* 24 (Hildesheim)

Flickinger, R.C. (1918) *The Greek Theater and its Drama* (Chicago)

Flory, S. (1993) 'The death of Thucydides and the motif of "land on sea" ', in R.M. Rosen and J. Farrell (eds.) *Nomodeiktes: Greek Studies in Honour of Martin Ostwald* (Ann Arbor) 113-23

Foley, H.P. (1993) 'The politics of tragic lamentation', in A.H. Sommerstein, S.

Halliwell, J. Henderson and B. Zimmermann (eds.) *Tragedy, Comedy, and the Polis* (Bari) 101-43
Fornara, C.W. (1966) 'The hoplite achievement at Psyttaleia', *JHS* 86, 51-4
——— (1971a) *Herodotus: An Interpretative Essay* (Oxford)
——— (1971b) 'Evidence for the date of Herodotus' publication', *JHS* 91, 25-34
Forrest, W.G. (1960) 'Themistokles and Argos', *CQ* 10, 220-41
——— (1963) 'Aristophanes' *Acharnians*', *Phoenix* 17, 1-12
——— (1966) *The Emergence of Greek Democracy* (London)
——— (1986) 'The stage and politics', in M. Cropp, E. Fantham and S. Scully (eds.) *Greek Tragedy and its Legacy: Essays Presented to D.J. Conacher* (Calgary) 229-39
Fowler, B.H. (1967) 'Aeschylus' Imagery', *C&M* 28, 1-74
Fowler, R.L. (1996) 'Herodotos and his contemporaries', *JHS* 116, 62-87
Francis, E.D. (1980) 'Greeks and Persians: the art of hazard and triumph' in D. Schmandt-Bessarat (ed.) *Ancient Persia: The Art of an Empire* (Malibu) 53-86
——— (1990) *Image and Idea in Fifth-Century Greece*, ed. M. Vickers (London)
——— and Vickers, M. (1985a) 'Argive Oenoe', *AC* 54, 105-15
——— (1985b) 'The Oenoe painting in the Stoa Poikile, and Herodotus' account of Marathon', *BSA* 80, 99-111
——— (1985c) 'The Marathon epigram in the Stoa Poikile', *Mnemosyne* 38, 390-3
Franco, C. (1986) 'I Persiani secondo Aristofane', *Orpheus* 7, 112-14
Freymouth, G. (1953) 'Zur MILÊTOU HALÔSIS des Phrynichos', *Philologus* 99, 51-69
Frost, F.J. (1968) 'Themistocles' place in Athenian politics', *CSCA* 1, 105-24
Frye, R.N. (1972) 'Gestures of deference to royalty in ancient Iran', *IA* 9, 102-7
Gagarin, M. (1976) *Aeschylean Tragedy* (Berkeley)
Gammie, J.G. (1986) 'Herodotus on kings and tyrants: objective historiography or conventional portraiture', *JNES* 45, 171-95
Garvie, A.F. (1969) *Aeschylus'* Supplices (Cambridge)
Gauthier, P. (1966) 'La parallèle Himère-Salamine au Ve et au IVe siècle av. J.-C.', *REA* 68, 5-32
Geddes, A.G. (1987) 'Rags and riches: the costume of Athenian men in the fifth century', *CQ* 37, 307-31
Georges, P. (1994) *Barbarian Asia and the Greek Experience* (Baltimore)
Germain, G. (1956) 'Le songe de Xerxès et le rite Babylonien du substitut royal (Étude sur Hérodote, VII 12-18)', *REG* 69, 303-13
Ghezzo, M.V. (1938/9) 'I Persiani di Eschilo', *AIV* 98, 427-48
Goldhill, S.D. (1987) 'The Great Dionysia and civic ideology', *JHS* 107, 58-76, reprinted in J.J. Winkler and F.I. Zeitlin (eds.) *Nothing to Do with Dionysos? Athenian Drama in its Social Context* (Princeton, 1990) 97-129
——— (1988) 'Battle narrative and politics in Aeschylus' *Persae*', *JHS* 108, 189-93
——— (1991) 'Comic inversion and inverted commas: Aristophanes and parody', in *The Poet's Voice* (Cambridge) 167-222

——— (1997) 'Modern critical approaches to Greek tragedy', in P.E. Easterling (ed.) *The Cambridge Companion to Greek Tragedy* (Cambridge) 324-47

——— and R. Osborne (1994) *Art and Text in Ancient Greek Culture* (Cambridge)

Gomme, A.W. (1945) *A Historical Commentary on Thucydides* vol. I (Oxford)

——— (1948) 'The Eion epigram', *CR* 62, 5-7

——— (1954) *The Greek Attitude to History and Poetry* (Berkeley)

Gow, A.S.F (1928) 'Notes on the *Persae* of Aeschylus', *JHS* 48, 132-58

Gredley, B. (1996) 'Comedy and tragedy – inevitable distinctions', in M.S. Silk (ed.) *Tragedy and the Tragic* (Oxford) 203-16

Green, P. (1996) *The Greco-Persian Wars* (Berkeley)

Gregory, J. (1991) *Euripides and the Instruction of Athens* (Ann Arbor)

Griffith, M. (1998) 'The King and Eye: the rule of the father in Greek tragedy', *PCPhS* 44, 20-84

Griffiths, A. (1987) 'Democedes of Croton: a Greek doctor at Darius' court', in H. Sancisi-Weerdenburg and A. Kuhrt (eds.) *Achaemenid History II. The Greek Sources* (Leiden) 37-51

——— (1999) 'Euenios the negligent nightwatchman (Herodotus 9.92-6)', in R. Buxton (ed.) *From Myth to Reason?: Studies in the Development of Greek Thought* (Oxford) 169-82

Hägg, T. (1985) 'Metiochus at Polycrates' court', *Eranos* 83, 92-102

Haldane, J.A. (1965) 'Musical themes and imagery in Aeschylus', *JHS* 85, 33-41

Hall, E. (1989) *Inventing the Barbarian: Greek Self-Definition through Tragedy* (Oxford)

——— (1993) 'Asia unmanned: images of victory in classical Athens', in J. Rich and G. Shipley (eds.) *War and Society in the Greek World* (London) 107-33

——— (1994) 'Drowning by nomes: the Greeks, swimming, and Timotheus' *Persians*', in H.A. Khan (ed.) *The Birth of the European Identity: the Europe-Asia Contrast in Greek Thought*, Nottingham Classical Literature Studies 2 (Nottingham) 44-80

——— (1996a) *Aeschylus* Persians (Warminster)

——— (1996b) 'Is there a *polis* in Aristotle's *Poetics*?', in M.S. Silk (ed.) *Tragedy and the Tragic* (Oxford) 295-309

Halliwell, F.S. (1997) 'Between public and private: tragedy and the Athenian experience of rhetoric', in C. Pelling (ed.) *Greek Tragedy and the Historian* (Oxford) 121-41

Hammond, N.G.L. (1956) 'The battle of Salamis', *JHS* 76, 32-54

Harmon, A.M. (1932) 'The scene of the *Persians* of Aeschylus', *TAPhA* 63, 7-19

Harrison, E.B. (1966) 'The composition of the Amazonomachy on the shield of Athena Parthenos', *Hesperia* 35, 107-33

——— (1972a) 'A new fragment from the northern frieze of the Nike temple', *AJA* 76, 195-7

——— (1972b) 'Preparations for Marathon, the Niobid Painter and Herodotus', *Art Bulletin* 54, 390-402

Harrison, T. (1997a) 'Herodotus and the ancient Greek idea of rape' in S. Deacy and K. Pierce (eds.) *Rape in Antiquity* (London) 185-208

——— (1997b) 'Herodotus and the certainty of divine retribution', in A.B. Lloyd (ed.) *What is a God? Studies in the Nature of Greek Divinity* (London) 101-22
——— (1999) 'Herodotus' conception of foreign languages', *Histos* 2
——— (2000a) *Divinity and History: The Religion of Herodotus* (Oxford)
——— (2000b) 'Sicily in the Athenian imagination: Thucydides on the Persian Wars', in J. Serrati and C.J. Smith (eds.) *Sicily from Aeneas to Cicero* (Edinburgh)
——— (forthcoming) 'Persian dress and Greek freedom: the representation of eastern decadence in Greek historiography from Hecataeus to Alexander'
Hartog, F. (1988) *The Mirror of Herodotus: The Representation of the Other in the Writing of History* (tr. J. Lloyd, Berkeley)
——— (1996) 'Fondements grecs de l'idée d'Europe', *QS* 43, 5-17
Hauvette, A. (1894) *Hérodote. Historien des Guerres Médiques* (Paris)
Hay, D. (1957) *Europe: The Emergence of an Idea* (Edinburgh)
Headlam, W. (1902) 'Ghost raising, magic, and the underworld', *CR* 16, 52-61
Heath, M. (1987) *The Poetics of Greek Tragedy* (London)
Hegyi, D. (1973) 'Historical authenticity of Herodotus in the Persian "Logoi" ', *AAntHung* 21, 73-87
Herington, J. (1986) *Aeschylus* (New Haven)
——— and Lembke, J. (1981) Aeschylus *Persians* (New York)
Hickman, R.M. (1938) *Ghostly Etiquette on the Classical Stage*, Iowa Studies in Classical Philology 7 (Dubuque)
Hignett, C. (1952) *A History of the Athenian Constitution to the end of the Fifth Century BC* (Oxford)
Hohti, P. (1974) 'Freedom of speech in speech sections in *Histories* of Herodotus', *Arctos* 8, 19-27
Holtsmark, E.B. (1970) 'Ring composition and the *Persae* of Aeschylus', *SO* 45, 5-23
Hook, L. van (1934) 'The praise of Athens in Greek Tragedy', *CW* 27, 185-8
Hornblower, S. (1987) *Thucydides* (London)
——— (1992) 'The religious dimension to the Peloponnesian War or what Thucydides does not tell us', *HSCP* 94, 169-97
Horsfall, N.M. (1974) 'Aeschylus and the Strymon', Hermes 102, 503-5
Ireland, S. (1993) 'Dramatic structure in the *Persae* and *Prometheus* of Aeschylus', in I. McAuslan and P. Walcot (eds.) *Greek Tragedy*, Greece and Rome Studies 2 (Oxford) 38-44
Jacobstahl, P. (1938) 'A Sybarite Hymation', *JHS* 58, 205-16
Jaeger, W. (1939) *Paideia* (tr. G. Highet, Oxford)
Jeffery, L.H. (1965) 'The *Battle of Oinoe* in the Stoa Poikile: a problem in Greek art and history', *BSA* 60, 41-57
Johnson, W.A. (1995) 'Oral performance and the composition of Herodotus' *Histories*', *GRBS* 36, 229-54
Jones, A.H.M. (1957) 'Athenian democracy and its critics', in his *Athenian Democracy* (Oxford) 41-72
Jones, J. (1962) *Aristotle and Greek Tragedy* (London)

Jouan, F. (1981) 'L'évocation des morts dans la tragédie grecque', *RHR* 198, 403-21

Jouanna, J. (1981) 'Les causes de la défaite des Barbares chez Eschyle, Hérodote et Hippocrate', *Ktema* 6, 3-15

——— (1984) 'Collaboration ou résistance au barbare: Artémise d'Halicarnasse et Cadmos de Cos chez Hérodote et Hippocrate', *Ktema* 9, 15-26.

Kakridis, J.T. (1975) 'Licht und Finsternis in dem Botenbericht der Perser des Aischylos', *GB* 4, 145-54

Kearns, E. (1985) 'Change and continuity in religious structures after Cleisthenes', in P.A. Cartledge and F.D. Harvey (eds.) *CRUX: Essays in Greek History presented to G.E.M. de Ste. Croix* (Exeter and London) 189-207

Keaveney, A. (1996) 'Persian behaviour and misbehaviour: some Herodotean examples', *Athenaeum* 74, 23-48

Kebric, R.B. (1983) *The Paintings in the Cnidian Lesche at Delphi and their Historical Context* (Leiden)

Kelley, K.A. (1978) 'Variable repetition: word patterns in the *Persae*', *CJ* 74, 213-19

Kent, R.G. (1953) *Old Persian. Grammar, Texts, Lexicon* (2nd. ed., New Haven)

Kitto, H.D.F. (1939) *Greek Tragedy: A Literary Study* (London)

——— (1950) *Greek Tragedy. A Literary Study* (2nd ed., London)

——— (1966) *Poiesis: Structure and Thought* (Berkeley)

Konishi, H. (1979) 'Cimon and the "Persian" tetralogy', *LCM* 4, 161-4

Konstan, D. (1987) 'Persians, Greeks and empire', *Arethusa* 20, 59-73

Korzeniewski, D. (1966) 'Studien zu den Persern des Aischylos', *Helikon* 6, 548-96

Kuhrt, A. (1988) 'Earth and water', in A. Kuhrt and H. Sancisi-Weerdenburg (eds.) *Achaemenid History III. Method and Theory* (Leiden) 87-99

——— and Sherwin-White, S. (1987) 'Xerxes' destruction of Babylonian temples', in H. Sancisi-Weerdenburg and A. Kuhrt (eds.) *Achaemenid History II. The Greek Sources* (Leiden) 69-78

Kurke, L. (1992) 'The politics of *habrosyne* in archaic Greece', *ClAnt* 11, 91-120

Lada-Richards, I. (1999) *Initiating Dionysus: Ritual and Theatre in Aristophanes'* Frogs (Oxford)

Lang, M.L. (1967) 'Scapegoat Pausanias', *CJ* 63, 79-85

Lateiner, D. (1977) 'No laughing matter: a literary tactic in Herodotus', *TAPhA* 107, 173-82

——— (1989) *The Historical Method of Herodotus* (Toronto)

Lattimore, R. (1943) 'Aeschylus on the defeat of Xerxes' in *Classical Studies in Honor of W.A. Oldfather* (Urbana) 82-93

——— (1958) *The Poetry of Greek Tragedy* (Baltimore)

Laurot, B. (1981) 'Idéaux grecs et barbarie chez Hérodote', *Ktema* 6, 57-68

Lavagnini, B. (1927) 'L'azione drammatica nei Persiani di Eschilo', *Athenaeum* 5, 295-301

Lavelle, B.M. (1993) *The Sorrow and the Pity: A Prolegomenon to a History of Athens under the Peisistratids c. 560-510* BC, Historia Einzelschriften 80 (Stuttgart)

Lawrence, A.W. (1951) 'The Acropolis and Persepolis', *JHS* 71, 111-19
Lawson, J.C. (1934) 'The evocation of Darius' (Aesch. *Persae* 607-93)', *CQ* 28, 79-89
Lazenby, J. F. (1988) 'Aischylos and Salamis', *Hermes* 116, 168-85
Lenardon, R.J. (1959) 'The chronology of Themistokles' ostracism and exile', *Historia* 8, 23-48
Lesky, A. (1965) *Greek Tragedy* (tr. H.A. Frankfort, London)
Lévy, E. (1984) 'Naissance du concept de barbare', *Ktema* 9, 5-14
Lewis, D.M. (1958) 'The Phoenician fleet in 411', *Historia* 7, 392-7
——— (1977) *Sparta and Persia* (Leiden)
——— (1985) 'Persians in Herodotus', in M.H. Jameson (ed.) *The Greek Historians: Papers Presented to A.E. Raubitschek* (Palo Alto) 89-105, reprinted in Lewis (1997) 345-61
——— (1987) 'The King's table' in H. Sancisi-Weerdenburg and A. Kuhrt (eds.) *Achaemenid History II. The Greek Sources* (Leiden) 79-87, reprinted in Lewis (1997) 332-41
——— (1992) 'Sources, chronology, method', *CAH* V^2, 1-14
——— (1997) *Selected Papers in Greek and Near Eastern History*, ed. P.J. Rhodes (Cambridge)
Lewis, R.G. (1997) 'Themistocles and Ephialtes', *CQ* 47, 358-62
Lewis, S. (1995) 'Barbers' shops and perfume shops. "Symposia without wine" ', in A. Powell (ed.) *The Greek World* (London) 432-41
——— (1996) *News and Society in the Greek Polis* (London)
——— (1999) 'Who is Pythius the Lydian?', *Histos* 2
Lloyd-Jones, H. (1956) 'Zeus in Aeschylus', *JHS* 76, 55-67
Lombardo, M. (1983) ' "*Habrosyne* e *Habra*" nel mondo Greco arcaico', in *Forme di Contatto e Processi di Trasformazione nelle Società antiche*, Atti del Convegno di Cortona (24-30 Maggio 1981) (Pisa, Rome) 1077-103
Long, T. (1986) *Barbarians in Greek Comedy* (Carbondale and Edwardsville, Illinois)
Loraux, N. (1973) 'Marathon, ou l'histoire idéologique', *REA* 75, 13-42
——— (1981) *L'invention d'Athènes: histoire de l'oraison funèbre dans la 'cité classique'* (Paris), tr. by Alan Sheridan as *The Invention of Athens: The Funeral Oration in the Classical City* (Princeton, 1986)
Lucas, D.W. (1950) *The Greek Tragic Poets* (London)
Macan, R.W. (1908) *Herodotus VII-IX* (London)
McCall, M.F. (1986) 'Aeschylus in the *Persae*: a bold strategy succeeds', in M. Cropp, E. Fantham and S. Scully (eds.) *Greek Tragedy and its Legacy* (Calgary) 43-9
Macleod, C. (1982) 'Politics and the *Oresteia*', *JHS* 102, 124-44, reprinted in his *Collected Essays* (Oxford, 1983) 20-43
——— (1983) 'Thucydides and tragedy', in his *Collected Essays* (Oxford) 140-58
Mallowan, M.E.L. (1972) 'Cyrus the Great (558-529 BC)', *Iran* 10, 1-17
——— (1985) 'Cyrus the Great (558-529 BC), *Cambridge History of Iran* 2, 392-419

Manganaro, G. (1960) 'La *Milêtou halôsis* di Frinico e l'oracolo epiceno per Argo e Mileto', *RFIC* 38, 113-23

Martin, V. (1952) 'Drame historique ou tragédie? Remarques sur le nouveau fragment tragique relatif à Gygès', *MH* 9, 1-9

——— (1965) 'La politique des Achéménides. L'exploration prélude de la conquête', *MH* 22, 28-38

Martorelli, A. (1977) 'Storia persiana in Erodoto: echi di versioni ufficiali', *RIL* 111, 115-25

Martyn, J.R.C. (1964) 'Aristophanes *Frogs* 1019-30', *CPh* 59, 178-81

Marx, F. (1928) 'Der Tragiker Phrynichus', *RhM* 77, 355-61

Masson, O. (1950) 'A propos d'un rituel hittite pour la lustration d'une armée', *RHR* 137, 5-25

Matheson, S.B. (1995) *Polygnotus and Vase Painting in Classical Athens* (Madison)

Mattingly, H.B. (1977) 'Poets and politicians in fifth-century Greece', in K.H. Kinzl (ed.) *Greece and the Eastern Mediterranean. Studies presented to Fritz Schachermeyr on the occasion of his eightieth birthday* (Berlin) 231-45

Mazzarino, S. (1960) 'Eschilo, Pericle e la storia dell' Areopago', *Rivista di Cultura Classica e Medioevale* 2, 300-6

Méautis, G. (1937) 'Eschyle et Polygnote', *JA* ser. 6 10, 169-73

Meier, C. (1990) *The Greek Discovery of Politics* (tr. David McLintock, Cambridge, Mass.)

——— (1993) *The Political Art of Greek Tragedy* (Cambridge)

Meiggs, R. (1972) *The Athenian Empire* (Oxford)

Melchinger, S. (1979) *Die Welt als Tragödie* vol. I (Munich)

Merck, M. (1978) 'The city's achievements. The patriotic Amazonomachy and ancient Athens', in S. Lipshitz (ed.) *Tearing the Veil. Essays on Femininity* (London) 95-115

Meritt, B.D, H.T. Wade-Gery and M.F. McGregor (1950) *Athenian Tribute Lists* vol. III (Princeton)

Meritt, L.S. (1970) 'The Stoa Poikile', *Hesperia* 39, 233-58

Metzler, D. (1966) *Untersuchungen zu den griechischen Porträts des 5 Jhd v.Chr.* (Münster)

Michelini, A.N. (1982) *Tradition and Dramatic Form in the Persians of Aeschylus* (Leiden)

Miller, M.C. (1988) 'Midas as the Great King in Attic fifth-century vase painting', *AntK* 31, 79-89

——— (1995) 'Persians. The Oriental Other', *Source: Notes in the History of Art*, 38-44

——— (1997) *Athens and Persia in the Fifth Century* BC. *A Study in Cultural Receptivity* (Cambridge)

Mills, S. (1997) *Theseus, Tragedy and the Athenian Empire* (Oxford)

Missiou, A. (1993) '*DOULOS TOU BASILEÔS*: the politics of translation', *CQ* 43, 377-91

Mitchell, L.G. (1997) *Greeks Bearing Gifts: The Public Use of Private Relationships in the Greek World 435-323* BC (Cambridge)

Mitsis, P. (1988) 'Xerxes' entrance: irony, myth, and history in the *Persians*', in P. Pucci (ed.) *Language and the Tragic Hero: Essays in Honor of Gordon M. Kirkwood* (Atlanta) 103-19

Moles, J. (1996) 'Herodotus warns the Athenians', *Papers of the Leeds International Latin Seminar* 9, 259-84

Momigliano, A. (1984) 'Persian empire and Greek freedom', in *Settimo Contributo* (Rome) 61-75, originally published in A. Ryan (ed.) *The Idea of Freedom: Essays in Honour of Isaiah Berlin* (Oxford, 1979) 139-51

Moreau, A. (1993) 'Le songe d'Atossa. *Perses*, 176-214. Éléments pour une explication de textes', in P. Ghiron-Bistagne, A. Moreau and J.-C. Turpin (eds.) *Les* Perses *d'Eschyle*, Cahiers du Gita no. 7 (Montpellier) 29-51

——— (1993b) 'La tétralogie des *Perses* a-t-elle une unité?' in P. Ghiron-Bistagne, A. Moreau, and J.-C. Turpin (eds.) *Les* Perses *d'Eschyle*, Cahiers du Gita no. 7 (Montpellier) 119-44

Morris, I. (1993) 'Poetics of power: the interpretation of ritual action in archaic Greece', in C. Dougherty and L. Kurke (eds.) *Cultural Poetics in Archaic Greece: Cult, Performance, Politics* (Cambridge) 15-45

Morris, S.P. (1992) *Daidalos and the Origins of Greek Art* (Princeton)

Munson, R.V. (1993) 'Three aspects of Spartan kingship in Herodotus', in R.M. Rosen and J. Farrell (eds.) *Nomodeiktes: Greek Studies in Honour of Martin Ostwald* (Ann Arbor) 39-54

Murray, G. (1940a) *Aeschylus: The Creator of Tragedy* (Oxford)

——— (1940b) 'The League of Nations: the first experiment', in H.A.L. Fisher et al. *The Background and Issues of the War* (Oxford) 49-75

——— (1953) *Hellenism and the Modern World* (London)

Murray, O. (1987) 'Herodotus and oral history', in H. Sancisi-Weerdenburg and A. Kuhrt (eds.) *Achaemenid History II. The Greek Sources* (Leiden) 93-115

Myres, J.L. (1908) 'Herodotus and anthropology', in R.R. Marett (ed.) *Anthropology and the Classics: Six Lectures Delivered before the University of Oxford* (Oxford) 121-68

Nenci, G. (1950) 'Per una interpretazione storiographica del proemio dei Persiani', *PP* 5, 215-23

Nickau, K (1990) 'Mythos und logos bei Herodot', in W. Ax (ed.) *Memoria Rerum Veterum: Festschrift ... C.J. Classen* (Stuttgart) 83-100

Nylander, C. (1970) *Ionians in Pasargadae* (Uppsala)

——— (1983) 'The standard of the Great King', *Opuscula Romana* 14, 19-37

Ober, J. (1996) *The Athenian Revolution: Essays on Ancient Greek Democracy and Political Theory* (Princeton)

——— (1998) *Political Dissent in Democratic Athens: Intellectual Critics of Popular Rule* (Princeton)

Olmstead, A.T. (1960) *A History of the Persian Empire* (3rd. ed., Chicago)

O'Neill, E. (1942) 'A Note on Phrynichus' *Phoenissae* and Aeschylus' *Persae*', *CPh* 37, 425-7.

Orlin, L.L. (1976) 'Athens and Persia ca. 507 BC: a neglected perspective', in L.L. Orlin (ed.) *Michigan Studies in Honour of G.G. Cameron* (Ann Arbor) 255-66

Osborne, R. (1996) *Greece in the Making 1200-479 BC* (London)

Paduano, G. (1978) *Sui Persiani di Eschilo: problemi di focalizzazione drammatica* (Rome)

Parker, R. (1983) *Miasma: Pollution and Purification in Early Greek Religion* (Oxford)

——— (1996) *Athenian Religion: A History* (Oxford)

——— (1997) 'Gods cruel and kind: tragic and civic theology', in C. Pelling (ed.) *Greek Tragedy and the Historian* (Oxford) 143-60

Patin, M. (1877) *Études sur les tragiques grecs I. Eschyle* (4th ed., Paris)

Payen, P. (1997) *Les Îles Nomades: Conquérir et Résister dans L'Enquête d'Hérodote* (Paris)

Pelling, C. (1997a) 'Aeschylus' *Persae* and History', in C. Pelling (ed.) *Greek Tragedy and the Historian* (Oxford) 1-19

——— (1997b) conclusion to C. Pelling (ed.) *Greek Tragedy and the Historian* (Oxford) 213-35

Perdrizet, P. (1912) 'La légende du châtiment de l'Hellespont', *REA* 14, 357-69

——— (1921) 'Le témoignage d'Eschyle sur le sac d'Athènes par les Perses', *REG* 34, 57-79

Perlman, S. (1976) 'Panhellenism, the polis and imperialism', *Historia* 25, 1-30

Péron, J. (1982) 'Réalité et au-delà dans les Perses d'Éschyle', *Bulletin de l'Association Guillaume Budé* (March, 1982) 3-40

Petre, Z. (1978) 'Eschyle, Salamine et les épigrammes de Marathon', *Revue Roumaine d'Histoire* 17, 327-36

Petrounias, E. (1976) *Funktion und Thematik der Bilder bei Aischylos, Hypomnemata* 48 (Göttingen)

Pickard-Cambridge, A.W. (1988) *The Dramatic Festivals of Athens*, 2nd ed. rev. by J. Gould and D.M. Lewis (Oxford)

Podlecki, A.J. (1966) *The Political Background to Aeschylean Tragedy* (Ann Arbor)

——— (1968) 'Simonides: 480', *Historia* 17, 257-75

——— (1971) 'Cimon, Skyros and "Theseus' Bones" ', *JHS* 91, 141-3

——— (1975) 'Theseus and Themistocles', *RSA* 25, 1-23

——— (1983) 'Aeschylus' women', *Helios* 10, 23-47

——— (1986) 'Polis and monarch in early Greek tragedy', in J.P. Euben (ed.) *Greek Tragedy and Political Theory* (Berkeley) 76-100

——— (1987) 'Solon or Peisistratus? A case of mistaken identity', *AncW* 16, 3-10

——— (1991) *The Persians by Aeschylus* (2nd ed., Bristol)

——— (1993) *'Kat' arkhês gar philaitios leôs*: the concept of leadership in Aeschylus', in A. Sommerstein, S. Halliwell, J. Henderson and B. Zimmermann (eds.) *Tragedy, Comedy and the Polis* (Bari) 55-79

Post, L.A. (1950) 'The *Seven against Thebes* as propaganda for Pericles', *CW* 44, 49-52

Pretagostini, R. (1998) 'Aristofane "etnologo": il mondo persiano nella falsa ambasceria del prologo degli *Acarnesi*', *Seminari Romani* 1.1, 41-56

Prickard, A.O. (1879) *The* Persae *of Aeschylus* (London)

Pritchett, W.K. (1959) 'Towards a restudy of the battle of Salamis', *AJA* 63, 251-62

——— (1993) *The Liar School of Herodotus* (Amsterdam)
Puech, A. (1932) 'Les trois récits principaux de la bataille de Salamine', *Mélanges Glotz* vol. II (Paris) 757-64
Pugliese Carratelli, G. (1966) 'Le guerre mediche ed il sorgere della solidarità ellenica', in *La Persia e il Mondo Greco-Romano*, Accademia Nazionale dei Lincei 76 (Rome) 147-56
Pulleyn, S.J. (1997) *Prayer in Greek Religion* (Oxford)
Quincey, J.H. (1962) 'Notes on the *Persae*', *CQ* 12, 182-6
Raaflaub, K. (1979) 'Polis Tyrannos: Zur Entstehung einer politischen Metapher', in G.W. Bowersock, W. Burkert and M.C.J. Putnam (eds.) *Arktouros: Hellenic Studies presented to Bernard M.W. Knox on the Occasion of his 65th Birthday* (Berlin and New York) 237-52
Redfield, J. (1985) 'Herodotus the tourist', *CPh* 80, 97-118
Rhodes, P.J. (1981) *A Commentary on the Aristotelian* Athenaion Politeia (Oxford)
——— (1992) 'The Athenian revolution', *CAH* V^2, 62-95
Richardson, L.J.D. (1952) 'The inner conflict in the *Persae*', in M. White (ed.) *Studies in honour of Gilbert Norwood* (Toronto) 55-62
Ridley, M.R. (1922) Aeschylus *Persae* (Oxford)
Riemann, K. (1967) *Das Herodoteische Geschichtswerk in der Antike* (diss. Munich)
Robertson, D.S. (1939) 'A Sybarite Hymation', *JHS* 59, 136
Robertson, M. (1975) *A History of Greek Art* (2 vols., Cambridge)
Robinson, C.A. (1939) 'The struggle for power at Athens', *AJPh* 60, 232-7
——— (1946) 'The date of Themistocles' ostracism', *AJPh* 67, 265-6
Rogers, J.D. (1903) 'On the *nomismata purgina* of Aeschylus, *Pers.* 859', *AJA* 7, 95-6
Roisman, J. (1988) 'On Phrynichos' *Sack of Miletus* and *Phoinissai*', *Eranos* 86, 15-23
Romilly, J. de (1983) 'Le thème de la liberté et l'évolution de la tragédie grecque', in *Théâtre et Spectacles dans l'Antiquité*, Université de Sciences Humaines de Strasbourg. Travaux du Centre de Recherches sur le Proche-Orient et la Grèce Antiques 7 (Leiden) 215-26
——— (1993) 'Les barbares dans la pensée de la Grèce classique', *Phoenix* 47, 283-92
——— (1994/5) 'Cruauté barbare et cruautés grecques', in *Festschrift Hans Schwabl*, *WS* 107/8, 187-96
——— et. al. (1974) *Les Perses* (Paris)
Rood, T.C.B. (1999) 'Thucydides' Persian Wars', in C. Kraus (ed.) *The Limits of Historiography* (Leiden) 141-68
Root, M.C. (1979) *The King and Kingship in Achaemenid Art* (Leiden)
——— (1980) 'The Persepolis Perplex: some prospects borne of retrospect', in D. Schmandt-Besserat (ed.) *Ancient Persia. The Art of an Empire* (Malibu) 5-13
——— (1985) 'The Parthenon frieze and the Apadana reliefs at Persepolis: reassessing a programmatic relationship', *AJA* 89, 103-20
——— (1991) 'From the heart: powerful persianisms in the art of the western

empire', in H. Sancisi-Weerdenburg and A. Kuhrt (eds.) *Achaemenid History VI. Asia Minor and Egypt: Old Cultures in a New Empire* (Leiden) 1-29

Rose, H.J. (1950) 'Ghost ritual in Aeschylus', *HThR* 43, 257-80

——— (1957) *A Commentary on the Surviving Plays of Aeschylus* vol. 1 (Amsterdam)

Rosenbloom, D. (1993) 'Shouting "fire" in a crowded theater: Phynichus' *Capture of Miletus* and the politics of fear in early Attic Theater', *Philologus* 137, 159-96

——— (1995) 'Myth, history and hegemony in Aeschylus', in B.E. Goff (ed.) *History, Tragedy, Theory. Dialogues on Athenian Drama* (Austin) 91-130

Roux, G. (1974) 'Eschyle, Hérodote, Diodore, Plutarque racontent la bataille de Salamine', *BCH* 98, 51-94

Rutherford, I. (1996) 'The New Simonides: towards a commentary', *Arethusa* 29, 167-92

Said, E. (1978) *Orientalism* (London)

——— (1993) *Culture and Imperialism* (London)

Saïd, S. (1981) 'Darius et Xerxes dans les *Perses* d'Eschyle', *Ktema* 6, 17-38

——— (1984) 'Grecs et Barbares dans les tragédies d'Euripide. La fin des différences', *Ktema* 9, 27-53

——— (1988) 'Tragédie et renversement: l'exemple des *Perses*', *Metis* 3, 321-41

——— (1993) 'Pourquoi Psyttalie ou comment transformer un combat naval en défaite terrestre' in P. Ghiron-Bistagne, A. Moreau, and J.-C. Turpin (eds.) *Les* Perses *d'Eschyle,* Cahiers du Gita no. 7 (Montpellier) 53-69

——— (1998) 'Tragedy and politics', in D. Boedeker and K.A. Raaflaub (eds.) *Democracy, Empire, and the Arts in Fifth-Century Athens* (Cambridge, Mass.) 275-95

Ste. Croix, G.E.M. de (1972) *The Origins of the Peloponnesian War* (London)

Salanitro, G. (1965) 'Il pensiero politico di Eschilo nei Persiani', *Giornale Italiano di Filologia* 18, 193-235

Sancisi-Weerdenburg, H. (1983) 'Exit Atossa: Images of Women in Greek Historiography on Persia', in A. Cameron and A. Kuhrt (eds.) *Images of Women in Antiquity* (London) 20-33

——— (1985) 'The death of Cyrus: Xenophon's *Cyropaedia* as a source for Iranian history', in *Papers in honour of Professor Mary Boyce*, Acta Iranica. Hommages et Opera Minora X-XI vol. II (Leiden) 459-71

——— (1987a) 'Decadence in the empire or decadence in the sources? From sources to synthesis: Ctesias', in H. Sancisi-Weerdenburg (ed.) *Achaemenid History I. Sources, Structures and Synthesis* (Leiden) 33-45

——— (1987b) 'The fifth oriental monarchy and hellenocentrism: Cyropaedia VIII viii and its influence', in H. Sancisi-Weerdenburg and A. Kuhrt (eds.) *Achaemenid History II. The Greek Sources* (Leiden) 117-31

——— (1989a) 'Gifts in the Persian empire', in P. Briant and C. Herrenschmidt (eds.) *Le Tribut dans l'Empire Perse. Actes de la table ronde de Paris* (Paris) 129-46

——— (1989b) 'The Personality of Xerxes, King of Kings', in L. de Meyer and

E. Haerinck (eds.) *Archaeologica Iranica et Orientalia. Miscellanea in honour of L Vanden Berghe* (Ghent) 549-61

——— (1994) 'The orality of Herodotus' *Medikos Logos* or: the Median empire revisited', in H. Sancisi-Weerdenburg, A. Kuhrt and M.C. Root (eds.) *Achaemenid History VIII. Continuity and Change* (Leiden) 39-55

Sansone, D. (1985) 'The date of Herodotus' publication', *ICS* 10, 1-9

Sartori, F. (1969-70) 'Echi politici ne "I Persiani" di Eschilo', *AIV* 128, 771-97

Schaps, D.M. (1977) 'The woman least mentioned: etiquette and women's names', *CQ* 27, 323-30

——— (1993) 'Aeschylus' politics and the theme of the *Oresteia*', in R.M. Rosen and J. Farrell (eds.) *Nomodeiktes: Greek Studies in honour of Martin Ostwald* (Ann Arbor) 505-15

Schmid, W. and O. Stählin (1934) *Geschichte der Griechische Literatur* I.2 (Munich)

Schmitt, R. (1978) *Die Iranier-Namen bei Aischylos,* Iranica Graeca Vetustiora I (Wien)

——— (1984) 'Perser und Persisches in der alten Attischen Komödie', *Acta Iranica* 23, 459-72

Scott, W.C. (1984) *Musical Design in Aeschylean Theater* (Hanover, New Hampshire)

Seaford, R. (1994) *Ritual and Reciprocity: Homer and Tragedy in the Developing City-State* (Oxford)

Sealey, R. (1967) 'The entry of Pericles into history', in his *Essays in Greek Politics* (New York) 59-74, originally published in *Hermes* 84 (1956) 234-47

Séchan, L. (1967) *Études sur la Tragédie Grecque dans ses rapports avec la Céramique* (2nd ed., Paris)

Segal, C. (1996) 'Catharsis, audience and closure in Greek tragedy', in M.S. Silk (ed.) *Tragedy and the Tragic* (Oxford) 149-72

Sheppard, J.T. (1911) *Greek Tragedy* (Cambridge)

Sider, D. (1983) 'Atossa's second entrance: significant inaction in Aeschylus' *Persai*', *AJPh* 104, 188-92

Sidgwick, A. (1903) *Aeschylus' Persae* (Oxford)

Simon, E. (1963) 'Polygnotan painting and the Niobid Painter', *AJA* 67, 43-62

Smyth, H.W. (1924) *Aeschylean Tragedy* (Berkeley)

Sordi, M. (ed.) (1986) *L'Europa nel mondo antico, Contributi dell' Istituto di storia antica* 12 (Milan)

Sourvinou-Inwood, C. (1989) 'Assumptions and the creation of meaning: reading Sophocles' *Antigone*', *JHS* 109, 134-48

Stadter, P. (1992) 'Herodotus and the Athenian *Archê*', *ASNP*[3] 22.3-4, 781-909

Stansbury-O'Donnell, M.D. (1989) 'Polygnotus' *Iliupersis*: a new reconstruction', *AJA* 93, 203-15

——— (1990) 'Polygnotos' *Nekyia*: a reconstruction and analysis', *AJA* 94, 213-35

Starr, C.G. (1962) 'Why did the Greeks defeat the Persians?', *PP* 17, 321-32

——— (1975) 'Greeks and Persians in the 4th century BC' (part 1), *IA* 11, 39-99

——— (1977) 'Greeks and Persians in the 4th century BC' (part 2), *IA* 12, 49-115

Stears, K. (1998) 'Death becomes her: gender and Athenian death ritual', in S. Blundell and M. Williamson (eds.) *The Sacred and the Feminine in Ancient Greece* (London) 113-27

Stern, J. (1989) 'Demythologisation in Herodotus: 5.92.η', *Eranos* 87, 13-20

Stinton, T.C.W. (1990) 'The scope and limits of allusion in Greek tragedy', in his *Collected Papers on Greek Tragedy* (Oxford) 454-92, originally published in M. Cropp, E. Fantham and S. Scully (eds.) *Greek Tragedy and its Legacy: Essays Presented to D.J. Conacher* (Calgary) 67-102

Stoessl, F. (1945) 'Die Phoenissen des Phrynichos und die Perser des Aischylos', *MH* 2, 148-65

——— (1952) 'Aeschylus as a political thinker', *AJPh* 73, 113-39

Straten, F.T. van (1974) 'Did the Greeks kneel before their Gods?', *BAB* 49, 159-89

Tanner, J. (1994) 'Shifting paradigms in Classical art history', *Antiquity* 68, 650-5

Taplin, O. (1972) 'Aeschylean silences and silences in Aeschylus', *HSCP* 76, 57-97

——— (1977) *The Stagecraft of Aeschylus* (Oxford)

Tarn, W.W. (1908) 'The fleet of Xerxes', *JHS* 28, 202-33

Thalmann, W.G. (1980) 'Xerxes' rags: some problems in Aeschylus' *Persians*', *AJPh* 101, 260-82

Thébert, Y. (1980) 'Reflections on the use of the foreigner concept: evolution and function of images of the barbarian in Athens in the classical era', *Diogenes* 112, 93-110

Thomas, R. (1989) *Oral Tradition and Written Record in Classical Athens* (Cambridge)

Thompson, D.B. (1956) 'The Persian Spoils in Athens', in S.S. Weinberg (ed.) *The Aegean and the Near East: Studies Presented to H. Goldman* (Locust Valley, NY) 281-91

Thomson, G. (1973) *Aeschylus and Athens* (4th edition, London)

Thomson, J.A.K. (1927) *Irony: An Historical Introduction* (Cambridge)

Tourraix, A. (1984) 'L'image de la monarchie Achéménide dans les *Perses*', *REA* 86, 123-34

——— (1993) 'Les *Perses*, la Géopolitique et l'Histoire', in P. Ghiron-Bistagne, A. Moreau, and J.-C. Turpin (eds.) *Les* Perses *d'Eschyle*, Cahiers du Gita no. 7 (Montpellier) 99-117

Tozzi, P. (1980) 'Salamina, l'obbedienza distrutta e la libertà dei Greci d'Asia nei *Persiani* di Eschilo', *Athenaeum* 58 (1980) 259-63

Tracy, S.V. (1986) 'Darkness from light: the beacon fire in the *Agamemnon*', *CQ* 36, 257-60

Trenkner, S. (1957) *The Greek Novella* (Cambridge)

Tucker, T.G. (1935) *The Persians of Aeschylus* (Melbourne)

Tuplin, C.J. (1994), 'Persians as Medes', in H. Sancisi-Weerdenburg, A. Kuhrt and M.C. Root (eds.) *Achaemenid History VIII. Continuity and Change* (Leiden) 235-56

——— (1996) *Achaemenid Studies*, Historia Einzelschriften 99 (Stuttgart)

Tyrell, W.B. (1984) *Amazons. A Study in Athenian Mythmaking* (Baltimore)

Ure, P.N. (1923) 'Themistocles, Aeschylus and Diodorus', *CR* 37, 64

Vanderpool, E. (1966) 'A monument to the battle of Marathon', *Hesperia* 35, 93-106

Verdin, H. (1982) 'Hérodote et la politique expansionniste des Achéménides. Notes sur Hdt. VII.8', in J. Quaegebeur (ed.) *Studia Paulo Naster Oblata II, Orientalia Antiqua* (Louvain) 327-36

Veyne, P. (1988) *Did the Greeks Believe in their Myths?* (tr. P. Wissing, Baltimore)

Vickers, M. (1985) 'Persepolis, Vitruvius and the Erechtheum Caryatids: the iconography of medism and servitude', *RA* 3-28

——— (1990) 'Interactions between Greeks and Persians', in H. Sancisi-Weerdenburg and A. Kuhrt (eds.) *Achaemenid History IV. Centre and Periphery* (Leiden) 253-62

Virgilio, R. di (1973) *Il vero volto dei Persiani di Eschilo* (Rome)

Vogt, J. (1972) 'Die Hellenisierung der Perser in der Tragödie des Aischylos: religiöse Dichtung und historisches Zeugnis', in R. Stiehl and G.A. Lehmann (eds.) *Antike und Universalgeschichte: Festschrift H.E. Stier* (Münster) 131-45

Wade-Gery, H.T. (1933) 'Classical epigrams and epitaphs. A study of the Cimonian age', *JHS* 53, 71-104

Walbank, F.W. (1951) 'The problem of Greek nationality', *Phoenix* 5, 41-60

Walker, H.J. (1995) *Theseus and Athens* (New York)

Wallace, P.W. (1969) 'Psyttaleia and the trophies of the battle of Salamis', *AJA* 73, 293-303

Wallinga, H.T. (1989) 'Persian tribute and Delian tribute', in P. Briant and C. Herrenschmidt (eds.) *Le Tribut dans l'Empire Perse: Actes de la table ronde de Paris* (Paris) 173-81

Walters, K.R. (1981) ' "We fought alone at Marathon": historical falsification in the Attic funeral oration', *RhM* 124, 204-11

Wardman, A.E. (1959) 'Tactics and the tradition of the Persian wars', *Historia* 8, 49-60

Waters, K.H. (1971) *Herodotus on Tyrants and Despots* (Wiesbaden)

Waters, M. (1996) 'Darius and the Achaemenid line', *AHB* 10, 11-18

Wees, H. van (1995), 'Politics and the battlefield. Ideology in Greek warfare', in A. Powell (ed.) *The Greek World* (London) 153-78

Weil, R. (1976) 'Artémise et le monde à l'envers', in *Recueil A. Plassart* (Paris) 215-24

West, S. (1985) 'Herodotus' epigraphical interests', *CQ* 35, 278-305

——— (1987) 'And it came to pass that Pharaoh dreamed: notes on Herodotus 2.139, 141', *CQ* 37, 262-71

West, W.C. (1970) 'Saviors of Greece', *GRBS* 11, 271-82

Whitby, L.M. (1999) 'Ion of Chios and the margins of the Delian League', in E. Dabrowa (ed.) *Ancient Iran and the Mediterranean World* (Krákow)

Wiesehöfer, J. (1990) ' "Denn es sind welthistorische Siege." Nineteenth- and twentieth-century German views of the Persian wars', *Culture and History* 11, 61-83

——— (1996) *Ancient Persia from 550 BC to 650 AD* (tr. A. Azodi, London)

Wilamowitz, U. von (1898) 'Unechte Briefe', *Hermes* 33, 382-9

——— (1914) *Aischylos Interpretationen* (Berlin)

Wilson, J.R. (1986) 'Territoriality and its violation in the *Persians*', in M. Cropp, E. Fantham and S. Scully (eds.) *Greek Tragedy and its Legacy* (Calgary) 51-7

Winnington-Ingram, R.P. (1983a) 'Zeus in *Persae*', in his *Studies in Aeschylus* (Cambridge) 1-15, originally published in *JHS* 93 (1973) 210-19

——— (1983b) 'A word in the *Persae*', in his *Studies in Aeschylus* (Cambridge), 198-9, originally published in *BICS* 20 (1973) 37-8

Woodford, S. (1974) 'More light on old walls', *JHS* 94, 158-65

Young, T.C. (1980) '480/479 BC – a Persian perspective', *IA* 15, 213-39

Zuntz, G. (1955) *The Political Plays of Euripides* (Manchester)

Index

Reference is made to notes only when these contain sustained discussion on a point which is not handled in the corresponding section of the main text.

www.ingramcontent.com/pod-product-compliance
Lightning Source LLC
Chambersburg PA
CBHW071527120726
47907CB00013B/1239

* 9 7 8 1 3 5 0 1 1 3 4 1 1 *